MURDER BY MAIL

MURDER BY MAIL

A GLOBAL HISTORY OF THE LETTER BOMB

Mitchel P. Roth and Mahmut Cengiz

REAKTION BOOKS

Published by
Reaktion Books Ltd
Unit 32, Waterside
44–48 Wharf Road
London N1 7UX, UK
www.reaktionbooks.co.uk

First published 2024
Copyright © Mitchel P. Roth and Mahmut Cengiz 2024

Printed and bound in Great Britain by Bell & Bain, Glasgow

A catalogue record for this book is available from the British Library

ISBN 978 1 78914 940 1

CONTENTS

Introduction

L etter bombs have existed for as long as there have been traditional postal services. If bombs 'are one of the oldest weapons of the political terrorist', then according to the terrorism expert Richard Clutterbuck 'the letter bomb is one of the meanest and most cowardly of all forms of attack.'[1] Those most likely to feel the wrath of the letter bomber are not the intended targets, but, rather, the everyday office clerk, secretary or postal worker – an individual that a perpetrator might consider collateral damage. Letter bombs can be lethal, but more often they maim and disfigure innocent recipients of mail, if they explode at all.

This book focuses on explosive devices sent via the postal service or some other delivery service with the intention of causing harm to a specific recipient. The text uses the terms 'letter bomb', 'mail bomb', 'infernal devices' and 'parcel bombs' or 'package bombs' interchangeably. No matter the mail transport, these infernal machines, packed into seemingly normal letters or packages, usually contain a small explosive charge and shrapnel designed to cause injury. One of the differences from improvised explosive devices (IEDs) is the fact that letter bombs are intended for a specific target rather than to cause widespread damage and disruption. Regardless of a letter bomber's motivation there is a terroristic quality to the act, 'characterized by the psychological immediacy of the explosion for the victims and the fear induced in those who are made aware of the attacks courtesy of the mass media'.[2] The serial mail bomb cases of the Unabomber (Ted Kaczynski, whose nickname came from the fact that he placed mail bombs in universities (Un) and an aeroplane (a)), the MAGAbomber (Cesar Sayoc Jr, who targeted critics of Trump and the MAGA world),

Walter Leroy Moody Jr and many others included in this book, such as Franz Fuchs and Mark Conditt, illustrate the hysteria a series of anonymous mail bombs can create among the public. Another way of looking at the impact of weaponized mail is that 'the very nature of the act leads to the disruption of confidence.'[3]

Books have been written about the history of IEDs, the machine gun, booby traps, torpedoes, landmines and other deadly devices.[4] The first substantial publication on the history of letter bombs is *The History of Mail Bombs: A Philatelic and Historical Study* by Dale Speirs, published in 2010. There are 324 citations from various newspapers between 1857 and 2004. Hence, through no fault of Speirs's, it was not written for a scholarly audience. As a leading member of the Wreck and Crash Mail Society, Speirs's book is more concerned with the study and collection of mail and envelopes damaged by letter bombs. Of its 127 pages at least 40 are devoted to photographs of these letter survivors. Truly fascinating stuff. We learned much from his book including the fact that most letter bomb injuries are to the left hand. Since most people are right-handed it would make sense that they are holding letters in their left hands while opening them with their right.[5]

Murder by Mail: A Global History of the Letter Bomb is the first comprehensive and scholarly history of parcel, package and letter bombs. Although most death-dealing devices have been given their due and are well chronicled by book-length treatments, murder by mail, package and letter bomb has never been given the historical attention it deserves (except for specific case studies).

When the authors began this project they were unaware of the global ubiquity of these devices over the past century. Virtually every continent has experienced singular or serial mail bomb outrages over the past 150 years. Motivations for these attacks are wide-ranging, including extortion, profit, psychopathy and other mental illnesses and terrorism. But more often than not, in the modern era, they are part of a strategy of personal revenge used against former employers, spouses and lovers. Since this book is focused on mail bombs, weaponized letter and package bombs bearing anthrax and sarin are beyond its purview.

Mail bombs, while numerous, make up a small proportion of overall tactics and weapons employed in domestic and foreign terrorist operations, but they remain a significant threat due to the relative simplicity of acquiring and assembling these devices as well as the ease of sending them undetected by mail and parcel services. Moreover, they have generated widespread fear and public anxiety over the past decades.[6]

Some mail bombers are serial offenders and have no common motive for their crimes. Serial bombers, such as the Unabomber Ted Kaczynski, who remains the gold standard of letter bombers for his eighteen-year spree that ended in 1996, can be motivated by any number of causes – religion, sadism, politics, finances or even moral codes (such as being pro-life). Along with poisoners, mail bombers are distinct from other criminals. They plan meticulously, nurse long grudges and retaliate far out of proportion to any injury they feel they might have received.

While it has been common for most people to believe that the mail bomber is a 'person motivated by radical political beliefs', according to the United States Postal Service, 'this stereotype is incorrect.' Former business partners or employees may seek revenge when a business relationship sours or when business reversals cause layoffs or firings. Law enforcement officers and members of the judiciary have been targeted by those seeking revenge for being investigated or prosecuted. 'Revenge is the motivation that most often triggers a letter or package bomb.'[7]

Letter bomb mechanisms have not changed much over the past century. Mail bombs are only limited by the availability of components and parts, the ability of a bomber to secure certain materials and the knowledge of how to use such materials as home-made explosives. 'Bombers are creatures of habit, if they become comfortable with a certain type of device and it accomplishes the mission, they'll continue to use it.'[8]

In the 1950s a journalist declared that putting an explosive device in a parcel-post package 'delivered by an unsuspecting postman to an equally unsuspecting victim is the sneakiest method of attempted murder known to man (with poison a close second)'.[9]

Poisoning by mail is a much simpler crime to solve since the 'poisoned missile is intact and available for inspection'. By comparison, in the case of explosive devices 'postal inspectors usually are only left with fragments of paper and string. If they are lucky, bits of carbon, small lengths of wire or distinctive scraps of paper give them small leads.'[10]

In the 1960s mail bombs became more common. In 1967 journalist Caryl Rivers wrote, 'each year dozens of people try to turn the unwitting postman from a bearer of messages into an instrument of violence.'[11] The head of the u.s. Post Office crime lab in Washington, DC, claimed that the choice of bomb varied by gender. Psychopaths, rejected suitors, men and women motivated by jealousy and lacking the courage or taste for personal violence decide to try 'murder by mail'. Rivers's gender pronouncement was based on his experiences over time. 'Men send bombs [explosives]' but women are likely 'to send poisoned cakes, cookies, brownies, and other goodies'.[12] Another unexpected observation about mail bombers in the United States was the fact that by the 1960s most murder-by-mail attempts took place in a specific geographic area, namely the 'hill country of Kentucky, Tennessee, and other southern states, where traditions of family feuds and vendettas are deeply rooted'.[13]

While researching and drafting this book over the past several years the authors found hundreds of mail bomb cases. While much has been written about this phenomenon in the United States, it turns out murder by mail has been a strategy adopted around the world for many of the aforementioned motivations. *Murder by Mail* examines the history of this tactic chronologically. Each chapter covers a variety of selected cases to tell the story. Some feature serial bombers and terrorists while others focus on revenge-motivated individuals. While the sixteen chapters run chronologically by decade, there are several stand-alone chapters on serial mail bomb cases that deserved deeper coverage, such as Ted Kaczynski, Walter Leroy Moody Jr and Cesar Sayoc Jr.

1

Mail Bombs: The Early Years

In the beginning, there was the infernal machine, shorthand for the precursors to the modern mail, package and letter bombs. 'Infernal machines' or 'devices' referred to any device sent through the mail or some form of postal delivery system to a recipient with the intention of causing destruction of life, limb or property when opened. In most cases early package bombs employed the devious use of some type of explosive, usually gunpowder. Package and mail bombs were preceded by the imaginative use of primed pistols, ready to fire at whoever had the misfortune of opening the box first. One of the oldest examples dates back to the early eighteenth century.

The Bandbox Plot

A number of accounts suggest that the first package bomb device (infernal device) was discovered on 4 November 1712. Although not a bomb per se, its use of gunpowder-charged pistols was lethally designed by the assassin to shoot the recipient, similar to how a modern-day parcel bomb might be set to detonate when opened. In this case the target was the Earl of Oxford and British Lord Treasurer Robert Harley. Once the recipient opened the box, it proved a close harbinger of bomb devices that would take centre stage in the centuries to come. The so-called 'bandbox plot' was facilitated using a lightweight hat box, containing two (or three, in some accounts) loaded and cocked pistols attached to a thread and primed to fire as soon as the box was opened.

How the box was delivered remains just as elusive as who sent it.[1] Harley had already received the lightweight hatbox, or bandbox, before he entertained a visitor, the Anglo-Irish novelist, pamphleteer and clergyman Jonathan Swift (1667–1745).[2] Best known for his later satirical works, *Gulliver's Travels* (1726) and *A Modest Proposal* (1729), Swift was still more than a decade away from reaching the apogee of his fame. The box sat unopened on the office floor near Harley's desk. As Swift and Harley chatted, something about the box caught Swift's attention. He espied a curious thread attached to the inside of the box. Inquisitive, and probably with the assent of his host, Swift cut the packthread fastened to the lid, unknowingly disarming the device. After cutting it, the lid of the box was lifted, revealing a clever apparatus comprising several pistols tied to a packthread fastened to the lid.[3] Some accounts have suggested that Swift interrupted the detonation of the world's first recorded parcel bomb. But it was not a bomb, or a detonation, in the conventional sense. However, it still might have resulted in the first victim of a package bomb. Publicity surrounding the fortuitous timing noted that Swift, 'perceiving the thread, seized the package and cut the thread thus disarming the device'.[4] Although it was never determined who sent the package, most observers laid the dastardly plot at the door of the opposition Whig party. Once this incident was widely publicized it generated plenty of support and sympathy for Harley.

Long forgotten by the twenty-first century, the incident was memorialized in a ballad entitled 'Plot upon Plot' around 1713:

> Two ink-horn tops your Whigs did fill
> With gunpowder and lead;
> Which with two serpents made of quill,
> You in a bandbox laid;
> A tinder-box there was beside,
> Which had a trigger to it,
> To which the very string was ty'd
> That was designed to do it.[5]

Almost all of Swift's works were published anonymously. In his letters to Stella, his dear platonic friend until her death in 1728, he wrote,

I wonder how I came to have so much presence of mind, which is usually not my talent; but so it pleased God, and I saved myself and him; for there was a bullet apiece. A gentleman told me that if I had been killed, the Whigs would have called it a judgement, because the barrels were inkhorns, with which I have done them so much mischief.[6]

Some contemporaries were of the mind that Swift was too keen to claim credit for his role in the incident; others even branded it a hoax. In one of the first accounts of this near miss, it was Harley who began to open the box when he spotted a pistol, whereupon Swift asked for the box, and opening it, by the window, 'found powder, nails, etc., so arranged that, if opened in the ordinary way, whole would have been fired, and two barrels discharged in different ways'.[7]

Another early account of a parcel bomb is mentioned in the eighteenth-century diary of a Danish official, Bolle Willum Luxdorph (1716–1788). In an entry for 19 January 1764, he mentioned a Colonel Poulson, living at Børglum Abbey, who was sent a box by mail. When he opened it, he found 'gunpowder and a fire-lock which sets fire unto it, so he became injured'. A later entry in the diary from 15 February notes that Poulson received another related letter written in German that read, 'soon the dose will be increased.'[8] Outside of Poulson being injured by the parcel, not much else is known about this incident. The Swift and Luxdorph accounts are the most frequently mentioned tales of mail bombs prior to the nineteenth century and coincide with the first seeds of a common postal service. If any lesson can be drawn from these two events it is that the modern letter bomb was not quite ready for primetime.

While the Swift case does not qualify as a bomb it did use explosive gunpowder, which is the most important ingredient of a letter device. The second important element is the existence of some sort of postal delivery system. Naturally, the first package bombs were delivered by hand to the address on the package. In the nineteenth century postal services became much more common and demonstrated characteristics recognizable in the modern postal system.

A Brief History of Postal Services

The first postal services pre-dated the inception of mail, letter and package bombs by more than two centuries. In the United Kingdom, King Charles I inaugurated the first public mail service in 1635. At the time, this service consisted of little more than letters transported from one mail transit point to another by carriers on foot or horseback. Up until then, the post system was reserved for the use of the king and his court. In 1653 Frenchman Jean-Jacques Renouard de Villayer (1607–1691) established a postal system in Paris, setting up mailboxes and having someone deliver the letters that were placed in them if they used postage-prepaid envelopes that he sold. However, according to one popular account, this did not last long after a prankster put mice in mailboxes, scaring off customers. In 1775 the U.S. Postal Service was created, one of the few government agencies explicitly authorized by the U.S. Constitution.

Despite these early developments in France, England and the United States, this does not mean that there were no previous systems for moving material communications from one designated place to another. For example, historian Mary Bellis suggests that the first documented use of a postal system might date back to 240 BC Egypt, when pharaohs used state-sponsored, designated couriers to transport royal decrees.[9]

Important developments in the prehistory of the letter bomb include the 1837 invention of the adhesive postage stamp by a schoolmaster in England named Rowland Hill (1795–1879). He was knighted for his efforts and through his contributions the first postage stamp system in the world began in England in 1840, making the prepayment of postage both possible and practical.

Nineteenth-Century Cases

The earliest recorded examples of explosive mail devices in the early nineteenth century include three cases in particular, heavily covered as they were by newspapers on both sides of the Atlantic. While there is no consensus as to the date of the first mail bomb, one account from 1833 makes an interesting claim for this distinction.[10] According to the 18 October 1833 issue of the *New York City Evening Star*, in June of that year the former Lieutenant-Governor of Rhode Island, Edward Wilcox, received a leather trunk 'by a sloop from New York'.[11] It had a label attached stating that it was sent by a relative. He was suspicious from the outset and thought it might not be 'a friendly present'. He cautiously picked up its lid and noticed some cords, which did little to assuage his suspicion. So he set it aside until he could find out more about what lay within. Several days later some young men opened the trunk, cutting the cords carefully, and found the box contained two horse pistols 'with muzzles buried in upwards of thirty pounds of powder'.[12] The cords, as in the 1712 Jonathan Swift affair, were attached to triggers in such a way that if the lid was raised a few inches, the whole trunk would have exploded. Wilcox probably recognized that the 'trigger cords were part of the firing mechanism', and quickly figured out 'not to put much pressure' on the cords. Bryan Burnett and Paul Golubovs suggest this is 'not only the first report of a mail bomb but also the defusing of a mail bomb'.[13]

What distinguishes the 1833 device is its ingenuity. If all had gone as planned the flintlock firing mechanism activated when the trigger was pulled would have caused the flint to strike the steel 'frizzen' (better known as the hammer or steel), igniting the flash pan when struck. The fine-grain powder in the flash pan would have been ignited and, via the touchhole in the weapons barrel, the powder would have been set off. In the event that the lid had been lifted off the trunk, it would have caused both pistols to fire. The fact that the device was carefully designed to withstand transportation without firing suggests that the perpetrator designed the internal configuration to preclude movement of any objects which could

ensnare the cords and cause premature firing of the weapons. It
suggests sophisticated mounts for guns, and if it had gone off it
would have spread parts of the trunk and guns like shrapnel over a
wide area.[14]

In October 1850 the *Morning Chronicle* in London reported the
discovery of another infernal machine. A man and his twenty-
something son were in a newspaper's counting house (financial
office) when the foreman handed them an oval box made of wood,
addressed to the older man. His son shook it first and commented
that it sounded as if it was filled with sand. The son looked closely
at the box, took out a knife and began to pry up the lid. His father
warned him to be cautious. His warning was prescient, for the
moment the lid was partially raised a small quantity of gunpowder
fell out on the desk. It became quickly apparent that the box contained combustible materials and that it was sent for the purpose of
destroying or mutilating the person who opened it.

The father told his son to cease his examination until they could
pour some water through the slit into the box, hoping to neutralize
'any combustible ingredient which it might contain'. The lid was
then opened without further worry. Now the men could see the true
nature of this infernal machine as it was exposed to view. The box
contained close to a pound of fine gunpowder 'with irregular pieces
of lead' and a number of 'lucifer matches and sandpaper placed in
such a position that the least amount of violence used in forcing the
top off must lead to an explosion of the whole contents of the interior'. An inquiry was then launched to try and determine who
instigated this 'destructive engine'. But with nothing besides the
addressee's name to go on, it was decided to publicize the particulars
of this incident in the hope of getting someone to come forward
with information.[15]

A policeman was dispatched to the post office to try and ascertain if anyone could identify the sender of the box. Demonstrating
the challenges of the modern English postal service, a postal
employee informed the policeman that the box was deposited along
with thousands of letters and parcels and that no one remembered
who left the package; as a result the investigation stalled. It was only

through sheer luck that the device did not explode in the post office. It was obviously prepared to explode if it fell or friction in the box set the contents off. Ultimately, the bomb targets and the postal employees took solace in their providential escape. It was hoped that the accompanying publicity would make the public more cautious when receiving unfamiliar packages. There is no evidence that anyone was arrested for this incident.[16]

No deaths, injuries or damage occurred in conjunction with the 1833 and 1850 package bombs. But in a case four years later, on 27 June 1854, a couple died a day apart in America's first deadly mail bombing.[17] The victims were a custodian and thirty-year-old resident medical student at the Cincinnati College of Medicine and Surgery, named Isaac Allison, and his twenty-year-old wife Catherine, a nurse. The story began when they started receiving packages in the mail at their college apartment. Each was identical to the others, 'a walnut box about 15" long, 6" wide, and 4" deep, wrapped in brown paper'.[18] There were rumours that the packages had something to do with the couple blackmailing a well-known burglar, who went by the alias William Connolly, in exchange for keeping quiet about a large theft of cash from a steamboat. What made this conjecture believable was the fact that the Allisons had been arrested for theft in the case but released when no one could identify them. The couple had been fired but were staying at the hospital until they were replaced.

On the morning of 26 June 1854 a stranger paid two teenage boys a dime to deliver another package addressed to the Allisons. Before sending the boys on their way to the hospital address, the stranger warned them to carry the package carefully. The boys handed it to a clerk, instructing him to deliver it to Dr John Baker at the hospital office. Baker figured it was just another package from the mystery man and promised to deliver it to Allison's apartment. Later the doctor told journalists and the police that the box weighed about 15 pounds and made a peculiar rustling sound when it was shaken.

About ninety minutes after the package made it to the Allisons' room, a 'massive explosion rocked the entire hospital building' and nearby structures, injuring some patients and employees. Dr Baker, who had delivered the package, rushed into the room to find both Allisons mortally injured. Baker asked the husband, who had been 'horrifically disemboweled and blinded, his clothes still on fire', what happened. All he could muster was, 'A torpedo in that box, Doctor.'[19] He would be dead within two hours. But before he took his last breath he was able to identify the two boys who delivered the package to the hospital and pointed to the aforementioned William Connolly as the likely culprit. However, Connolly provided alibis that cleared him.[20]

Baker next tried to assist Catherine. She was in extreme agony, her clothes still alight, with 'the flesh . . . blown from the sides of her face' and her arm 'horribly mangled'. She died the next day in 'great agony'. In the words of the *Cincinnati Times* on 27 June, 'It was no less a deed than the destruction of two lives . . . by what is generally known as the infernal machine.' According to the newspaper account, such a device 'had never been seen before'. It was described as:

> a piece of steel pipe about 12" long with a pistol-lock trigger. It was drilled with holes and packed with black powder, 22 chunks of iron, steel slugs, and steel balls . . . ingeniously designed so the opening of the box would explode the cap and ignite the powder.[21]

A Short History of Explosives

It is instructive here to trace the development of gunpowder and explosives to gain a better understanding of why it took so long to develop mail bombs. Although 'letter bomb' is the preferred rubric for discussing these devices, they come in many shapes and sizes and have been referred to as mail bombs, parcel bombs, package bombs, note bombs, message bombs, gift bombs, delivery and surprise bombs and postal bombs.

The most common ingredient in mail bombs is some type of explosive. Explosives can be traced back to the first primitive black powders created in China 'in the form of firecrackers and smoke signals, as early as the tenth century'.[22] The development and history of explosive black powder is rather unsure and incomplete. Indeed, historians continue to debate whether the Chinese were merely toying with a combustible smoke-producing powder or had actually discovered it.

By the time Marco Polo visited China in the late thirteenth century gunpowder was still unknown to the West, while the Chinese had been using it for fireworks and the like for close to three centuries. Ultimately, its use would transform European warfare as 'armies exchanged their lances, swords, and crossbows for cannon, portable harquebuses, and pistols.'[23] Mongol armies invading Poland and Hungary during the late thirteenth century reportedly used primitive bombs of bamboo tubes loaded with black powder and sharp stones as projectiles.

In AD 900 the Chinese invented the so-called 'fire-lance', a bamboo (later metal) tube with one opening, packed with sulphur, charcoal and small amounts of the 'fire chemical': 'explosive saltpeter or nitrate salts, a key ingredient of gunpowder'.[24] A historian of dynamite points out that the 'earliest black powder' was a blend of 'three naturally occurring substances', sulphur, charcoal and saltpetre, 'unreliable and difficult to use'.[25] These three ingredients, according to historian Stephen R. Bown, were usually impure, separated during transportation or storage and easily became damp. Moreover, since black powder was uniformly ground it could be packed into a weapon too tightly, 'slowing down combustion and causing misfires (in guns)'.[26]

Having been mentioned in the writings of Roger Bacon (1214–1292), the Arabic writer Abd Allah (seventh century) and Count Albertus of Bollstadt (1200–1280), it is fair to say that the thirteenth century was the likely time period for the entrance of black powder onto the world scene since it is fairly certain that it was known to Arabs and Europeans by then.[27] 'Black powder' is a modern term, and according to one historian, 'it stems from the fact that the first Smokeless Powder was a lighter color, a gray, in comparison to the commonly dark black of the propellant it would largely supplant.'[28]

In the fifteenth century the development of corned powder, using a technique known as corning, improved the quality and strength of black powder. By mixing the ingredients as uniformly as possible and then wetting it into clumps, the mixture was changed to a form in which the elements would not separate. These clumps were then mechanically broken up (a dangerous task) into kernels, thus the term 'corning'.

From Gunpowder to Dynamite

As noted above there were few mail bombs prior to the great surge in their use in the late 1800s. Gunpowder was the only explosive readily available until Alfred Nobel (1833–1896) patented dynamite in 1867, making explosives safer to transport and more dependable. Prior to Nobel's advances in explosives one of the biggest strides forward in the development of parcel bombs was the creation of nitroglycerine. In 1847 an Italian studying chemistry at Turin University, Ascanio Sobrero (1812–1888), experimented with a mixture of sulphuric and nitric acid, which he combined with glycerine. Explosives were far from his mind and, like many inventions and discoveries, his experiments had unexpected consequences that would prove revelatory.

As he worked at devising new medicines he made the mistake of heating the sulphur, nitric acid and glycerine together in a test tube. Fortunately for him the test tube only contained a small quantity of the ingredients, because as soon as it was held over a flame a loud crack could be heard and it exploded. He only suffered minor injuries from flying glass. But it was soon recognized that the oily liquid he had produced was actually nitroglycerine.[29]

The Italian continued to experiment with the unpredictable new compound. For some reason he fed some to a dog, which died quickly. When he dissected the animal he made an important discovery, one that augured less for bomb-making and more for prolonging life. Once he noticed the blood vessels in the dog's heart were hugely dilated it occurred to him immediately that it just might be a new remedy for angina and other circulatory problems. In the twenty-first century it remains one of the most widely used treatments for circulatory problems involving the heart.[30]

Sobrero understood another potential use for the new compound: in larger quantities it had potential as a weapon of war. At this time the only known explosive was gunpowder, a compound of charcoal, sulphur and saltpetre, which had been the go-to explosive for at least a millennium. As the writer Simon Webb has noted, in reality, 'gunpowder is not really an explosive at all. It is simply a substance which will burn very fast and only explodes if it is enclosed in a container such as a gun barrel or bomb casing.'[31] Indeed, if someone is tempted to fill a saucer with gunpowder and then touch it with a red-hot needle – no explosion. The powder may flare up, singeing one's eyebrows, but you would be expected to survive relatively unscathed. If you tried this with a saucer of nitroglycerine you would most likely blow off your hand, whether or not it was enclosed within a container. In the cant of explosives, 'it would be considered a high explosive'; by contrast gunpowder then was a 'low explosive'.[32]

There was surely a market for this product, especially considering the limits of gunpowder, and it was soon in great demand. However, one challenge to its popular use still remained – it was too sensitive and liable to explode if banged, splashed, dropped or even shaken too hard. What is more, it deteriorated over time into unstable compounds, which could explode spontaneously without any warning. A fortune was in the offing for anyone who could find a way to make the compound stable and harness its power for general commercial use. This fortune would be amassed by a Swede who coincidentally shared a professor at Turin with Sobrero.

The Swedish chemist and manufacturer Alfred Nobel was experimenting with nitroglycerine in 1863, attempting to make a more powerful industrial explosive. The following year his brother and four others were killed when a shed used for the production of volatile nitroglycerine exploded. Nobel then decided to experiment with mixing nitro (nitroglycerine) with a fine, porous powder, and in 1867 he took out a patent for dynamite.[33] He found a way of absorbing nitro into a type of clay called kieselguhr, making it safer to handle, and in 1867 he patented the process and product that became known by the trademark 'dynamite'. There is a certain irony in the fact that a discovery that resulted in life-saving medication would also become known as 'the poor man's artillery', and it was not long before it became the perfect tool for what would be known in anarchist circles and among political extremists as 'propaganda by deed'.[34]

2

Opening Salvos of the Infernal Machines

New advances in explosives came at just the right moment for burgeoning groups of extremists and lone criminal actors seeking more violent methods for waging war on society and each other. As postal services improved the 1880s and 1890s witnessed a major uptick in mail bomb incidents. On 13 April 1881, for example, an unidentified person posted the first Australian letter bomb at the Adelong Post Office. By the time it reached its destination its recipient 'found [it contained] a quantity of dynamite with a tin tack inserted in a percussion cap'.[1] Mail bomb historian Dale Speirs located a notice of this case in the 13 April 1881 *New South Wales Police Gazette*. Despite a £50 reward and the offer of a free pardon to any accomplice to the individual who sent the dynamite, no one was ever charged in this case. It is interesting that there was already a statute in the Victorian statute book:

> Whoever shall enclose in or with any letter packet or newspaper or shall put into any post office or newspapers into any pillar or box for the receipt of letters packets or newspapers to be sent by post any explosive dangerous or destructive substance or liquid or any matter or thing likely to injure any person shall be guilty of felony and shall be liable on conviction . . . to be imprisoned with or without hard labour for any term not exceeding seven years.[2]

Mail bombs continued to plague postal systems around the world in the late nineteenth century. However, legislation protecting anyone using the American mail service also protected the potential bombers. One of the barriers to checking for letter bombs in the United States was the 1878 Supreme Court case *ex Parte Jackson*, which prohibited opening a piece of mail without a warrant. According to the decision, 'Letters and sealed packages . . . in the mail are as fully guaranteed from examination and inspection, except to their outward form and weight, as if they were retained by parties forwarding them in their own domiciles.' Indeed,

> The constitutional guarantee of the people to be secure in their papers against unreasonable search and seizures extends to their papers, thus closed against inspection wherever they may be . . . No law of Congress can place in the hands of officials connected with the postal service any authority to invade the secrecy of letters, and such sealed packages in the mail.[3]

Motivations and Targets

There was no prototypical mail bomber or target in the 1880s. A number of high-profile cases were linked to routine motivations, including blackmail, extortion and, of course, revenge. One case that was particularly newsworthy involved a former artist at Madame Tussauds venerable wax museum. In 1889 the *London Times* reported that 61-year-old Edward White was charged with sending a parcel bomb to John Theodore Tussaud, the manager of Madame Tussaud & Sons Waxworks, after being fired.[4] The so-called infernal device immediately aroused suspicions and a report was made to the local Marylebone Lane police station. A constable was sent to examine the box. Demonstrating a familiarity with mail bombs, he 'cautiously opened from the bottom' where he found 'an infernal machine of the most dangerous character'. Each side of the package

> was lined with a thick cake of dynamite, the interior space being full of fine sporting gunpowder. Attached to the top of the lid was a strip of sandpaper arranged to play against

two fuses, which, on the lid being opened, would have ignited the powder and caused a frightful explosion.

For safety, the police took control of the bomb and alerted postal authorities. From the beginning a former employee was suspected of sending the device owing to the fact that Tussaud had recently fired long-time employees, or as the press put it, 'made a general clearance of all the old hands'.[5]

The targets of postal bombs came from all walks of life, especially in Gilded Age America, where titans of industry became richer and the poor grew poorer. Politically motivated letter bombers adopted the postal service as a low-risk delivery system for their infernal devices. In December 1895 attempts were made via mail infernal machines to George M. Pullman and P. D. Armour. However, as the mail was being collected in the morning mailbox, two packages caught the attention of Captain Stuart of the Postal Inspection Service. One was addressed to Pullman's private residence in Chicago and another to Armour's home address. There was already a protocol for handling suspicious packages at this time. In this case the superintendent was told to submerge Pullman's package in water before trying to open it. Once the danger seemed to have passed, further inspection revealed a bomb consisting of a section of lead pipe filled with match heads and a white powder believed to be dynamite. Both packages were described as rectangular, measuring 6 inches long, 2 inches deep and 2 inches wide and weighing 24 ounces each. Each was wrapped in light brown paper and addressed in rough hand by pencil. In the margins was written 'contons [contains] wire'. Likewise the street addresses were misspelled.[6]

You did not have to be a captain of industry to receive a mail bomb. The same year Armour and Pullman were sent letter bombs, a Miss Mattie of Centralia (Tacoma, Washington) received an infernal machine in a box addressed to her by the Reverend B. F. Fuller, a Christian Church minister who had been jilted by her a year previously. He had promised to go away, and had done so until he heard she had paired up with a new beau. He wrote her several letters before constructing a box to hold a physician's thermometer with a piece of sandpaper under the lid. A fulminating cap, a parlour match and a bit of rubber band were arranged so as to ignite the match and cap and cause a large dynamite bomb just beneath the cover to explode when the lid was withdrawn. However, a country postmaster's curiosity saved her life when he pried open the box after he saw the edge of the sandpaper protruding through a break in the package.[7]

In the early years of the twentieth century postal authorities in the United States and elsewhere were kept increasingly busy trying to flag the delivery of infernal machines. Sometimes, even in the criminal underworld, imitation can be the greatest form of flattery. A variety of actors resorted to letter bombs to promote causes, solve relationship issues, exact revenge or just create havoc. Mail bomb incidents made the news from Prussia, Stockholm and Berlin to London, New Orleans and beyond.

1904–10: Dr Martin Ekenberg, Letter Bomb Pioneer

Numerous articles have credited Dr Martin Ekenberg as the inventor of the letter bomb. It would be convenient to know who the creator of this diabolical device was. But it was certainly not him. On 24 January 1910 Ekenberg, 'the Swedish man of science', was extradited to London's Bow Street Police Court to stand trial for the attempted murders of four people in Sweden by sending them postal bombs. Born Martin Birger Natanael Ekenberg in Töreboda, Sweden, on 12 March 1870, he earned a doctorate in philosophy from the University of Königsberg, Germany.[8] He returned to Sweden, where he developed a process for drying milk. According to a contemporary account dried milk could be 'transported anywhere or kept as long as desired. Warm water added to the powder produced a fluid closely resembling fresh milk.'[9] In 1896 he founded a business based on his invention for refining fish oil into engine oil. It failed.

Ekenberg continued to start businesses but relied on financial support from wealthy businessmen. When each business failed, he had to find a new source. It reached the point where he saw these men as 'traitors' who 'abandoned him'. He went about getting even by sending mail bombs to the targets of his anger. His first letter bomb was sent on 19 August 1904 to a Stockholm director named Karl Fredrik Lundin, who had been involved in his failed fish oil scheme. One writer claimed that this bomb shattered 'the age of postal innocence'. It was sent from a well-known department store in Stockholm but Lundin survived the parcel bomb with minimal injuries. Like the other explosive devices it was initially blamed on the usual suspects of the era – anarchists and nihilists. However, the next day Lundin received a postcard with a cryptic message that ended with, 'A former employee of yours has decided that you're ripe for the picking.'[10]

He sent his next bomb a year later to Alfred Valentin. Valentin refused to accept delivery because it still had postage due. It exploded back at the post office, injuring several workers. A third bomb was sent five years later but it was intercepted by the police.[11] The fourth reached the hands of John Hammar, the director of the Swedish Export Society. It tore off his thumb and forefinger. For those with macabre tastes, the thumb now resides in Stockholm's Museum of Police History.

Between 1904 and 1909 Ekenberg seemed to be unravelling financially and mentally, disappointed by the lack of success he felt he deserved. He took out his rage on former business partners. In an attempt to deflect attention from himself he simultaneously addressed letters to Swedish newspapers from a supposed anarchist group. The letters accused one of the victims of abusing his workers and the victim was sentenced to death for his crimes.

Initially the attacks were blamed on Swedish Social Democrats. It was not long before the chemical scientist came under scrutiny. Suspicion arose after Swedish police ran photos of his handwritten letters in the newspapers. Someone recognized his writing and was able to trace him to London. In his residence investigators found the typewriter used for some of the letters. Swedish newspapers had been used for packing the mail bombs and police found a perfect match between a torn-off piece of paper in a bomb and the original newspaper in his house. The bombs had been affixed with a seal that had a distinct stylistic design and was identified by an employee as coming from Ekenberg. Another employee identified some of the bomb parts as coming from his lab in London.[12]

It was clear on his arrest that the scientist was not firing on all cylinders. Newspaper reports described him as suffering from overwork but in any case, he died on 7 February 1910 in London's Brixton Prison while awaiting extradition to Sweden. An autopsy revealed he died from a heart attack. The coroner ruled that his death was from natural causes. Still others believed he committed suicide.

Seeking Attention and Getting Even

Bomb construction by attention seekers and revenge-motivated bombers ranged widely in ingenuity. In most cases they proved nonlethal, that is, if they worked at all. In September 1906 an infernal machine was addressed to Jacob H. Schiff of Kuhn, Loeb & Co. on the floor of the New York Stock Exchange. It was found under a letterbox by a young African American man who turned it over to the mail carrier. It was similar to one mailed to the Stock Exchange office the previous year. The more recent bomb was rigged up in a small tin box while the one sent the previous year was in a wooden box. The wrapped package was intended to be mailed, but to the curious substation superintendent something seemed off and he decided to take a closer look at its contents within the manila wrappings. He slashed a hole in the bottom of the package. Once he saw powder streaming through the hole, he wasted no time covering it with a bucket of water. After soaking it for a while, several inspectors and Secret Service men examined it. It measured about 10 inches long, 4 inches wide and 1½ inches high. On the cover there was fifteen cents' worth of postage stamps arranged quite neatly.

Similar to other bombers from this era, the sender refrained from addressing the package in his own hand. He had clipped Mr Schiff's name from a commercial directory of sorts, and after the name he pasted a slip with the words, 'K, L & Co., floor of New York Stock Exchange, New York'. Trying to link the package to a particular person or group, the postal inspector remembered that a member of the 'Russian Hebrew colony' had called at the Federal building and told him of a secret meeting of a radical section held ten days earlier. At the meeting the speaker roundly denounced Schiff, who had recently arrived from Russia, for allegedly giving secret aid to the Russian tsar during the recent Russo-Japanese War.[13] It just so happened that K, L & Co. had floated the Japanese bond. However, the speaker openly declared that Schiff was in constant correspondence with the tsar's ministers. The Russian antagonist at the meeting made a similar charge against the Rothschild family. In fact, a year earlier, on 18 August 1905, Baron Alphonse de Rothschild was at his summer retreat when his office in New York received a mail bomb. That same day another bomb was sent to M. Guggenheim's Sons & Co. by the same person. Both packages were covered in brown paper and contained an arrangement of matches, powder and bullets. A sliding lid, moving in grooves, was the device intended to explode the powder. Police eventually concluded that the bomb was sent by some crank who had a tough time on Wall Street and wanted to blow up a couple of financiers to get even.

In late November 1906 A. C. Marsh (Burgess of Washington County, Pennsylvania) was targeted by a mail bomb. Despite being carefully packaged and containing three sticks of dynamite fastened together with a wire and attached with a percussion cap, it failed to explode. Local officials thought it might have been sent by the local Black Hand society, which had been active in the Pennsylvania locale after Marsh tried to break it up.[14]

In another inconclusive incident the following year, on 5 September 1907 a package containing a large percussion cap was found at a Philadelphia substation addressed to Secretary of the Treasury George B. Cortelyou. Authorities described it as about 4 inches long, 2 inches wide and ¾ inch thick. The clerk received the package and brought his steel cancellation die down on it, which exploded and shredded the package into pieces. The clerk was unhurt. This device used pieces of paper put together and placed in a package with Cortelyou's address in Washington, DC, cut from a newspaper and pasted on the package. It just so happened that the target's brother was Chief Postal Inspector James B. Cortelyou. The apparent lack of enough explosives to do much harm led authorities to believe it was mailed as a practical joke. However, authorities would not reveal what was inside the package besides the explosive cap.[15]

In 1908 postal authorities intercepted an infernal machine sent to New Jersey governor John Franklin Fort. It contained enough explosives to blow him apart but, fortunately for him, it lacked sufficient postage. Fort authorized the postal service to open the package. It was described as

> an ingenious contrivance of matches, powder, and bullets . . . sealed in such a manner that the greatest caution was necessary in removing the cover . . . The machine was mailed in an ordinary 2-cent government stamped envelope . . . Inside was a second blue envelope on the outside of which was pasted a strip of red paper. The blue envelope contained a tinfoil tube, and one made of paper in which were the explosives. Pasted all over the explosive were any number of inscriptions such as: 'And the gun against this rotten government,' 'Get right with God,' and 'You will know me better after we are acquainted.'. . . All but the first of these, and a number of others had been clipped from newspapers. One was printed in ink on a long thin strip of cardboard, to which was attached a button such as worn on a regular army uniform. There was also a piece of red, white, and blue ribbon. Pasted on one of the tubes were the names of several trusts, including the whiskey, rubber, and tobacco trusts.[16]

That same day Philadelphia postal inspectors investigated another device sent to Fort. It had been mailed on 23 August, the day after the New Jersey governor issued a proclamation regarding the sale of liquor in Atlantic City on Sundays.

The following year a schoolmaster in Prussia on his way to Schillersdorf was stopped by a man who courteously asked him to deliver a letter to Baron Albert Rothschild, who was at his 'hunting

seat' in Silesia. He agreed to do so and after riding some distance
the letter exploded, grievously wounding the schoolteacher.[17] That
same year Ion Hammer, the director of the Swedish Export
Association, was injured by a bomb neatly concealed in a package.
It exploded as the wrapping was being removed in his office.
Although he survived, the explosion blew off the thumb and forefinger of his right hand and painfully gashed his face. The bomb was
delivered with a letter stating that the packet with its very valuable
contents was a gift to him. The inner wrapping around the bomb
was a copy of the Socialist newspaper *Brand*.[18]

The Black Hand Bombs

In the years before Italian-American organized crime became synonymous with the word 'mafia', it was given a handful of other
identifiers, including the *mano nero*, or Black Hand. More like small
gangs or cells of extortionists than any form of organized crime, this
phenomenon popped up in Italian neighbourhoods of several
American urban centres, beginning in the late nineteenth century.
Between 1902 and 1910 a series of 'Black Hand Bombs' exploded in
New York City's Little Italy. Unlike mail and postal bombs, these
bombs were usually made of nitroglycerine, ignited manually and
left out in public places. In some cases dynamite was positioned in
olive oil cans and ignited by a time fuse which the so-called
dynamiter lit, after which they walked away.

By 1906 the Black Hand attained a sinister reputation for its
use of extortion and death threat letters in several American urban
centres. Black Hand gangs typically consisted of six to ten members
operating under one leader. The term 'Black Hand' was by most
accounts introduced by a *New York Herald Tribune* writer in 1906. It
soon became shorthand for 'Italian criminals' (no matter who the
actual malefactors were).[19]

It was not long before religious groups and law enforcement
launched a crusade to get these gangs under control. In the process,
the Black Hand adopted package and mail bombs as a method for
getting their messages across and obtaining extortion payments

from local Italian-American merchants and families. As this scourge continued, in 1909 a Baptist minister targeted Sicilians in sermons raging against the sins of gambling and other vices. The day after one of his sermons a Reverend Robbins received a package from a mail carrier. He opened the package to find a drawing of a human skull on the box inside, a classic Black Hand letter. In place of the usual skull and crossbones the sender had drawn eye sockets with human eyeballs. The letter advised the cleric to end his sermons 'against our employer or you will suffer ... Beware. I hope this will blind you.' As he opened the box it ignited a charge packed with flash powder, exploding and burning his face and hands. Postal investigators linked the bomb to the Society of the Banana (yes, the banana), a business owned by Salvatore 'Sam' Lima outside Columbus, Ohio.[20]

In another related incident that same year, on 20 January Teresa Amicon had just prepared her children for the day's activities when she found a package on the back porch. It was similar to one her brother had received, enclosed in a Pittsburgh newspaper. She shuddered as she unwrapped the package. Inside she found a stick of dynamite and a letter. Teresa sent her son to get her husband, who was working at a warehouse. He read the letter that his wife had avoided reading and after realizing its threatening contents he went to the police.[21]

A New Decade: The 1910s

The 1910s saw an increase in mail bombs, especially in the United States. It would later seem like a harbinger of the deadly anarchist letter bomb campaign that began as the decade ended. In Germany, in December 1911, a formerly wealthy German paper manufacturer named Fredrich Prietzsche was arrested for trying to dynamite a judge and two prosecuting lawyers who had recently convicted him of perjury. On 9 December all three received through the mail, 'as printed matter, bombs 10 inches long, containing 100 grammes of the explosive and brass and lead slugs'. Police were certain that Prietzsche sent them.[22]

On 3 February 1912 Mrs Grace Taylor (aka Walker) was killed by a letter bomb in her New York City flat. A neatly wrapped parcel was delivered to her in the late afternoon. It had passed through the postal system and was left by a letter carrier who rang her doorbell. She went to answer and then hurried back with the package. Pulling the string from the parcel and ripping off the paper, she thought it might have been a box of confectionary. The removal of the string released a spring that detonated the bomb, sending the slugs and iron pieces inside it through the air. The explosion rocked the whole building and Mrs Taylor was killed immediately. Despite several suspects the case went cold until the following year.

The following month an attempt was made to kill New York judge Otto A. Rosalsky with a bomb that missed killing him by a hair's breadth. Like a number of mail bombs in the early twentieth century, it malfunctioned. In this case an accumulation of dirt got into the mechanism of the infernal machine. The bomb came by mail and was delivered by a postman to his apartment in the late afternoon. Rosalsky's maid accepted the delivery and placed it on a table in the judge's library. It didn't immediately seem suspicious. The package measured 6 inches long, 4 inches deep and 4 inches wide, and was neatly done up in yellowish-brown paper wrapping bearing the picture of a well-known department store. The address was typewritten. It was common for mail bombers to use a typewriter or some other method of addressing a label since they knew their handwriting could be recognized by the targets in some cases.

When the judge returned home an hour later, he was speaking with his wife as he began to open the package. Taking off the wrapper revealed a plain white pasteboard box. When he first glimpsed the contents of the box he backed out of the room and yelled to his wife and brother, 'Why, it's a bomb! It's a bomb.' He prevented them from putting it in water and insisted on an expert coming to his lodging, noting that there were some machines that go off when submerged in water. When the veteran bomb expert, Combustibles Inspector Owen Eagan, arrived he decided he couldn't wait and cautiously proceeded to examine the device. 'He took out a little wad of tissue, which [he] believed contained a fulminating substance.' The judge was called out of the room to receive a telephone call and a moment later heard the bomb go off. He rushed into the room and found Inspector Eagan bleeding profusely.[23] The judge's tampering with the device before Eagan got there had near-fatal consequences for the inspector. Eagan had been opening bombs for many years and by 1924 had opened over 7,000 of them. This was the only major physical injury he received during his career, losing his right forefinger in the process.

In a newspaper article written seven years later, looking back on the case, it was explained that, by the time Owen Eagan got his hands on the bomb sent to Rosalsky, either the judge or the police had tampered with it beforehand and upset his usual modus operandi for opening bombs. When the bomb went off in his hand,

> Grains of antimony were blown into his forehead and even into the lid of one eye, leaving queer little lumps that are still [in 1919] perceptible. His face, nose and chest were laid open and still exhibit a filigree of scars.[24]

Besides the loss of his right forefinger he lost all feeling in his thumb. Like the aforementioned Taylor letter bomb this case would not be solved until the following year, when it was connected to Rosalsky's decision in a separate case in which a Folke S. Brandt was sentenced to thirty years in prison for burglary. The cases were linked to the same bomber in what turned out to be one of New York City's most sensational mail bomb cases.

Also in March 1912, three bombs were discovered in Chicago's postal system. Until 1912 mail bombs mostly consisted of some form of explosive concoction. However, in this case Secret Service investigators revealed 'a new kind' of bomb. The three devices did not contain explosives but 'worked with a spring and were intended to blind the recipients with a powdered drug'. One of the bombs included 'a vile letter' addressed to the chief of the Chicago division of the u.s. Department of Justice Charles F. DeWoody, 'Chief of Staff of Hades'. The other two bombs never reached their destinations. The note was signed, 'A worse anarchist than Emma Goldman'.[25]

Not all mail bombs were intended to kill; in fact there are instances when letter bombs were adopted as part of extortion plots. On 19 April 1912 Alexander R. Peacock, a millionaire former partner of Scottish-American industrialist and philanthropist Andrew Carnegie, received a letter wrapped around a bomb threatening him with death unless he agreed to the demand for $5,000 from an unknown blackmailer who signed the letter 'Black Hand'. The bomb was 'a stick of dynamite about 7 inches long'. Attached to it were two percussion caps and two time fuses.[26] The stick of dynamite was 'the largest stick made' and was large enough to destroy the Peacock mansion. Until the extortionist was caught almost ten days later, the Peacock family was assigned police protection.

The perpetrator of this plot proved to be William Pastorius. Born in Ohio, the 24-year-old former student of the universities of Heidelberg and Budapest was described as 'an accomplished musician and law student'. He might have spoken five languages and been 'a clever artist and accomplished musician', but he was maybe not so clever an extortionist. At the time of his arrest he was broke and down on his luck, 'selling gum drops in the city in five languages' and reported to be a frequent attendee at anarchist meetings.

In a letter Peacock was told he would be given details about where to leave the money. Investigators received another letter several days later instructing where the money should be left. The very detailed instructions ended with a warning, 'Do not attempt to have our members arrested who may happen to take the money for us.' The Achilles heel of most extortion, ransom and kidnapping plots in this era was how to exchange the payment without the perpetrator being caught. Following a string of leads detectives arrested him as he stepped off a bridge. On 25 May 1912 he was convicted in a Pittsburgh courtroom of attempted blackmail and sending a bomb to Peacock and sentenced to four to six years in prison doing hard labour. It took a jury only 23 minutes to find him guilty.[27]

1913

The following year, 1913, proved to be the high-water mark of the decade for apolitical mail bombers. The year was marked by a variety of letter bomb cases, many motivated by revenge. Until the end of the decade there was a steady decline in mail bomb cases, especially after the First World War began in 1914 and consumed the attention of the entire world.

One of the more bizarre bombing cases was brought to an unexpected conclusion in 1913 when a New York City clerk named Harry J. Klotz was severely injured while making a bomb in his apartment. Authorities were called to his building, where the mortally wounded clerk confessed to three mail bombings, including two with fatalities, after he was severely injured by what turned out to be a bomb of his own making. He took responsibility for the February 1912 Taylor killing and that of Mrs Madeline Herrera months earlier. Moreover, he confessed to having sent the bomb that exploded in Judge Rosalsky's library.[28] He died just moments later.

Before he succumbed to his injuries, he explained that he had sent the bomb to Rosalsky because 'he didn't like him.' He was especially agitated over his unsuccessful effort to obtain the release of Folke S. Brandt, who was serving a thirty-year sentence for burgling the home of Mortimer Schiff. When asked why he sent one to Grace Taylor, he replied, 'I do not know why; that's all.' Later he admitted he had a quarrel with her. Police believed he was enraged over having been forbidden to enter Mrs Taylor's home after a young woman who had lived with her had rejected his attentions. Pressed for an explanation about the Herrera bomb, he said he sent it 'for experimental purposes', although he never explained what the experiment was. The Klotz family lawyer stated that the account of the dying man's confession was 'preposterous'. No other suspect was ever connected to the bombings.[29]

Years later Inspector Owen Eagan still remembered the craftsmanship of these bombs. He recounted,

> His productions were marvels of the unexpected . . . I still have in my bomb chamber a harmless looking wooden box whose cover bears a very handsome Japanese inlay of pearl design of clasped hands and crossed swords, woven through

these as to be nearly imperceptible is the outline of a skull and crossbones. The eyes of the skull were matches which were ignited by the lifting of the lid. The pearl hilts of the swords were set with matches which acted similarly. There was a minute electric battery connected with the hinges so that if the matches failed the battery would work when contact was made by the cover being laid all the way back. This fellow Klotz was an inventor of the first class.[30]

On 16 September 1913 a 'machine' arrived in the mail at the house of General Harrison Gray Otis filled with enough high explosives to destroy his house. It was similar to a bomb found on his lawn in September 1910, which had been sent at the same time his *Los Angeles Times* newspaper building was destroyed by Ortie McManigle and the McNamaras.[31] Otis sent the machine to the police, who took it to a riverbed where it was buried and exploded, 'tearing a great hole in the riverbed'.[32]

Some mail bombings remained unsolved. One such was a case on 17 June 1913 which Canadian law enforcement described as 'unprecedented'. On that day a simple package was delivered to the home of Alphonse Bilodeau in Sherbrooke, Quebec. It appeared to be made of cardboard, about 6 inches long and 2 inches wide, wrapped in brown paper. Once it was delivered by the postman, Bilodeau's wife opened it in the presence of her sister-in-law. After she removed the outside wrapping 'a blinding flash and explosion' killed her and seriously injured her companion. In an instant their wooden two-storey house was destroyed. Experts believed the infernal machine contained nitroglycerine and nitric acid. Like most of these devices, it was packaged cleverly so that when it was opened the two contents came together, causing the blast. More than twenty years later, journalists continued to revisit this unsolved incident.[33]

In December there were several letter bomb cases that targeted women. On 12 December 1913 Ida Anusewitz was working as a shorthand typist at the O. K. Bottling Company in New York's Bowery. That morning a small pasteboard box was delivered to the business by the Adams Express Company. She briefly laid it aside until she got round to opening all the mail. Once she began her typical opening of letters and parcels she finally came to this package. It would be the last piece of mail she would ever handle. Ida cut the string to open the infernal machine and it exploded as designed, wrecking the office and hurling her to the corner of the room. She died within thirty minutes. It seemed at first that 'because of the peculiar direction of the force of the explosion ... the explosive used was dynamite and it had been set off by connection with a small electric battery.' On further investigation, pieces of glass were found on the floor unlike any used by the bottling business. At this point it was assumed that the explosive was some 'liquid chemical enclosed in a heavy glass retainer and connected with a battery'. Also recovered were 'fragments of fine insulated copper wire' and other debris from the 4-pound package. From the start it was believed that the culprit was a recently discharged worker who was targeting the proprietor of the bottling company. The man who delivered the package to the mail was described by an express employer in the parlance of the day as a 'slouchy Italian, wearing wrinkled clothing, a black slouch hat and a black sweater'. The package was loosely wrapped. The witness said he thought the man was a 'black hander' on first impression. The owner told authorities he did not know of any disgruntled employees. Like so many other cases concerning mail bombs, the case went cold.[34]

The day before Christmas 1913 another infernal machine made its way through the postal system. When it arrived at the home of Mrs Marie Taranto it exploded in her front room, narrowly missing her and her child. Her escape was nothing less than miraculous. She had taken the package at the front door from the postman and initially thought it was a small book. Almost immediately she began tearing off the wrapping like a child opening a Christmas gift. Just prior to the delivery she had 'been beating milk for her child, whom she held in her arms'.[35] The child cried for milk as she opened the package. Fortuitously, she set it down briefly on a parlour table and moved towards the kitchen to fill the baby's bottle. Before she reached the kitchen the house shook as the bomb exploded and wreaked havoc in that part of the house. She had released the 'percussion mechanism when she removed the outer cover'. She escaped injury but the house was severely damaged. Windows were blown out and china ornaments shattered.

Speaking to police after the fact, she told them that she had become suspicious when she saw the handwriting on the wrapper. She suspected it was from her husband, who she had been separated from for two years. A similar package had been sent to her by messenger previously but she had refused delivery.[36] She reasoned that he 'may have tried to kill her with the bomb because she had declined his proposal of reconciliation'.[37]

Further examination of the device led investigators to reconstruct what they thought was an 'outside shell' composed of light wood, octagon-shaped. It was about 6 inches long and 2 inches in diameter. Inside the parcel was a 'varied assortment of wire, nails, tacks, broken bits of glass, tin and various bits of metals'. These ingredients were clearly supposed to act like shrapnel. It was not determined whether the explosive was nitroglycerine or gunpowder. In the infernal machine was a box of matches. The machine was devised so that there would be 'friction against the matches as soon as an attempt [was made] to open the box'. Investigators were unsure whether the bomb was in the letter box or in the parcel post mail. At this time period the penalty for sending an infernal machine through the postal system was a maximum fine of $5,000 or ten years in prison, or both.[38]

The only thing Mrs Taranto was sure of was that the address looked like it was in her husband's handwriting. She said it could have been one of his relatives who were also her 'enemies'. Once her husband heard of the bombing and of the suspicions swirling around him, he turned himself in to the police. He adamantly insisted he had nothing to do with it and was let go by the police.

The First World War Years

In 1914 a Frederick W. Mennerich was killed in Sullivan, Illinois, 'by the explosion of an infernal machine' that he received in the mail. He deduced from the appearance of the parcel that it might be some type of 'explosive apparatus' and initially refrained from opening it.

He wrote to his estranged wife in Springfield about the package. He told her he decided to open it because he knew how to do so without it exploding, if the box contained dynamite. However, the letter was not mailed and was found unsealed in the yard after the explosion. This fact led the sheriff to suspect that he had made the machine himself to cover up his suicide. Mennerich then tried to open the package after deciding 'that his ability as an expert repairman' of some sort would prevent the ignition of the explosive. The dynamite mutilated the repairman and he took two painful hours to die. The couple had been separated for several months and the wife was taken into custody as a witness but later released.[39]

Beginning in 1914 letter bombings declined. One explanation might be that the First World War began in 1914 and until the end of the decade captured the attention of the Western world. Explosives and the new engines of warfare had taken tens of thousands of lives. Compared to the infrequent letter bomb killings that sporadically made the news, tanks, poison gas and mass casualty events seemed more newsworthy and threatening than postal bombs back at home. Perhaps the petty vendettas and relationship squabbles that often led latent bombers to plot revenge by mail were overshadowed by the terrifying nature of modern warfare.

In 1916 there were several letter bombing cases in the western United States. In June a bomb was addressed to Utah's Governor Spry but it exploded as it was being transferred between mail cars near Butte, Montana. The car was completely wrecked. Authorities believed the bomb was sent to the governor in revenge for the recent execution of Joseph Hillström, an active member of Industrial Workers of the World (IWW).[40]

Five months later F. C. Wehmeyer, an orange grower from Porterville, California, found a package in his mailbox containing an infernal machine. Fortunately for him, he was suspicious and turned the package over to the local police. The only motive for such an attack was that there was 'some neighborhood feeling because of Saturday night dances held at his country home'.[41]

Shortly before the end of 1916 Milton A. Morgan was arrested in Portland, Oregon, by postal inspectors for sending a bomb through the mail to a man in Albany, Oregon, named John F. Meisner. There was still debate over his alibi but what was certain was that Morgan had served a stint in the Oregon Penitentiary and while there became friends with another inmate named Otto Hooker. Hooker had escaped from prison and was hiding under Meisner's house. Hooker was shot when Meisner alerted the authorities to his presence.[42]

The first two decades of the twentieth century began with a series of letter bomb cases, many taking place in America. This chapter has provided a sample of some of the most serious and perplexing incidents. Murder by mail was still a rare event outside the Western world, but all that would change in the decades ahead as wars of liberation against colonization broke out in far-flung regions of the globe. However, one of the greatest bombing campaigns of the era took place in the British Isles, where by the 1910s women had been fighting for the right to vote since the late nineteenth century. Indeed, suffragettes were using weaponized mail before groups such as the Irish Republican Army (IRA). The 1910s in Great Britain were marked by a postal bomb campaign by the suffragettes, who experimented with different types of mail bombs between 1913 and 1914. It is these campaigners who are the focus of the next chapter.

3

Suffragette Bombers

M embers of the Women's Social and Political Union (WSPU) in Great Britain were popularly referred to as 'suffragettes'. The organization was founded in 1903 by Emmeline Pankhurst and her daughters with the single goal of gaining votes for women. Its chosen motto was 'deeds, not words', eerily reminiscent of the Russian anarchists of the era (the People's Will) who adopted the 'propaganda by deed' bombing and assassination strategy in the 1880s.[1] The implementation of this slogan was indicative of a call to action, and within two years the WSPU became increasingly militant, targeting both property and people.

There are some scholars who suggest that their bombings and other violent activities were inspired by the Fenian dynamite campaign of 1881–5. But the suffragettes used more sophisticated devices. In some cases they used high-explosive nitroglycerine that was probably produced for them in their own labs by followers.[2]

Emily Wilding Davison

Beginning in 1909 the suffragettes became progressively violent, going as far as committing property damage, ranging from breaking windows in London's West End to setting fire to pillar boxes (free-standing post boxes found on the street). But over the next few years their actions became even more aggressive. In 1911 their violent activities sporadically targeted British civil servants. That same year a suffragette named Emily Wilding Davison (1872–1913) launched several solo attacks in London.[3] She first targeted the postal service in December 1911 when she went to a Fleet Street post office with a specially prepared package containing cloth soaked in kerosene in a paper envelope. She then dropped it through a post office slot and set fire to it. However, it went out quickly. Davison's original method for starting fires in letter boxes proved ineffective due in no small part to the fact that burning kerosene rags tended to die out in enclosed spaces such as a pillar box, using up available oxygen quickly. She was arrested and imprisoned after several arson attacks on pillar boxes.

Once freed she was back at it. On 29 January 1913 Davison was linked to a package addressed to David Lloyd George, minister for munitions during the First World War and future prime minister, which burst into flames in a mail sorting room before it could reach him. Likewise, she placed a device in a sorting box in Croydon around the same time. In this case, the package contained glass tubes filled with phosphorus. While no one was injured it was not as innocent as it seemed since the chemical can cause permanent lung damage.

Terrorism historian Simon Webb dubbed Davison the 'suffragettes' most famous heroine'.[4] She achieved a certain martyrdom in June 1913 when she ran out into the middle of the Epsom Derby horse race and was trampled to death by a horse. There is still a debate over whether it was suicide or just a foolhardy attempt to pin something to the horse or just grab it. As a postscript, the horse's jockey was so haunted he committed suicide years later. Newsreel cameras captured the death of the first suffragette arsonist and bomber.[5]

The First Campaign

Women in Great Britain and Ireland had been fighting for the right to vote since the nineteenth century and by the new century a number of groups were actively promoting their cause. 'From the beginning, the suffragettes were more militant than previous groups. They favoured direct action of a public nature, rather than quietly working behind the scenes, as had been the tactic of the suffragists.'[6] Although British women had campaigned peacefully for suffrage for decades they had little to show for it and turned increasingly militant beginning in 1912–13. In fact the British suffragettes would beat the IRA to the punch when it came to the adoption of letter bombs and other infernal machines. Although they targeted several post office buildings, pillar boxes were more attractive targets since there was less risk or chance of police involvement. Well into 1913 these attacks usually consisted of pouring ink, oil or black varnish through letter slots to make letters and addresses unreadable. But in 1913 they adopted mostly letter bombs.

While the IRA is often credited with introducing terror to the British Isles the first terrorist bomb to explode in Ireland in the twentieth century was planted by suffragettes. Some sources assert that they invented the letter bomb, a postal missive designed to maim or kill those with whom they disagreed. Moreover, 'their combination of high explosive bombs, incendiary devices and letter bombs . . . provided a pattern for IRA campaigns in the 1970s and '80s.'[7]

Few chronicles on terrorism, bomb-making or explosives cover the campaign of the suffragettes in Great Britain between 1913 and 1914. Better known for their hunger strikes and noble goals, some historians have suggested that their violent campaign seemed to 'have been airbrushed from history'.[8]

In July 1912 Christabel Pankhurst 'began organising a secret campaign of arson' that began in November 1912 when post boxes were booby-trapped across England during a five-day-long pillar box sabotage campaign. It involved the pouring of hazardous chemicals into some boxes. In London there were accounts of letters igniting while in transit at post offices, and paraffin and lit matches being placed in pillar boxes.[9]

Between 1912 and 1915, the WSPU left hundreds of bombs on trains and in theatres, post offices, churches and other public sites. Few accounts of terrorism mention their campaign. Over the past century suffragette supporters have tried to 'sanitise their own history' by conveniently taking out references to their violent actions from documents, memorabilia and memoirs.[10] The suffragettes and their accomplices were always experimenting, creating more ingenious methods. For example, moving on from kerosene fires they used phosphorus and sulphuric acid to set off fires which tended to smoulder and then burst forth when the pillar box was opened, or when letters were emptied out of the sack in the sorting office and exposed to air.[11]

Suffragette Bombing Tactics

Unlike their use of explosives and arson in targeted attacks on the offices and homes of prominent British statesmen, the suffragettes' adoption of letter bombs and attacks on postal facilities increased the likelihood of deaths and injuries of innocent working men and women.

According to one historian of the letter bomb, the suffragettes were 'unlike any other mail bombers before or since', since most of their mail bombs were intended to burn in street letter boxes, or pillar boxes.[12] Several suffragettes were hurt by spillage or backfire through letter slots. To alleviate this risk they began sending bombs through the postal system.

Earlier bombs were placed into pillar boxes without any address, but often marked with slogans such as 'Votes for Women'. Occasionally a package was addressed to a particular politician or other official and marked with threatening slogans such as 'Something to go on. Better in Store.' While these types of devices did little physical harm to intended targets, their inherent danger was to the business sector, due in no small part to the fact that suffragette action caused fewer people to use the post during this period. Affecting normal business correspondence, their use 'struck directly at the heart of the mail order trade', disrupting normal invoicing and payments for business while also stifling charities that relied on mail donations.[13]

The suffragettes experimented with different types of mail bombs. Staining bombs were typically letters that were 'open at one end or containing an open tube or bottle of oil, ink, black varnish, or potassium permanganate (stains deep purple)'. In some cases they used a waterproof envelope containing the fluid with one end left open. This was more common during the initial pillar box attacks mentioned above.[14]

During the first half of the 1913 bombing campaign incendiary bombs were added to the arsenal. As letter bomb historian Dale Speirs described them, these were typically 'packets or long envelopes containing one or two test tubes of liquid phosphorus, with no padding to protect them'. These were prone to leaking. The terrorists used paraffin as an incendiary because it did not spontaneously burst into flames as does phosphorus, limiting collateral damage. These bombs burst into flames when the tubes were broken during processing, if not when a postman was emptying a pillar box then while in his mailbag; there was always potential for injury when mailbags were dumped onto sorting tables at the post office, with fires sometimes damaging or destroying letters or burning postal workers.[15]

Other mail bombs included corrosive bombs sent in plastic bags inside ordinary envelopes or a test tube in an unpadded packet. Similar in construction to phosphorus bombs, they contained sulphuric acid or less commonly some other type of corrosive chemical.

Of all the mail bombs that would presage the more deadly era to come, explosive bombs were the rarest and 'not typical of their campaign'. Nonetheless, there were several incidents when a kerosene bomb and a shrapnel parcel bomb were sent to magistrates hearing cases against them.[16] During 1913 the suffragettes ratcheted up their violence by occasionally using explosive devices inside packages packed with nuts and bolts, designed for maximum damage. During the Belfast Troubles in the 1970s the IRA used a similar method of bomb preparation dubbed 'Belfast confetti'.[17]

A Reign of Terror

On 5 February 1913 four postal workers were seriously burned in Dundee, Scotland, as they emptied mailbags in the sorting office. Some of the hazardous mail was addressed to Prime Minister Herbert Asquith and contained phosphorus and other chemicals.

When exposed to air they would burst into flames. The attacks continued through the month. On 18 February a bomb exploded in a house under construction for Lloyd George. Other attacks followed on wood yards and empty buildings. Several days later another postman was burned at a South London post office when a letter he was handling suddenly caught fire.[18]

Emmeline Pankhurst accepted the blame for the Lloyd George bombing and on 13 April 1913 was sent to prison for three years, leading members of the WSPU to promise a 'reign of terror' that 'would stagger humanity'.[19] This was not an idle threat. One thing was clear: the suffragettes were rarely lacking for bomb-making materials and seemed to have a ready supply of explosives, gunpowder and nitroglycerine. Soon after Pankhurst's incarceration, postal staff at London's Borough High Street office were sorting parcels on 5 May when one caught their attention because it was 'so heavy and rattled curiously when shaken'.[20] At this point postal employees were on the lookout for any type of infernal device. Workers took the package to a police station, where officers discovered a substantial quantity of gunpowder and lead shot along with a tube of nitro.

On 6 May 1913 a bomb containing enough nitroglycerine to blow up a London newspaper office was found among the packages collected by the parcel post service at the southeastern district post office. The metallic clink of the parcel aroused suspicion among the employees, several hundred of whom were on duty at the time. The package was plunged into water and the police, who were called, opened it and found it filled with gunpowder, a quantity of slugs and a tube of nitroglycerine. Police suspected it was suffragettes. One official branded them as 'irresponsible lunatics who are carrying on the militant movement'.[21]

The following day another package bomb was uncovered in London at St Paul's Cathedral when a church caretaker traced the source of a loud ticking sound to a brown paper parcel placed under a choir chair. He plunged it into a bucket of water and called the police. Once opened it was found to be a bomb consisting of a charge of dynamite attached to an ingenious timing mechanism made from a cheap wristwatch and a battery.[22] Set to explode at midnight, the circuit failed to detonate the device after the soldering on one of the terminals came loose. Police would describe it as 'small, fiendishly powerful'. Most of the parts required for manufacturing a bomb were easy to obtain without drawing suspicion. Watch batteries and various containers were everyday items. The most common explosive charge used by suffragettes was gunpowder, which 'has relatively low explosive power' and 'can be accentuated under compression'.[23]

While the suffragettes were quite keen on planting bombs, most did not explode, explaining the lack of fatalities and serious injuries. Since the 1860s nitroglycerine had been used in the form of dynamite, the explosive substance absorbed by a porous clay called kieselguhr. Nitro was easy to manufacture at home or in the lab as long the process and proportions of ingredients were correct. Otherwise it would result in a manufacturing explosion.[24]

On 14 May 1913 the suffragettes tried to assassinate barrister and Conservative politician Sir Henry Curtis-Bennett with a parcel bomb. His staff suspected the package almost immediately when it arrived at his Bow Street office. Inside, police found an

ingenious letter bomb – a tin full of gunpowder with a round of ammo attached so that it pointed to an explosive charge. A nail was held in place over this, with the point resting on a percussion cap of cartridge. Just a sharp tap would detonate it.[25]

Between 1913 and 1914 there was at least one suffragette-instigated bombing every month across the UK. By some accounts there were a total of 337 arson and bomb attacks during this period. The researcher C. J. Bearman counted 21 bombing and arson attacks per month in 1913.[26]

Bombings and arson continued through to the end of 1913. On 19 July six letter box fires were reported in Birmingham. A postman suffered serious burns on his hand while clearing a postbag and coming into contact with acid that had been poured over letters.

Besides using acids as incendiary agents, suffragettes began pouring sulphuric acid or spirits of salt (hydrochloric acid) into boxes to destroy letters. On 22 December 1913 mailbags in Nottingham caught fire, burning several workers.

In 1914 there was a further escalation of violence as dangerous chemicals and explosives were sent through the post to politicians, including Prime Minister Herbert Asquith. Since Pankhurst's call to arms in January 1913 pillar boxes had been seen as easy and accessible targets. These attacks were more a nuisance than danger. Nonetheless, their numbers were considerable. Between June 1913 and April 1914 five hundred post boxes in the London area were attacked with chemicals or explosives.[27]

Historian Simon Webb suggests that the use of letter bombs as a terrorist weapon marked 'the beginning of the present practice whereby the mail of politicians is routinely screened for suspicious packages. Most of these were crude devices, little more than glorified fireworks with primitive fuses made from matches.'[28] But the intention to injure the recipient was unmistakable.

Another tactic involved sending containers of sulphuric acid through the post to those thought to be opposed to the extension of voting to women. One package addressed to the prime minister broke open at a sorting office, injuring four members of staff when they were splashed with acid. Likewise a mail carrier in Fulham, London, was out of work for a fortnight with acid burns as a result of another incident.[29]

As the bombings and acts of vandalism mounted, more of the victims were postal employees just doing their jobs. Occasionally incendiaries ignited while mail was being transported by letter carrier or mail van. Bomb attacks and arson continued through July 1914. On 12 July a bomb exploded in a mailbag on a train travelling between Blackpool and Manchester. The suffragettes became more adept at bomb-making as time wore on. One of their standard methods was sending letter bombs made from phosphorus through the post. It was assumed they were responsible for several fires in mail vans, sometimes setting the wooden carriage of the train alight. In July 1914, as a train passed through the Lancashire village of

Salwick, postal workers were sorting letters in a mail van when the mailbag exploded, starting a fire, and the side of the wooden carriage began to burn. Someone was alert enough to throw the bag from the train. Investigation revealed that a package in the burned mailbags had contained a bottle of sulphuric acid and a quantity of magnesium which apparently broke and started the fire.

The Last Bombs

The last recorded suffragette bomb attacks took place on 1 August 1914 outside Christ Church Cathedral in Lisburn (now in Northern Ireland), damaging stained glass and masonry on what turned out to be the same day Germany declared war on Russia. Two days later Germany attacked France and Belgium and on 4 August Britain declared war on Germany. It was at this point that Pankhurst ordered a suspension of the suffragettes' bombing campaign, which coincided with a general amnesty given to imprisoned suffragettes. One historian claimed the letter bomb campaign in part provided inspiration for the IRA's future bombing and terrorist campaigns in Britain, including the S-Plan of 1939–40 which used incendiary attacks on pillar boxes and planting of devices.[30]

To the detriment of the cause, the Pankhursts seemingly specifically sanctioned attacks on postal workers. Acts that targeted pillar boxes and post offices were viewed as cowardly attacks on working men who, like the suffragettes, did not have the parliamentary vote yet since they were not members of the establishment, just ordinary workers in routine menial jobs.[31] Ultimately, once the suffragettes turned to violence and innocent citizens were victimized it actually harmed their cause, perhaps even setting back their goal by more than a decade.

In one 2005 study C. J. Bearman found that their bombings and arson attacks were more numerous than previously accepted, and the economic costs for the destruction even higher.[32] In 1918 women in the UK were granted the right to vote, but only in Parliamentary elections, part of a growing trend that saw many countries extend the right to vote to women.[33] It was not until the passage of the

Equal Franchise Act of 1928 that British women achieved the same voting rights as men in elections.

Were the suffragettes of 1913–14 terrorists? Most of their violent activities would fit the modern definition although there was no legislation against terrorism at the time. Moreover, their campaign would be considered single-issue terrorism, like eco-terrorists and abortion clinic bombers today. Most of the charges fell under the rubric of the Malice Damage Act of 1861. With their frequent use of explosive devices and dangerous chemicals it is a miracle they didn't kill anyone. However, their actions were merely a harbinger of the bloodshed yet to come.

4

May Day and the Nationwide Package Bomb Plot

etween 1919 and 1920 a national hysteria over political radical-
ism led various American states to introduce laws that
surpassed the federal government's suppression of non-
conforming and perceived threatening behaviours. Prior to 1919
several states had such legislation on their statute books targeting criminal anarchy. As early as 1902, in the wake of President
William McKinley's assassination the previous year, at least one u.s.
state had passed a criminal anarchy law. Other states followed suit.
Midwestern and western states, including Idaho, Minnesota,
Montana and South Dakota, enacted similar legislation to facilitate
the prosecution of Industrial Workers of the World (iww, or
Wobblies) members.[1]

The fear of anarchism spread in the United States and abroad in
the late nineteenth century. Anarchists supported the creation of
cooperative societies without any centralized government. Some
turned to violence and terrorism. The most successful anarchist
campaigns were carried out in Russia in the years leading to the
Bolshevik Revolution. American anarchism was linked to labour
violence and the legions of impoverished European immigrants
who felt oppressed by nativist American elites.

Newspapers inflamed public opinion by branding anarchists as
'dynamarchists' and 'bomb throwers'. From then on, the word
'anarchist' became synonymous with communism, terrorism and
dynamite.[2] Likewise after the May Day mass mail bomb attacks
in 1919, which we will go on to discuss, newspapers referred to
the plotters with such sobriquets as 'dynamitards' and 'human
vermin'.[3] The anarchist (Galleanist) newspaper *Cronaca Sovversiva*

(Subversive Chronicle) went even further, launching an avalanche of invective at its foes, cataloguing them

> as bandits, pirates, mercenaries, mobsters, above the law bigshots, systematic scammers, hypocrites, charlatans, thieves, criminals, blackmailers, murderers, sewer trash, Pharisees, bible thumpers, shameless conmen, spies, imposters, thugs, fetid carcasses, assassins, butchers, slave drivers, scabs, pigs, cows, pygmies, sheep, fools, idlers, vultures, shrews, proselytizing neophytes, tyrants, and on and on.[4]

The Galleanists

Perhaps no radical group in America was more associated with bombing during the early twentieth century than the Galleanists, named after the movement's leader, Luigi Galleani (1861–1931). Born in Italy, he arrived in America shortly before the 1901 assassination of President McKinley. Beforehand he had agitated for anarchist objectives in Italy, France and Switzerland. According to a leading authority on the group his arrival 'would change the dynamics of anarchist terrorism' in the United States.[5]

The Galleanists can best be described as a decentralized political action group with independent cells operating throughout much of the Western world. Their leader advocated the use of dynamite and assassination to overthrow governments and capitalism. In the early 1900s he published a bomb manual 'calling for vengeance against tyrants, enemies of the people'. He had adapted an earlier version of a guide to explosives that a chemist friend had previously compiled. The group's bombings began in 1914 and culminated with the May Day 1919 bombing plot. As the threat of deportation loomed large the Galleanists resorted to a new way of delivering bombs, combining their expertise in making bombs with dispatching them through the postal system. Knowing full well that authorities typically staked out traditional bomb targets such as police stations, churches, courthouses and so forth, it was thought that the subterfuge of using the postal system offered a safer delivery system. The May 1919 plot was probably most influenced by the German anarchist Johann Most (1846–1906), who had been in America since 1882. He became an advocate of using dynamite in the pursuit of anarchist objectives. He, along with other likeminded extremists, sought to upend capitalism and the state through a series of fatal blows. In doing so he 'helped transform the neutral substance of dynamite into a great political symbol, shorthand for the vengeance of an aggrieved immigrant working class'.[6] In time Most would become recognized as a leading proponent of 'Propaganda by Deed', or, in his words, 'Shoot, burn, stab, poison and bomb'.[7]

The package bombs were all posted between 22 and 26 April 1919 with the intention that their arrival would coincide with 1 May, a date synonymous with working-class camaraderie. It was also meant to memorialize Chicago's bloody Haymarket Square bombing on 4 May 1886, which saw anarchists and others stage a rally in favour of the eight-hour working day. An unknown anarchist then threw a bomb into a crowd of Chicago policemen on Haymarket Square, killing seven of them. According to one historian, after the bombing a 'reign of terror swept over Chicago'.[8] In any case, 1 May, or May Day, was designated as a day in support of workers by an international federation of socialist groups and trade unions.

Authorities were confident that the motive behind the plot was 'three fold in scope', according to one reporter for the *New York Times*. This theory is substantiated by the fact that all the bombs were sent to officials heavily involved in the deportation of several radical agitators in the West. So, in effect, the devices were aimed against enforcement of deportation provisions of immigration laws. Moreover, there was an increasing prospect of the passage of these provisions by the next Congress and further restrictions on immigration.[9]

The Package Bomb Plot

If the May 1919 plot was to succeed as planned, it was imperative that all of the bombs arrived at their destinations at the same time.

It would only take one parcel to arrive early for authorities to issue an alert and probably intercept the rest. And this indeed is what happened. There is only a rough consensus on the actual number of bombs with some accounts ranging as high as 36 and others as low as 22. But what is not in doubt was when the first bomb arrived. They were all supposed to arrive on 1 May. Anyone who has been reliant on the vicissitudes of mail services past and present would probably not be surprised at how this went. On 28 April 1919 a bomb sent from New York City to Seattle's mayor Ole Hanson arrived at his office. Fortuitously for him he was out of state on a speaking engagement. He had attained some national prominence recently for opposing a general strike in Seattle and evidently that was enough to put him on the anarchist hit list. A member of his staff removed the brown paper covering the parcel and found the cardboard box wrapped in green paper. Opening the cardboard box from the top should have loosened a coil spring, causing the acid to leak and detonate the explosives. However, the aide opened the box from the wrong end. As a result, the bottle of acid dropped out intact on the table and did not trigger the fulminating caps. Police said that the bomb had sufficient power to blow out the entire side of the building.[10]

This failed attack was followed by a much more serious incident in the u.s. state of Georgia the following day. On 29 April a package arrived at the Atlanta home of ex-u.s. senator Thomas Hardwick, who was not there at the time. His main offence in the minds of the anarchists was in co-sponsoring the anti-radical Immigration Act of 1918, which made the deportation of anarchists possible. Hardwick's housekeeper opened the package and both of her hands were blown off. Mrs Hardwick was nearby and suffered burns to her face and neck. Several of her teeth were loosened and a piece of shrapnel cut her lip.

Just as the Galleanists feared, these mistimed arrivals alerted postal authorities and put a significant dent in the nefarious plan. On 30 April New York City postal worker Charles Kaplan came across a newspaper description of the first bomb. It dawned on him that there were sixteen exact replicas waiting for first-class postage.

They were being held in the short payment department on the main floor of the post office, and had not yet been delivered because of insufficient postage. Kaplan remembered they had all been addressed to various political and business world luminaries. Each weighed 6 ounces and had small red seals closing the ends of the wrapping. At three cents an ounce, each should have had eighteen cents of postage, but none had more than six cents.[11] His diligence and that of other postal employees probably saved many lives. Police investigators found that these were identical to the ones sent to Seattle and Atlanta.[12] Savvy postal inspectors were alerted across the United States and were able to intercept several others, although some arrived at destinations but were not opened by the targets, who had learned of the scheme through news accounts. Meanwhile, fourteen mail bombs were held up at post offices on the West Coast.[13]

There was no shortage of suspects during the 1919 letter bomb campaign. Between the agitators of the iww in Western states, especially where miners were struggling against mine owners, and the Galleanists, the postal service was overwhelmed with tracking package bombs and the like. The whole country was on edge after more than thirty mail bombs were either intercepted or arrived at destinations in late 1919. They were addressed to some of the most prominent people in America. One investigator labelled the bombs as 'booby trap dynamite filled bombs'. Another observer suggested that 'all evidence points to the alien anarchist element of New York City as the agents of the plan.'[14]

The targeting of so many high-ranking officials meant that the scale of the May Day plot was unprecedented. Each bomb was 'wrapped in brown paper with similar address and advertising labels'. Inside each package,

wrapped in bright green paper and stamped 'Gimbel Brothers – Novelty Samples', was a cardboard box containing a six-inch by three-inch block of hollowed wood about one-inch in thickness, packed with a stick of dynamite. In addition, the words 'NOVELTY' and 'SAMPLE' were

Theodore G. Bilbo, Mississippi governor	Albert Johnson, Washington congressman
Frederick Bullmers, editor of *Jackson Daily News*, MS	William H. King, Utah senator
Albert S. Burleson, Postmaster General	William H. Lamar, solicitor of the Post Office Department
John L. Burnett, Alabama congressman	J. P. Morgan, financier
Anthony Caminetti, Commissioner General of Immigration	Kenesaw Mountain Landis, U.S. district judge, Chicago
Edward A. Cunha, San Francisco assistant district attorney	Frank K. Nebeker, special assistant to the Attorney General
Richard E. Enright, New York City police commissioner	Lee S. Overman, North Carolina senator
T. Larry Eyre, Pennsylvania senator	A. Mitchell Palmer, U.S. Attorney General
Charles M. Fickert, San Francisco district attorney	John D. Rockefeller, industrialist
R. W. Finch, special agent, Bureau of Investigation	William I. Schaffer, Pennsylvania Attorney General
Ole Hanson, Seattle mayor	Walter Scott, Mississippi mayor
Thomas W. Hardwick, former Georgia senator	Reed Smoot, Utah senator
Oliver Wendell Holmes Jr, U.S. Supreme Court associate justice	William C. Sproul, Pennsylvania governor
Frederic C. Howe, Commissioner General of Immigration, Port of NY (Ellis Island)	William B. Wilson, Secretary of Labor
John F. Hylan, New York City mayor	William M. Wood, president of the American Woolen Company

stamped in red letters on separate areas of the packages. Next to the typed name of the addressee was an emblem of a mountain climber with a pack on his back and an alpenstock in his hand. A small vial of sulfuric acid was fastened to the wood block, along with three fulminate-of-mercury-blasting caps.[16]

If a recipient opened the end of the box marked 'open' it 'would release a coil spring that caused the acid to drip from its vial onto the blasting caps; the acid ate through the caps, igniting them and detonating the dynamite.'[17] Once the acid was released and the fulminate of mercury caps ignited, the bomb detonated, sending shrapnel from metal slugs contained within the cylinder in every direction.

It did not take long before authorities linked the bombs to the Galleanists, the most active Italian anarchist group at this time. This group was considered the 'first to introduce the use of package bombs on a wide scale' and was the first to detonate a 'vehicle bomb in the United States in the form of a horse and wagon'.[18] The core group of anarchists was no more than sixty people. As the two bombings made banner headlines across the country, the Galleanists were wondering what happened to the other bombs.

The *New York Tribune* offered a begrudging admiration for the May Day package bombs in an editorial, describing the expertise of the bomb-makers as 'ingenious, almost too ingenious'. The editorial described the bomb-makers as 'clever mechanics, clever chemists, persons with certain demonic carefulness, neatness, almost artistry' exemplified by 'that polished, hard, basswood, carved cylinder in the bright green cardboard box' that testified to 'skillful and patient labor'.[19] Echoing the editorial in the *Tribune*, the New York *Evening World* published a diagram of a bomb and marvelled at its craftsmanship. Postal inspectors declared that the 'workmanship was so exquisite and expert as to suggest the craft of an Oriental . . . the very model of neatness.' The description of the bomb was well documented with newspaper articles noting 'the greenish cartons, stamped with small figures, the cylindrical wooden containers, made especially for the purpose, turned on a lathe and polished with varnish until they had taken on the mirror like polish of mahogany'.[20]

The Bombs and the Bomb Expert

When Charles Kaplan discovered the sixteen bombs in New York City's post office basement, both he and the night-time superintendent immediately knew who to call – Owen Eagan of the Bureau of Combustibles at the New York City Fire Department. Over a 24-year period the 62-year-old had opened at least 7,000 bombs of all sizes. Only two exploded during that time, with the only permanent damage to himself being the loss of his right forefinger and permanent damage to a thumb (during the Rosalsky case, discussed earlier).

Eagan gave the most comprehensive description of the bombs in a newspaper interview with the *New York Herald* on 10 May. After finally getting to see the first of the sixteen bombs now being held, he opened the one addressed to Postmaster General Burleson. The bomb was described as

> a neat affair enclosed in a pasteboard box about the size of a *Uneeda* biscuit holder, and that the box was covered by yellow-white wrapping paper sealed with little red seals and bearing the fraudulent label, 'Gimbel Brothers' and that inside the pasteboard carton was a lacquered and tightly capped wooden tube containing a small vial of acid, 3 fulminate-of-mercury detonating caps and a 'mush' of dynamite which has been nitrated to make the mixture more powerful.[21]

Once Eagan had removed the package to another room for safety he soaked it in a pail of water for twenty minutes. This allowed the red seals to peel off and 'the gum with which the wrapper was edged softened and permitted the edges of the paper to roll up. Gently and slowly running his thumbs along the loosened edges he detached the wrapper and exposed the pasteboard container.' Back went the parcel into the pail of water for another half an hour, enough time to loosen the opening end of the carton. Barely touching this end, Eagan 'lifted the pasteboard flaps and then skinned the carton away from the wooden tube, much as one would skin a rabbit'. Now for the real job.

> The wooden tube was naked and accessible . . . he could see one end was capped with a wooden top which fitted very snugly and was meant to be loosened and removed by twisting. He did not twist . . . He decided to take a safer approach to opening it and over two hours loosened the wood cap enough to permit lifting it off the tube. There stood exposed a small vial, its corked neck even with the top of the tube, its base set in putty.

Two brass screws were revealed,

> one on each side of the frail vial and so arranged that they would have fractured the bottle had any attempt been made to twist off the wooden cap. He detached the screws one at a time, first loosening them at the base with a knife and then drawing them straight away, horizontally from the tube. With the vial out, crystals of chlorate of potash and the fulminate of mercury caps were exposed in their cotton packing, and it was a simple matter to detach these and come upon dynamite mush with which the bottom of the tube was packed.[22]

Several months later Eagan concluded that the bombs were all similar in composition, describing them as 'composite bombs of the nitroglycerine, alkaline, metallic, chlorate type, manually, mechanically, and chemically ignited'. He was confident that whoever concocted these devices was 'a trained, experienced expert, who knew explosives and the psychology of his victims'.[23]

Eagan, a well-respected authority on infernal machines, 'expressed astonishment at the ingenuity of the contrivances'. He went further, commenting:

It does not resemble any machine I have ever come across. It is the neatest and from the standpoint of mechanical arrangement, the cleverest I have ever seen. Whoever perfected the thing must have been an expert mechanic and chemist.[24]

The Investigation

The precursor to the Federal Bureau of Investigation (FBI), the Bureau of Investigation (BOI), was handed the task of detecting weaponized mail sent to government officials and private citizens. Indeed, on 28 April 1919 the BOI at the Department of Justice was given 'an entirely new field of operations'.[25] The demand for bomb investigators was predicted in September 1918 after a bomb exploded in a federal building in Chicago, killing four. With BOI offices in the building it was assumed to be the work of the IWW getting back at the government for a recent trial of IWW leaders who were housed in the building waiting to be released on bail. However, like so many other bombing campaigns, including that of the Galleanists, it backfired. The leaders remained behind bars. Following this bombing the task of detection was shared by the two federal detective forces, the BOI and the Post Office Department's investigators. On 1 August 1919 J. Edgar Hoover became the first chief of the BOI anti-radical division. The bombings so alarmed the public that the news press pushed the government into action. Congress was quick to respond, with Senator King of Utah preparing a bill making it a federal crime to send mail or package bombs between states or belong to an organization supporting the overthrow of the government.

On 1 May 1919 the Washington, DC, *Evening Star* published a photo of one of the mail bombs under the headline, 'Man Who Uncovered Bomb Plot, and Views of the Death Dealing Device'. On the same page under another headline it described anarchists being hunted down as the May Day plot failed to gain victims. Law enforcement was kept busy with the time-consuming job of combing Bertillon cards – identification cards used by police, on which were photos, measurements and fingerprints of known criminals – for fingerprints. Meanwhile, detectives were sent out to canvass the paper trade, hoping to narrow the source of the wrappers of the bombs to just a few businesses. Likewise, police in all precincts were tasked with making enquiries of dealers in glassware, wooden tubes and cardboard boxes, trying to come up with matches for the bomb parts. In addition, a closer inspection was made of the wooden boxes that held the explosives and fulminate caps to ascertain whether they had been store-bought. As to who the bombers represented, one police chief did not think the iww was involved since they had 'too much to lose'. He believed, incorrectly, that the bombs were the work of some 'crank, for the sender lacks cunning', since whoever sent them 'was not smart enough to use a wrapper or to make sure the postage was sufficient'.[26]

However, naval intelligence officers were not so sure it was a mere crank. The New York Police Department was informed by the intelligence service that the bombs 'showed a startling resemblance in operation and principle to a type of German mine found by the Navy off the coast'. Moreover, there was a definite plan to have them all arrive on 1 May. The crank hypothesis was quickly put to rest. Ultimately, the package bomb plot was as unsuccessful as the hunt for the perpetrators: 'the combined police forces of the nation failed once again to trace the origin of a single bomb.'[27]

The nationwide package bomb plot of April 1919 has been considered one of the 'most ambitious terrorist plots in history'.[28] Moreover, terrorism historian Jeffrey D. Simon suggested that 'Terrorists had demonstrated an ability to launch a coordinated nationwide attack by using what had previously been considered a safe and reliable means of communication – the postal system.'[29] The *New York Times* called it 'the most widespread assassination conspiracy in the history of the country'.[30]

In many respects the 1919 anarchist mail bomb plot was ground-breaking. Mail bombs were not new, as previous chapters have demonstrated. But in this case the Galleanists introduced the new tactic of sending out a multitude of bombs to many targeted luminaries at one time. Banner headlines across America chronicled this newfound strategy. May Day 1919 introduced this tactic on a grand scale and proved a harbinger for the mass mail bomb campaigns to come.

5

The Roaring Twenties

After the May Day letter bomb campaign, as the 1920s began it was hoped that the threat of weaponized mail had receded for the time being. But political extremists began to experiment with more powerful explosive devices, avoiding the postal system altogether in order to maximize terror. The future beckoned on 16 September 1920 when a bomb detonated in a horse-drawn carriage in front of the banker J. P. Morgan's office on Wall Street.[1] At least 38 people were killed and dozens injured in the deadliest terrorist attack in American history prior to the Oklahoma City bombing in 1995 that took 168 lives. The explosion was so powerful that an automobile was blown 20 feet into the air. One of Morgan's bank clerks was beheaded by the blast. Initially, Secret Service chief William J. Flynn assumed the Wall Street bomb was directed at J. P. Morgan because he had been targeted the year before by a mail bomb and he was considered one of the stalwarts of American capitalism. Flynn eventually concluded it was actually targeting the financial heart of American society rather than specific individuals.

The Secret Service chief based his conclusions on his intuition that the bombing was connected to the perpetrators of the May Day plot the previous year. The department received five circulars signed 'American Anarchist Fighters', which were found in a mailbox. These 'furnished the first tangible clue' of who was behind the attack. The circulars were printed on the same type of cheap paper used to wrap bombs sent the previous June and signed 'Anarchist Fighters'. Flynn surmised there was a 'striking similarity between the circulars found after the nationwide bomb plot in 1919 and those found in the mail box'.[2] The detective agency head and soon-to-be chief of the BOI William J. Burns saw these devices as a resumption of the 1919 mail bomb plot from the previous summer. He believed the 1920 bombing was by the same organization but 'instead of repeating their former tactics, they just made bigger bombs.'[3]

The fear of exploding packages receded in the 1920s as radical groups adopted other strategies. However, letter bomb attacks continued, with most related to personal vendettas, revenge and extortion. For example, on 15 March 1921 in a small town in Maine a wealthy physician by the name of Dr John L. Pepper was seriously maimed by an infernal device delivered to his office. The dynamite bomb blew off his right hand, shattered fingers on his left and lacerated his face. He was critically injured and delivered to a hospital 6 miles away. The bomb wrecked his office – windows blown out, walls stripped of plaster and furniture destroyed. Investigators traced the device to a post office in a town across the Kennebec River from Madison. It had sat in the post office overnight. After the package was delivered it exploded in the doctor's office just after 11 a.m.

A postal employee remembered the package and described it as being 14 inches long, 3 inches wide and 6 inches deep. It was wrapped in brown paper and was heavy. It carried fifteen cents in stamps, more than enough to pay for its delivery; however, it was not mailed as parcel post for there was no return address of the sender, as would have been required under parcel post regulations. The source of the bomb was a mystery.[4]

The Yule Bomb Outrage – John Magnuson Case, December 1922

By the 1920s postal bomb investigators had a much better understanding of package bomb construction and components. However, the bombers' motivations still perplexed them since they came in all manner of contexts – personal vendettas, revenge and extortion, politics and many other reasons. In July 1922 'a parcel purported to contain sardines' was actually an infernal machine sent to a socialist advocate. In the absence of the target his secretary opened the parcel and 'was blown to pieces, while the socialist's wife and child were badly injured'.[5]

The case of John Magnuson and a feud between farmers in December 1922 offers a lesson in improved investigation tactics. Investigators used ink, wood, metal and handwriting experts to make a strong case. On 30 December John Magnuson and his eighteen-year-old son were arrested in connection with a dynamite bomb that exploded and killed Mrs James A. Chapman, wife of the chairman of the County Board of Supervisors. The deadly parcel had the appearance of a Christmas package and when Mr Chapman hastened to cut the strings and unwrap it, the bomb exploded. She died from her injuries on 27 December following the blast at her home in Cameron, Wisconsin. Her husband was seriously injured, losing his left hand as he opened the mail bomb. A property dispute ultimately led to the deadly affair. Chapman had sponsored a drainage ditch project and Magnuson was among the farmers adamantly opposed to it. A dredge that had been associated with digging the ditch was destroyed, followed by the torching of a farmer's barn. The bombing was the culmination of the feud between the factions.[6]

The mail carrier remembered picking up the parcel on 26 December from one of the boxes on his route. In fact, he remembered the exact box where he picked it up, not far from where a dredge had been blown up the previous year. Initially there were several theories about the provenance of the bomb parcel. However, once picric acid was detected it narrowed the list of probable suspects down to members of the farming community. Picric acid was a common material used throughout the county because of its efficacy as a land-clearing explosive. Before the dredge reached Magnuson's property it was blown up – Magnuson was known to have threatened Chapman over the project, telling him it would never cross his property. He was arrested three days later. A subsequent search of his property uncovered TNT, iron filings and shavings of wood similar to that used in the bomb. The bomb's trigger was held back by the string that, when untied or cut, discharged the explosive. Handwriting often played an important role in solving mail bomb cases. At Magnuson's trial experts testified that the handwriting on the bomb wrapping and samples of his handwriting were identical. Other specialists helped build the case against the bomber. Metalographists from the University of Wisconsin testified that the metal parts of the bomb and metal filings found in Magnuson's shed were from the same source, explaining that heat and pressure in the rolling mills differ and that metal from the same piece is easy to identify. Building the case, a noted wood expert opined that the bomb jacket and shavings found at the farm were the same, made from swamp oak. It didn't help Magnuson's case that he had previously denied having any of this wood on his property. Finally, ink experts testified that the ink used in addressing the bomb and the ink found in fountain pens at his residence were identical, easily distinguished because foreign matter had been added to it. In May 1923 Magnuson was found guilty of first-degree murder.[7]

'To Open Pull Knob'

Around the same time as the Magnuson affair, on the other side of the Atlantic, Scotland Yard was maintaining secrecy as best it could after a third postal bomb showed up in London. Harking back to the 1712 attempt to kill a Tory official who was meeting with Jonathan Swift, 'a parcel containing a loaded revolver' was posted at the Coburn Road Post Office to 74-year-old Miss Childs. She was the daughter of Mr Thomas Childs, who received the first 'death trap parcel' on 11 February 1923, the day before his daughter received hers. The small wooden box contained a revolver plugged in such a way that it would go off upon opening the lid. It had been placed on the floor of a waiting van for delivery. A loud explosion rent the air and a bullet hole was found in the sack in which the parcel had been positioned with other mail. No one was hurt and the rest of the parcels were undamaged.

Investigators examining what was left of the mail sack detected the presence of a mysterious parcel which was similar to the previous parcel sent to Mr Childs. The package was wrapped in brown paper and addressed in block letters. A bomb protruded from the box and on the lid were the words 'To open pull knob'. The postal office clerk who received the parcel was able to give a description of the individual who handed it in. Inside the box was the mechanism of a revolver, the barrel of which had been plugged and a string attached to the trigger so when the knob was pulled the weapon fired in the direction of the knob.[8] Official pictures of the device revealed the ingenious method of construction, apparently modelled on infernal machines that were frequently discovered in the dugouts and trenches vacated by Germans in the First World War.

In 1924 Grand Rapids Police asked the Detroit Italian Squad to assist in determining the author of a Black Hand letter demanding $5,000, received on 11 November 1924 by Samuel Baucina, an East End fruit dealer. The letter had threatened the lives of the Baucina family if they did not pay the extortion money. Federal agents investigating the explosion in a post office the following day, which killed three and wounded twelve, believed the parcel had also been intended for Baucina.[9] Law enforcement began scouring the Italian section of Grand Rapids almost immediately in an attempt to locate the source of the bomb.

The following month, shortly before Christmas, a bomb exploded and blew off the left hand of Ernest M. Torchia in Glendale, California. The only evidence remaining was small bits of wrapping paper. Further examination of the bomb site revealed that a small explosive device was placed in a phial, which had been exploded by a percussion cap or by contact with a spark from a battery. Parts of it including bits of carbon and a piece of zinc were found in the woodwork of the room. The container was described as a 'two-pound box, the edges of which were dovetailed'.[10]

Midway through the 1920s an individual attempted to recover money which he believed he had been defrauded of. Walter W. Graebner of Philadelphia confessed to sending bombs and close to one hundred threatening letters to his former defence counsel. The bombs were powerful enough to wreck a post office building and were described as ingenious, and strong enough to blow a train off the tracks if one exploded in a mail car.[11]

'Turn Here for One Cigar'

A trade war and conflict over patents led to the arrest of John T. Peterson, president of the Combination Blow Torch Manufacturing Company, after he was picked up in connection with sending a bomb through the mail. The device contained enough explosives to destroy the plant of the Everhot Manufacturing Company, located in a Chicago suburb. The bomb had been sent to Everhot sales manager A. C. Flotow, who reported that the week before he had received a letter signed by R. M. Guidano telling him to look out for a present to be sent by mail the following day. The package arrived as promised and the curious recipient opened it to find a box which had written on it, 'Turn here for one cigar'. Six female employees watched him turn the knob as instructed. However, his fingers were burnt when a dynamite cap became loose in the package and failed to ignite the bomb, which was filled with 'guncotton, slugs and "giant powder"'. The bomb's container was identified as that of a blow torch made by Peterson's company. As it turned out Peterson had formerly been an official for Everhot, the targeted company, and claimed that the patents it used were his. He said that a trade war between the two resulted but denied the charges of sending a bomb through the mail and that his arrest was the result of the long drawn-out battle to deprive him of his share in the profits of the patents he had developed for the Everhot torch.[12]

It was not uncommon for disgruntled residents to use postal bombs against small-town rural politicians. In 1926 constable Asa K. Bartlett of Blue Lake Township, Michigan, was convicted of killing three people at the Three Lakes tavern a month earlier. According to a newspaper account, political enmity was the motive. This was a rare case where the target was actually killed along with multiple non-targeted individuals. Bartlett had been nursing a grudge for several years by his own admission, dating back to when he unsuccessfully challenged 48-year-old August Krubaech, losing by one vote, in a bid to become the new township supervisor. The rancorous election saw charges and countercharges and one conviction for illegal voting. Bartlett only expressed sorrow for killing

Janet Krubaech, 19, and her fiancé William Frank, 22, in the same blast in the lobby of her father's resort tavern on 27 May 1926.[13]

This case had several elements in it that gave it maximum attention. The perpetrator was not just a political opponent and a constable active in enforcing the prohibition law, but the leader of the local Ku Klux Klan (KKK). Postal inspectors pieced together the remnants of the paper wrapping the bomb. The box was similar to one that would be 'used in sending a box of cigars'. Krubaech had faced rigorous opposition from the KKK. The package was delivered by a rural mail carrier as the family prepared for the marriage of the daughter. But sadly, Janet had run out to greet the postman, 'excited as a child', figuring it was an early wedding gift although it was addressed to her father. Her fiancé soon appeared from his family home just a mile away, expecting to take Janet to Muskegon to get their marriage licence. But she insisted that they delay leaving until her father opened the package. August opened it on the counter of the lobby and was met by a blast that could be heard 2 miles away, which tore off his right arm and dug a hole in his side. His wife ran in when she heard the blast and saw that Janet had both eyes blown out as she bravely told her mother to remain calm. Frank was mangled almost beyond recognition and clearly dead. August succumbed after two hours and Janet lingered for two days, only regaining consciousness sporadically and calling out for her father and her groom, whom she called by his pet name 'Opie'.[14]

Duds, Cranks and 'Scare Bombs'

As the 1920s came to a close, letter and package bombs were still causing havoc across America. Mail bombs were not just the tool of revenge seekers and political enemies in the 1920s. As in other eras, oddballs were drawn to this method of committing mayhem. One so-called eccentric inventor and bachelor, 26-year-old Francis Cadwell, was linked to a bomb sent to Clark Scott in Townsend, Tennessee, on 26 November 1929. Cadwell was confined to a psychopathic ward when he confessed and subsequently admitted to a plan to manufacture another dozen devices and mail them across the country. He didn't have much of an explanation for why he sent the bomb but told investigators that he sent it to Scott, whom he described as a friend he made while living in Tennessee, as 'an experiment to test the advisability of using the mail in bomb distribution'. As events played out his target opened the package postmarked Los Angeles at his boarding house and was seriously injured, losing his left hand and suffering severe burns, along with three bystanders, including an eight-year-old girl. Just half an hour after the blast Scott received a telegram from Los Angeles warning him not to open a package from that city. The message said, 'Do not open the package. It will explode. Throw it in river.' It was appropriately signed 'Dementia'. It was rather simple for detectives to trace the telegram to Cadwell together with postmarks on the package. The bomber told authorities he had forgotten the names of his other potential targets but assured them he had 'no motive for the plan and said he held no grudges against the persons'. His eccentricity had blossomed as he languished unemployed for some time and had been using his spare time to create 'freak machines'. In addition he bragged about inventing a 'coffin-like box containing an air pump'. Perhaps highlighting why he was being held in a psychiatric ward following his confession, Cadwell said he created the coffin device for himself: 'I get in when I'm not feeling good and pull the lid down. Then I pump out part of the air. It is just as good as going to the mountains.'[15]

Most of the postal bombs in this era did not result in deaths. In fact many never exploded. In February the federal building housing the New Haven Post Office was saved from destruction when a post office employee discovered a time bomb shortly before it was supposed to go off. Investigators claimed there were enough explosives in the package to destroy the building, which had one hundred employees. The bomb had all the hallmarks of other mail bombs from the 1920s. Authorities described it as 'a small paper wrapped parcel without address which had been deposited on the package chute'. Lacking an address, it caught the eye of an employee and it was handed over to federal agents.[16]

As the decade ended the public was alerted to a mail bomb sent to New York governor Franklin D. Roosevelt. Fortunately it was a dud. Otherwise it might have changed the course of history considering the trajectory of FDR's subsequent years. This was actually the second mail bomb attempt on Roosevelt's life while he was in public service. When he was assistant secretary of the Navy during the First World War he was sent another but it was intercepted before reaching his office.

The mail bomb was 'thwarted by the narrowest of margins', when a porter accidentally touched with his foot a parcel labelled 'candy'. The parcel contained an infernal machine meant to kill whoever opened it. When he knocked the package with his foot 'the jolt set off the matches and some smoke curled through the wrapper.' It was the second postal bomb scare over the past two months.

During the investigation, four bombs, a sawn-off shotgun and a clip of machine gun bullets were found inside a package mailed at the Grand Central Terminal Branch Post Office in New York. After the initial excitement authorities discovered that the bombs were filled with putty and that the whole collection was used as stage props in connection with lectures on crime.

A subsequent investigation described the bomb as being constructed 'after the manner of a child's jack-in-the-box and to be about as dangerous'. The bomb was essentially a 4-inch length of 1-inch pipe 'half filled with black powder, but recently sealed at both ends, indicating that the maker enjoyed complete ignorance of the ways of combustibles'. The bomber had crafted the device so that it was 'laid in a tin box, in which a little more black powder was scattered, and three matches were attached in such a manner that opening the box would ignite them'. The verdict, when all was said and done, was that if the device got through to its intended target it might only have 'singed his eyebrow, when the matches burned the loose powder. But there would be no explosion.' Detectives dubbed the bomb a 'scare bomb'.[17]

Investigators believed the bomb was broken by the porter who knocked it and that this sequence of events prevented a possible disaster. As it turned out there was no fuse on it and it could not have exploded. However, rather than a devious plot to kill the rising New York politician it turned out to be an attempt by the porter,

Thomas J. Callegy, to earn a promotion by 'discovering it'. Days after 'finding' the bomb, the porter was arrested. Authorities had become familiar with a case in Chicago where a porter was promoted after finding a bomb among the mail in the post office. Investigators searched Callegy's home in New Jersey and recovered 'coils and wire similar in size to that used in the bomb'. The porter insisted he was innocent and that he used these as materials to repair radio sets. His explanation was less than compelling and he soon confessed that 'he engineered the Roosevelt bomb plot' to help get a raise to support his family. The 45-year-old employee had worked for the post office for eight years and hoped he would finally be recognized for his work after this incident. One other bit of investigative work revealed that the package bore uncancelled postal stamps, a red flag that pointed to a postal employee who would have access to these.[18]

The Roaring Twenties began with the deadliest terrorist attack in American history up until then. However, the use of improvised explosive devices (IEDs) meant much more collateral damage in terms of lives lost and physical damage. Thanks to the very nature of postal systems, letter bombs were much more effective at reaching specific targets, whether at home or at work. Over the following decades attempted murder by mail was the preferred method for anonymously attacking targets. While most postal bombs in this era were less than lethal, they were as feared as any tool in the assassin's toolbox. But no one could have predicted the scale of bloodletting over the next two decades.

6

The 1930s: War Clouds on the Horizon

The 1920s seemed like an interregnum decade, taking place between the May 1919 bomb plot, also known as the Red Scare (marked by a widespread fear of far-left movements), and the rise of fascism in the 1930s, when mail bombs saw a resurgence with the rise of political conflict. It was not long into the 1930s that anti-fascism raised its head in the guise of weaponized mail bombs in the United States and Italy. From heads of state and mine union leaders to jilted spouses and business concerns, no one was off limits to mail bombers in the 1930s. As the decade began authorities suspected, but were not positive, that the Irish Republican Army (IRA) had added the letter bomb to its arsenal of terror. On 3 October 1930 powerful postal bombs exploded in London. One bomb addressed to Buckingham Palace detonated in a mail van, injuring four postal employees. One theory held that it was an assassination attempt; others suggested that the bombers had actually intended the bomb to explode earlier on the water crossing from Belfast, Northern Ireland, so that it would wreck the Irish mail steamer carrying the mail.[1] Nonetheless, authorities would link the IRA to a mail bomb strategy by the end of the decade.

Death of the Millionaire Newsboy

On 6 December 1930 Tony May, better known locally as the Millionaire Newsboy, died from injuries caused by a black-powder bomb delivered by mail in a box arranged so that it exploded when he lifted the cover. May had moved to America from Italy before his teenage years. For more than thirty years he was a prominent figure on the North Side in Chicago. He signed many bail bonds in Chicago and later in federal courts. He was also a money lender. Before attaining prominence he sold flowers in cabaret establishments. However, after being forced into bankruptcy after losing money on bond forfeitures and real-estate deals he was back to selling flowers in nightclubs and running his news-stands by day. This brought him back into a more comfortable financial situation and at the time of his death he owned four apartment buildings, one of which had thirty flats.

The bomb that killed May exploded as he opened it in his fourth-floor Chicago office. May might have been expecting a present for his 64th birthday when a box wrapped in heavy brown paper and bearing the label of a mail order house arrived at his home. The box was 13 inches long and 3 inches square. According to his son the box had actually arrived earlier in the week and May waited until the day before his birthday to open it. The blast could be heard for blocks. No trace of the box or wrappings remained. While bombs were common in Chicago during the Prohibition gang wars, murder by mail was uncommon in this era. One police officer observed, 'it was the first time in many years that a bomb or infernal machine had been sent through the postal system in Chicago.'[2]

The police pursued a motive for the bombing, focusing on May's news-stand business. He had stands at numerous Chicago locations including city hall. One of the stands formerly belonged to a gangster named John 'Peno' Donahue who had gone to prison for robbery in 1922. There were some reports that he had been out of prison at the time of the bombing and perhaps there was a connection, but this was never substantiated.

The victim had an interesting backstory that included being a millionaire until he became a bondsman and signed bonds for the former heavyweight boxing champion of the world, Jack Johnson. Johnson had been charged by the authorities with violating the federal Mann Act, which made it a crime to bring unmarried lovers across state lines for immoral purposes. Johnson's bond was $75,000; however, May was stuck with it when it was forfeited after the boxer fled to Europe. This forced him to return to his news-stand business.

An Anti-Fascist Plot, 1931

On 22 May 1931 a 'crude letter bomb made of inflammable powder and crushed glass' was sent to the superintendent of police in Cawnpore, India.[3] However, it only gained a passing mention in the press. This mail bomb and most others in 1931 were overshadowed by an anti-fascist mail bomb plot in America. A nationwide investigation of anti-fascist activities in the United States followed a bomb plot that left two mail clerks dead and claimed the life of a bomb expert.

In December 1931 at least six bombs had been mailed – to four prominent Italians, an Argentine vice-consul and a reform school official. Inspectors working the cases of the targeting of Italian supporters of the fascist government in Easton, Pennsylvania, sought to link the bombs to other recent bombings in Italian communities, especially on the east coast. Inspectors left for Philadelphia to seek links with bombings of twelve Italian stores over the previous two months.

Two young 'foreign looking' men had mailed the packages from a post office in Easton.[4] They argued with one of the post office victims over postage but paid and hurried away. Suspicious as to what was in the packages, postal office employee Edward W. Werkheiser, 29, decided to examine them as co-workers stood by. He placed one on the scales and, as he tried to open it, the package exploded, detonating a second package as well, knocking him and his co-workers to the floor. Werkheiser was mortally wounded, dying in a hospital shortly after. A fellow clerk had both arms and a leg blown off and one of his eyes blown out. He too died in the hospital. The packages were estimated to have been 10 inches long, 5 inches high and 5 inches wide. The interior of the parcel post room was heavily damaged.

Police took control of the four remaining packages. An explosives expert named Charles V. Weaver, sent from the Dupont Powder Company, took the packages to a quarry outside town and decided to explode them there. He successfully fired one and was trying to explode another when it failed to go off. He went over to the parcel to check it and it detonated, mortally wounding him as well.

Meanwhile, investigators were trying to figure out why two of the infernal machines were sent to targets without Italian connections: the Argentine vice-consul in Baltimore and an individual connected to a reform school in Huntington, Pennsylvania. What the four Italian targets had in common was that they were 'powerful supporters of the Mussolini regime' and what linked the bombs was the 'similarity in size and difference of contents noted on insurance receipts'.[5] Authorities began almost immediately to investigate anti-fascist groups because most of the packages were addressed to Italian newspapers. However, the owners denied any connection with the fascist or anti-fascist movements.[6] Authorities suspected one package was intended for the owner of an Italian newspaper and a friend of the New York City mayor; another for the editor of Generoso Pope's New York Italian newspaper, *il Progresso Italo Americano*; another for the Italian consul-general in New York City, Emanuele Grazzi; and the last for another Italian target.

While authorities debated the motivations of the mail bomber, some investigators saw the hand of the anti-fascist movement gathering strength in the United States and Italy. One bomb expert with the New York Police Department surmised Russian Soviet sympathizers might have mailed the deadly parcels.[7]

Bombers linked to this plot seemed to have altered their strategy on 31 December 1931, changing the transportation method of the bombs from the postal services to express companies. One bomb was delivered by express to the home of the Italian consul-general in New York City. Experts exploded it without any damage after a secretary alerted the police. A bulky package was delivered to a public-school official in Huntington, Pennsylvania, but suspicions were aroused and they refused to accept the box. The expressman put the parcel back in his truck. Police were able to catch up with the truck and recover the package. 'Inside the wrappings was a wooden box with a piece of insulated wire hanging from it.' Bomb squad members planned to shoot it with a rifle to see whether it was explosive while post office and police officials across the country took precautionary steps to avert further attacks.[8]

A package addressed to Oscar Durante, the vice president of the Chicago school board and editor of a pro-fascist newspaper in Chicago, was intercepted and exploded in a stone quarry on 1 January. Authorities were certain they were on the right path hunting for the bomb-makers, who sent sixteen packages of powerful bombs from New York and Easton, Pennsylvania. Three had been killed thus far in Easton. Federal agents seemed certain it was, like the 1919 anarchist campaign, 'a national terrorist plot'. Five bombs had been sent by express on 29 December 1931 from New York City to Italian officials in Chicago, Youngstown, Detroit and Cleveland.[9]

The scale of the plot widened on 10 January 1932 after three packages believed to contain bombs intended for Italy's king Victor Emmanuel and premier Mussolini were removed from the steamer *Excalibur* in Naples. There were 126 bags of parcel mail on the steamer bound from the United States. The sacks were unloaded onto mail boats and taken to an isolated spot for further investigation by bomb experts.[10]

It was not until March that police arrested a viable suspect: Columbo Boeri, 47, a Chicago anti-fascist currently wanted for deportation. He was captured at his home. He had been 'masquerading as a small grocer'. Authorities believed he was the ringleader of the nationwide distribution of mail and express bombs, which began with the post office deaths in Easton in December. Boeri's house was a complete chemical lab and evidence linked to the mail bomb plots as well as anti-fascist leaflets attacking the pope and Mussolini were found.[11] The following day, without explanation, authorities announced that they were convinced that Boeri had nothing to do with the bomb plot. Nonetheless, it was reported that the Department of Labor had begun deportation proceedings against him.[12]

While America was the focus of most mail bombings during the 1930s they took place sporadically in other parts of the world, from Italy to Ireland and even in the Caribbean. In late November 1932 three men were condemned to death in Cuba by a military court after being convicted of having sent a mail bomb that killed Lieutenant Diez Diaz at Artemisa in the summer. Under Cuban laws meant to control explosives the men were also sentenced to fourteen years, eight months and a day's imprisonment each on five additional charges of having sent bombs through the post.[13] It's unclear whether they served these sentences before being executed.

There seemed to be an uptick in mail bomb cases in 1933. It was the last year of Prohibition in America when several men, including a former deputy sheriff and his brother, were arrested for sending an infernal machine through the mail to the chief of police Henry C. Blakemore in Huntsville, Alabama. The brothers had been incarcerated since 31 December 1932, when the package, containing a home-made bomb consisting of 'a small automobile grease gun loaded with giant powder, surrounded with chipped steel and bullets, the mechanism designed to fire when opened', arrived at its destination. But it wasn't until the arrest of another accomplice that the full extent of the plot was revealed. The accomplice claimed he was hired by the Moon brothers to help make and send the bomb. He pleaded guilty to sending explosives through u.s. Mail.[14]

Target: Franklin D. Roosevelt

In one of the more bizarre mail bomb cases the chief of police of Watertown, New York, was investigating a letter sent to him hoping it would lead to the arrest of a fifteen-year-old Italian boy in connection with sending a bomb to president-elect Franklin D. Roosevelt in February 1933. Postal clerks intercepted the bomb. The boy was not arrested but was put under surveillance until his handwriting could be linked to the note sent with the bomb. The letter was signed, 'Paul Antonelli of Italy'. It read:

> Chief Singleton: Sir: I am friend of Zangara and I want to take up work that he fail [*sic*] to do. I kill all Presidents, Governors and Millionaires ... I hate policemen and kill all your officers who I see on street at midnight. I am one who killed Kansas City millionaire, so I kill police.[15]

The bomb was found in the post office the previous month and was addressed to Franklin D. Roosevelt, Washington, DC.[16]

The years 1933–4 were a particularly eventful time for the mailing of infernal devices in the United States, targeting a president, a civil rights lawyer and a newspaper editor. But like most other attempted parcel bomb cases there were no fatalities. In fact, as in some other high-profile cases, the FDR bomb plot would be revealed as a hoax several months later. On 29 March 1933 President Franklin D. Roosevelt was sent the third in a series of mail bombs. Like the others it was crudely made and was addressed indirectly to the president. The bomb was contained in a package addressed to an aviation company in New Jersey and the company was asked to forward it to Roosevelt. The writing on all three packages was similar to others sent to FDR.[17]

In June the Roosevelt bomb plot was revealed to be a hoax committed by Joseph Doldo, 20, who had left school in fourth grade. He told the police when arrested that he sent two 'crudely fashioned bombs' to the president 'just for fun'. Authorities were satisfied that with the arrest of the so-called 'Watertown crank' the case had been cracked. Not only did the jokester send the bombs but he sent a cheque for an impossible $750 million 'to cover the British war debt payment' that was due on 15 June. Doldo was arrested after he went to a bank to get a timetable similar to the one enclosed in a recent letter to the president. His first bomb was discovered in a Washington post office on 22 February 1932. Like the others it was made of shotgun shells.[18]

One of the most sensational American trials of the 1930s was that of the Scottsboro Boys in Alabama. It began on 25 March 1931 when nine Black youths aged thirteen to twenty were arrested in Alabama, accused of raping two white girls as they travelled as hoboes on a freight train. The subsequent trial and sentencing of the young men focused international attention on the segregated Jim Crow South. Rape was a capital crime in Alabama, even more so when the perpetrators were Black and victims white. Their lives were saved thanks to the defence given by their lawyer Samuel S. Leibowitz but not before the Jewish attorney from New York

was targeted for death by mail. At the end of April 1933 he was
sent an infernal device. He recounted his narrow escape to a
packed crowd at New York City's Holy Trinity Baptist Church:
when the parcel arrived in the mail his assistant put it in a pail of
water as soon as he saw its Alabama postmark. When it was finally
opened its contents included gunpowder and some type of timing
device. This was just one of many threats he had received and he
declared it would have no effect on his continuing defence of the
Scottsboro Boys.[19]

In November the *Mansfield News Journal* plant was bombed just
eight hours after the editor received a warning 'to lay off or you'll get
yours'. At roughly 4 a.m. the bomb exploded in the mailing room,
ripping up its floor and blowing out windows in the plant and
nearby buildings. The editor, G. H. Kochenderner, had been a thorn
in the side of racketeering of all kinds. In a series of editorials he had
requested more punitive punishment and for the eradication of
bootlegging, slot machines and other rackets. The plant had been
targeted two years earlier. The night watchman had just walked
through the mailing room when the bomb exploded. Except for
shock he escaped injury.[20]

The following year saw a number of high-profile cases, more
bizarre than deadly. In one 1934 case, a postal employee at a Washington, DC, post office came across a copy of the book *Uncle Tom's
Cabin* in the dead letter department, where parcels without adequate
postage are held. When he opened the book it exploded. One source
at the time described it as 'one of the most delicately balanced
bombs ever put into the mail'. The postal clerk, Myrton Genung,
was critically injured as he removed wrapping from the parcel, the
fingers from his left hand being torn off. 'Flying glass from the shattered top' of the clerk's desk seriously injured a messenger standing
behind the clerk.[21] The detonation blew the wrapping and postmark
to smithereens.

Other mail bombers have used this ruse before and since. The
bomber had hollowed out the book, discarding the pages, leaving
only the cover and the flyleaf with the book's subtitle, *Life among
the Lowly*. The bomb was adjusted so that opening the cover set off

the trigger. There was no consensus as to who had sent it or to whom it was sent. Rumours included anarchists targeting a high-level government official.[22]

On 10 June police arrested a coal miner, Big Blonde John Lukas, in Pittsburgh for sending the Washington post office mail bomb. Although Lukas maintained his innocence authorities were confident that he had mailed the bomb 'to injure or kill' his wife in what was then Czechoslovakia and that it exploded when Genung attempted to open a copy of the book in the dead letter room.[23] Lukas withstood four days of questioning and was unable to make bail. He had been in the United States for twenty years and was a naturalized citizen.[24]

'Three Judges of Hell': Paris 1934–5

Beginning in June 1934 the self-proclaimed 'Three Judges of Hell' began a bombing campaign that lasted well into the following year. Each bomb parcel contained a letter signed by the three judges from Greek mythology responsible for meting out justice in hell (Minos, Aeacus and Rhadamanthus). Three of the first bombs failed to explode. On 14 June the 'fantastic terrorists' sent the latest bomb to the government broadcasting station in Paris. It was 'a glass cylinder containing a quarter of a pound of powder arranged to explode on removal of a rubber band'.[25] However, it was intercepted by postal workers. The previous day a bomb exploded in a post office, injuring three postal clerks. Another infernal machine addressed to a book publisher was also detected on 13 June – in this case a young clerk noticed a faint metallic sound as she started to open the package but realized it had a spring intended to cause an explosion and stopped. Investigators found the same powder and loaded mechanism in the broadcasting station's bomb as in the book publisher's device. Others were spotted and destroyed before causing any damage or casualties.[26]

The Three Judges of Hell targeted a variety of individuals and firms. It became of greater concern to the police after the bomber threatened the lives of the French premier and other high officials.

On 16 June a bomb exploded in the office of André Citroën, the so-called Henry Ford of France, in a campaign of terror in Paris. It had been addressed to Citroën but a librarian at the motor plant opened it. His hands were 'badly torn and the office was damaged'. Three other infernal machines, which failed to explode, were received in the morning mail, bringing the total to nine mailed in the previous three days. Four were injured. One was received by the Venus Pencil Company, the French branch of the American firm, the second at Tokalon, a large American beauty firm controlled by E. Virgil Neal. Other 'missiles' were received at the Pathé film office and at a boarding house.[27]

On 16 June special precautions were taken to guard President Lebrun and Premier Doumergue against the bombs of terrorists. Over the past four days scattered infernal devices had been detected in the Paris postal service. These coincided with an outbreak of violence in the provinces. By 16 June ten bombs had been detected with only two exploding. In each case the bomb was delivered through the mail inside a rolled arms catalogue. Only alert employees prevented more damage and carnage. Twenty bombs had been sent, each containing a tube of dynamite to be exploded by a cap when the package was opened. Authorities opined that the bomber must be 'a man of some education, since he signs one of his letters, Minos, Aeacus, Rhadamanthus'.[28]

Authorities were hopeful that the 'maniac who has filled the French mails with deadly bombs in an insane, one-man war on the French people' had stopped his activities on 17 June as law enforcement mobilized.[29] However, just five days later the bomb campaign continued with another device located in the mail. 'Authorities are convinced an insane person, brooding over the Stavisky scandal [a financial scandal in France in 1934] is responsible.'[30]

The Three Judges of Hell revived their 'campaign of bomb terrorism' in December 1935 with a series of package bombs addressed to Parisian barbers. Each one contained a 'piece of sawed-off curtain rod filled with magnesium and a phosphorus compound at the end, which would ignite with the opening of the parcel'. The parcels each contained letters signed with the familiar names of the three judges, declaring that 'since the French people do not dare to apply the law to all with equal severity, we have assumed the noble mission of subjecting them all to it.'[31]

In 1935 the populist Louisiana senator Huey P. Long was the target of several mail bomb threats and he insisted that his protection was ramped up. He gave the post office permission to open any packages addressed to him, especially after a crude, home-made bomb was mailed to him from Oregon.[32]

As the European political climate became more heated in the run-up to the Second World War, on 20 September 1935 Austrian police intercepted explosive parcels mailed from suburban Urfahr to high government officials in Linz and Vienna. The Vienna device was stopped and destroyed while the Linz package was delivered to the city police chief, injuring the hand of a detective. Police blamed communists.[33]

Labour Violence: Pennsylvania 1936

The United States 'has had the bloodiest and most violent labour history of any industrial nation in the world'.[34] Industrial violence reached its zenith between 1911 and 1916 but sporadic incidents continued into the 1930s and beyond. In the second half of the decade letter bombs were used during mining union conflict in the coal country of Pennsylvania. On 10 April 1936 one man was killed and two seriously injured as a 'wave of mail bombings' in the Wyoming Valley anthracite area of the northeastern part of the state ratcheted up the tension in the region. At least six bombs were sent through the mail disguised as Easter gifts, killing one and injuring five. Few doubted this represented a revival of mining labour discord. Police and every available postal inspector in the east spread a dragnet over the area, fearing still more bombs to come. A judge, a former sheriff, an umpire of the anthracite conciliation board and a mine superintendent were among those believed marked for death.

In one of the union-related bombings a victim was 'literally blown to bits as the bomb let go'. His son-in-law, standing nearby, was badly hurt. One bystander said that the victim thought the package was a box of cigars. Rumour at the time was that it was probably addressed incorrectly and intended for another person with the same name who was involved in a recent mine dispute.[35] In a few hours, his death was followed by the explosion of an identical bomb that killed Thomas Maloney, a 'former insurgent union leader', and his four-year-old son.

Maloney received his bomb at home on Good Friday, 11 April 1936. He had gone outside to collect the mail and found a parcel marked 'Sample'. Inside he placed it on the kitchen table, took out his penknife and removed the wrapping to reveal what he thought was a box of expensive cigars, a gift from another union official. Opening the lid detonated the bomb, hurling him and his two children across the room. His sixteen-year-old daughter survived but his four-year-old son died five hours later. What they could not have known was that the bomb was part of a campaign of terror unleashed by a 'disgruntled 52-year-old German immigrant coal miner' named Michael Fugmann.

On 9 April Fugmann had mailed six cigar box bombs to six different recipients. The boxes contained dynamite and were electrically wired so they exploded when the lids were pried off. Fugmann's motives have always remained in question but there is evidence that he was disenchanted with the United Mine Workers of America and the United Anthracite Miners of Pennsylvania. In any case both men were familiar with each other before the blast.[36]

Simultaneously two more mail bombs were discovered. One failed to explode in the hands of Luther Kniffen, the former Luzerne County sheriff. Another was intercepted before it reached a county judge.[37] Each of the bombs were cleverly constructed out of cigar boxes and contained a stick or two of explosives and loose dynamite. Wrapping was festive with white paper and string; addresses were printed in pencil and the packages were marked 'Sample'.

The bomber was not apprehended until 29 September 1936 when Pennsylvania authorities linked Michael Fugmann to the cigar boxes fashioned into mail bombs. The manager of a local Schulte store testified that the previous March he gave Fugmann three empty cigar boxes. The store manager was brought to the jail after Fugmann's arrest. The defendant actually confirmed that he was the one who gave them to him. The federal forensics expert Arthur Koehler testified that the wood used in making the bomb compartments in the cigar boxes was similar to fragments found in Fugmann's home.[38]

During Fugmann's trial a replica of the mail bomb was displayed. It was divided into three compartments. In the right-hand compartment there was

> a flashlight battery glued to some small pieces of wood which in turn had been glued to the bottom of the box. A wire was attached to the battery and extended to a detonator placed in or near a stick of dynamite resting in the center compartment. There was also a quantity of loose powder or dynamite in the center compartment. In the lefthand compartment were portions of newspaper. A piece of copper wire was glued to the inside of the lid of the box and was so arranged that when the lid was lifted slightly the wire near the battery would make contact with the latter, set off a spark which would be carried to the detonator, and thus cause an explosion.[39]

Fugmann was convicted and executed on 18 July 1938.

Bombing sporadically made headlines over the rest of the decade. In July 1936 a parcel bomb killed a farmer and injured his wife in Cape Charles, Virginia. Curry Thomas opened the parcel thinking it was harmless as he and his wife, Elsie, sat in their car in front of their house. His body absorbed the brunt of the explosion but a fragment of the bomb penetrated Elsie's side and her left hand and wrist were mangled. The couple had picked up the package as they returned home from a golf outing. The box was about 4 inches square but powerful enough to hurl parts of the car a hundred yards away. They had just been married a month earlier.[40] In October a North Carolina dentist, Dr H. R. Hege, Elsie's former lover, was charged with the bomb murder. Once behind bars he wasted no time committing suicide, cutting his jugular vein and the radial artery in his left wrist with a broken piece from his glasses.[41]

The IRA: Balloon and Acid Letter Bombs

During the Spanish Civil War (1936–9) close to four hundred members of the IRA served in the International Brigade. British officials hoped this might 'distract IRA leadership from launching attacks in England'.[42] That is, until 1938. At a convention of the IRA that year there was staunch support for a bombing campaign in England.[43] In May the IRA Council adopted the strategy for a bombing campaign in England but first they had to find someone experienced in handling explosives. For this they found Seamus O'Donovan, who had resigned from the IRA when he was released from prison in 1924. He produced the S-Plan for widespread organized bombing and sabotage in England. He carefully selected suitable targets. There was some suggestion that German intelligence had assisted the IRA but this remains unsubstantiated.[44]

The IRA's lack of experience with explosives was illustrated on 28 November 1938 when three operatives set out to blow up a Customs post but the mine went off prematurely, killing the three operatives. In December major explosions occurred in England at electrical installations and power stations in London, Manchester, Birmingham and Northumberland. The bomb campaign mostly used high explosives and planted bombs. But they would shortly add a mail bomb component.

Before the outbreak of the Second World War, the IRA launched the British Isles' biggest mail bomb campaign. On 16 January 1939 seven bombs were detonated and others followed. Several raids by the Special Branch uncovered bomb-making factories including one that had more than one thousand rubber balloons. The IRA contributed a new bombing tactic that used balloon and acid letter bombs. The Glaswegian bomb-maker Peter Walsh, better known as Peter Stuart, has been credited with manufacturing what he called 'airships', essentially 'balloons filled with an ingenious incendiary formula which ignited as soon as the acid content had eaten away at the rubber protection and exposed the mixture to air'.[45]

It is unknown whether the IRA was inspired by the suffragette campaign from almost thirty years earlier but there were some strategic similarities, such as the targeting of pillar boxes. On 12 May 1939 explosions shook various shop letter boxes in Manchester. Police were soon searching letter boxes at the city's shops as well as other public spaces. In August explosions rocked mail stations in five English cities. A parcel exploded while mail was being transferred from a van to the station, injuring three people. At the Halifax main post office hundreds of letters burst into flames inside a mailbag. Police found 'the remains of rubber incendiary balloons', the telltale signs of the new IRA bombing devices.[46]

That same month tear gas bombs exploded in Liverpool cinemas and others detonated in London and Coventry. Some were delayed action incendiary devices which started fires in hotels across England. On 29 May magnesium bombs exploded in a Birmingham cinema. This terrorist campaign in England continued with sporadic pauses between explosions.

On 9 June the IRA struck postal services in five English cities, injuring twelve. They posted letter bombs which, when they exploded, splattered postal employees with acid in sorting offices and on a mail train going from Birmingham to London. In Manchester post-office workers were seriously injured when a bomb exploded in a post bag, and in Lincoln an envelope exploded in a sorting room, spraying acid on several workers.[47]

On 24 July 1939 the British home secretary stated in Parliament that there had been 127 terrorist outrages in England that had left at least one dead and 55 injured. Come 25 August the largest explosion to date killed five and injured sixty in Coventry. Two men were convicted and hanged for this in February 1940. In August the attacks continued. Letter bombs impacted four more towns and cities: Blackburn, Preston, Huddersfield and Bradford. Letters and parcels were damaged, as was at least one postman when one detonated in his mailbag. His reflexive movement to throw the bag on the ground saved him but set a nearby pillar box on fire. Fragments of rubber balloon and traces of acid were found in the detritus as well as a small envelope containing a balloon holding acid inside the envelope.

Once the war broke out on 3 September 1939 there was a sign of changed attitudes and reactions when it came to violence against England, and the planned terrorist campaign in wartime England ran into more obstacles. It was hoped that tighter wartime security and general alertness for spies might have put a stop to the IRA attacks. But shortly before Christmas in 1939 mail bomb attacks took place in the cities of Birmingham, Wolverhampton and Crewe. Meanwhile, in London three balloon-type incendiary bombs detonated at the Eversholt Street Post Office in the northwest sector of the city. Except for a slight injury to a postman who was involved in sorting the post, most of the damage was to the Christmas mail.[48] Similar bombs exploded at the Paddington and Kingsway post offices, damaging mail and little else. On 21 December five IRA incendiary devices exploded on a table at Birmingham's General Post Office. Workers were able to smother the flames with mailbags, but hundreds of letters were damaged. The 21 December letter bombs were posted in the city centre shortly before the last collection from the pillar boxes. Officials feared more bombs might have already been mailed with longer delayed action and could now be in transit to other parts of the country by train. Police described the bombs as of the balloon-and-acid type.[49]

On the night of 21 December attempts were made to burn out pillar boxes at Crewe. The first inkling of the incendiaries was when a passer-by noticed smoke coming out of 'the mouth of a box at the sub-post office'. The postmaster knew how to respond, pouring a bucket of water through the box aperture. Hundreds of letters were damaged. A similar case took place at a pillar box on Mill Street. Flames burst out but were extinguished with a mailbag. Ultimately, the 21–22 December mail bomb attacks damaged holiday mail and left several employees with only minor burns.[50]

The violent convulsions of the 1940s made murder by mail seem rather quaint. Newspapers and journalists covered bombs and bombings like never before but letter bombs seemed to fade from the headlines. With the exception of a couple of cases – such as one on 18 June 1942 when a parcel bomb was delivered to the public prosecutor of Dijon, France, with other mail in court, causing serious injuries – mail bombs were at their nadir.[51]

However, the last year of the war featured one of the more bizarre letter bombings of the era, in the case of one Maurice Knapp. He was the focus of a headline that announced that a 'Blind Man Mails Bomb to Woman'. On 23 October 1945 a federal grand jury indictment was filed charging a 'blind Cleveland, Ohio war worker with sending a home-made bomb by mail' to a woman in Beaumont, Texas. He pleaded not guilty to sending the bomb to Doris Peveto on 2 July 1939.[52] The bomb contained 'shot gun shells rigged to a fuse' but failed to explode when the package was opened.[53] He changed his story before sentencing claiming that he 'sent the bomb rigged with shotgun shells as a prank'. His *mea culpa* and physical disability carried little weight with the federal jury, and he was sentenced to twenty years in prison.[54]

7

The Stern Gang Parcel Bomb Campaign and the Post-War World

Following the end of the Second World War, among the immediate preoccupations of the London Metropolitan Police Special Branch was the growing threat of Jewish terrorism in Palestine and at home. The British mandate in Palestine by 1947 had the unintended consequence of bringing a postal bomb campaign home to London and beyond.

The London Metropolitan Police Special Branch took a special interest in Jewish terrorism at home after terrorists planted a bomb in the British embassy in Rome in April 1947. It failed to work. The bomb did not go off because the hands of its wristwatch timer were not set properly. But it did allow Special Branch operatives to identify the thumbprint of the Stern gang member Yaacov Eliav.[1] The Branch sent a stop-and-detain order for Eliav and arrested him and a young woman on the Paris–Brussels express in Mons. They had twenty sticks of gelignite in their possession. Several clues linked them to the Colonial Office in Rome, including a false French passport in the name of Elizabeth Lazarus, stamped in Dover shortly before the bombing. Normally they would have been extradited to the UK for trial. But it turned out she was actually a heroine of the French Resistance named Betty Knout (her maternal grandfather was the prominent Soviet leader Vyacheslav Molotov's brother). She had been decorated with the Croix de Guerre. Her companion claimed no knowledge of explosives. They were tried in Belgium for illegal importation of explosives after an examination of Knout's suitcase revealed a false bottom which contained similar letter bombs. Eliav was sentenced to twelve months and Lazarus to eight. Although their arrests and convictions were initially associated with a different bombing, it did enable the Branch to close the file on a series of letter bomb attacks they carried out from France.[2]

The Dynamite Man: Yaacov Eliav aka Levstein

Born in Russia in 1917, Yaacov (Ya'akov) Eliav aka Levstein moved to Palestine with his parents in 1925.[3] He joined the Jewish underground ten years later and by 1938 he was considered the director of its Jerusalem operations. His fellow extremists revered him as the 'Dynamite Man' for his expertise with explosives. In his autobiography Eliav claimed to have invented the letter bomb in 1947,[4] although, as the previous chapters have shown, infernal devices had a long history by the time Eliav came on the scene.

In 1939 he was sent to Poland for training in a guerrilla warfare course taught by the Polish army. He returned to Palestine the following year and assisted Abraham Stern in the founding of what became known as the Lehi. In 1942 Stern was killed by British forces in Palestine but his right-wing followers, including Eliav, continued the underground war for the creation of a Jewish state. The Stern gang was just one facet of a movement that included Haganah (more moderate) and the Irgun/Lehi (more militant). Fortunately for the Palestinian police these groups spent as much time battling each other as they did plotting against the 100,000 peacekeeping troops in the region.

Once Stern was killed Eliav took over as operations chief. In late 1945 he convinced the underground high command to allow him to establish a European base of operations in Paris.[5] From there he took the fight against the British to London in the following years. Also known by his 'nom de guerre *Yashka*',[6] the Dynamite Man was responsible for killing several police officers with a bomb and had already served two stints in prison before escaping in 1943.

British authorities tightened security in London in the wake of several high-profile bombings of government buildings in the spring of 1947. By 1947 Eliav had concluded that the best way to punish the British leadership was through a series of letter bomb attacks. He recounted in his memoir that he was 'going to send an official letter addressed to a government member, with enough explosives to kill him'.[7] Without a working lab in Europe he managed to come up with a letter bomb formula that would become known to the British Special Service and the Federal Bureau of Investigation (FBI) in due course. The elements he used were simple – high-quality blasting gelignite with an explosive force of nine to ten thousand per second, enough to kill at least one target. The bomb would weigh between 0.05 and 1 pound and be shaped like a candle. It could 'then be flattened and put inside an envelope and remained soft so no one could suspect there was anything inside besides paper'. He then acquired 'fresh material that was easy to work with and did not emit poisonous gas that endangered the worker'.[8]

When it came to the detonator, as a safety precaution, he used direct current detonators. He assessed each one with a voltmeter and used Eveready batteries because they were 'small and flat and can be easily hidden inside an envelope'. To be sure each would detonate he used two detonators and two batteries, which he always checked beforehand.[9]

The most crucial component of the letter bomb was the firing device. The Dynamite Man went into great detail explaining his protocol: 'When the envelope was opened the device connected the circuit from the batteries to the detonators and caused the explosion.' He claimed that he

invented a rudimentary mechanism which remained open inside the envelope and would close as soon as the envelope was opened. All the components were attached to a thin sheet of cardboard so [they could] easily insert them into the envelope. The explosive charges were also attached to the cardboard. Inside the charges were also attached to the cardboard. Inside the charges were attached the detonators.

Finally, 'we then attached the batteries to the cardboard and underneath them we tied the firing device, with the spring pointing

to the bottom of the envelope.' Once someone opened the letter
the spring was released, 'the circuit was closed, and the envelope
exploded.'[10]

The series of actions from bomb-making to target made up a
'delicate operation'. Steps were taken to prevent the device from
exploding as it was placed in the envelope. The bomber would
detach the detonators and substitute in their place a 'small electric
bulb that could be lit by the batteries'. The next step was to put the
device into the envelope along with the disconnected detonators
and the lit bulb. If the device was to work as planned, the 'installed
bulb would go off since the circuit inside the envelope was open'.
The envelope was then closed, all the while making sure the firing
device stayed disconnected. Finally, one of the bomb-makers held
the envelope open so the accomplice could take out the lightbulb
and connect the detonators to the electric current. Once this was
done, it 'now became a deadly trap'.[11]

Every detail for the bombing campaign was considered, from
the making of the bomb to the stationery. In order to blend in with
typical mail they used 'grey official British envelopes' that included
a government heading. Eliav was convinced this provided safe cover
'since officials expected to get mail from embassies in all parts of the
world'. The outer envelope was marked with the address and an
inner envelope bore the name of a minister or other target with the
words 'Private and Confidential'. By this subterfuge the secretary
was expected to open the first envelope and give the boss the second
to be opened.[12]

The bombers found the names and addresses of their targets
from a variety of sources including official government publications
and the British press. Ultimately, they collected seventy names and
addresses. In order to facilitate the bombings a large quantity of
explosives and detonators was needed. Thanks to a French Jew who
supported the independence campaign, Eliav was loaned the
materials. As a cover Eliav brought his pregnant wife with him on
the twelve-hour train trip to Marseilles to pick up the materials and
return to Paris. He brought back a suitcase full of explosives and she
carried the one with detonators.

Eliav was well aware of the political ramifications of launching attacks against the British directly from France. Not wanting to compromise French neutrality in the conflict, not only did they not use French stamps but they mailed the letter bombs from neighbouring countries, mostly Italy. One agent familiar with the French-Italian border took a knapsack of weaponized letter bombs to Turin and mailed them right away.[13] More than twenty were mailed from Italy to members of the British establishment, including Prime Minister Clement Atlee; Lieutenant-General Sir Evelyn Barker, former commander in Palestine; foreign secretary Ernest Bevin; MP Winston Churchill; Sir Stafford Cripps, president of the Board of Trade; General Alan Cunningham; former foreign secretary Anthony Eden; Major John Freeman, under-secretary to the War Office; Arthur Greenwood, Minister without Portfolio; Sir Harold MacMichael, former high commissioner in Palestine; colonial administrator Sir John Shaw; Major-General Sir Edward Spears, former minister to Syria and Lebanon; MP Oliver Stanley; and others.[14] Postal services were alerted to the plot. While several reached intended targets, they did not explode. The others were intercepted and defused. Authorities in Italy cooperated with Scotland Yard in an attempt to trace the letter bombs to their senders. Stamps and postmarks all indicated they came from specific towns in Italy but investigators remained tight-lipped about the evidence and whether the postal bombs were connected to the Palestine crisis.

The first batch contained no messages. Addresses were typewritten, as were the words 'Private and Confidential' on the inner envelopes. On 4–5 June more weaponized letters from Italy were handed over to Scotland Yard, including one addressed to Foreign Secretary Bevin. Two of the postal bombs arrived on 5 June but police would not disclose the recipients. Former foreign secretary Anthony Eden carried a letter bomb in his briefcase for over a day. He said he did not notice anything suspicious. 'It looked very dull, just like a circular; otherwise I might have opened it on the way home.' The day before, the Yard had warned him and he still did not check his briefcase. It took the foresight of his secretary the following day to 'pounce on the letter bomb'.[15]

The closest one of these potentially lethal packages came to injuring someone was the one sent to Sir Stafford Cripps. His secretary opened the outer envelope and noticed it was becoming hot, 'indicating that the detonating mechanism was beginning to work'. A messenger then put it into water. Meanwhile authorities continued to concentrate on Milan as the epicentre of the letter campaign and believed it to be one of the centres for Palestine terrorists operating out of Italy.[16]

On 5 June Scotland Yard reported that the British embassy in Paris had also received one of the 'ingenious bombs of gelignite, a pencil-sized battery, and a detonator, all packaged in a cream coloured envelope'. However, a spokesperson for the embassy said 'there was absolutely no truth to this report.' It is unclear whether this was simply a hoax.[17]

The following day postal workers intercepted nine more letter bombs, addressed to the prime minister, Winston Churchill, and other former and present British cabinet officers.

A new bag of mail brought to twenty the number of explosive letters received in London from Turin . . . in a murder by mail campaign which the Stern Gang proclaimed as its project. Italian police were still trying to trace the senders, none exploded except by police tests.[18]

On 7 June a Yard spokesman announced new precautions anticipating that the 'would be assassins have something else up their sleeves'. Due diligence was directed now towards package devices. The Yard took a new tack, deciding not to notify targets if bombs were discovered before reaching them. They did not want conspirators to know how many bombs arrived and were intercepted by the authorities.[19] That same day Turin police chief Dr Luigi Mazzagano announced that the Irgun 'without a doubt' had 'a powerful organization among the displaced persons in the area, which passes out anti-British propaganda among other Jews and the Italian populace'. At the time an estimated 10,000 displaced Central European Jews lived in the area.[20]

On 8 June a self-proclaimed member of the Stern gang reported that he was the one who mailed 24 letter bombs to prominent Britons and that he had posted them at the central post office in Turin. This individual, who called himself Ami Kam, was about forty years old. He was described as tall and well-built and was passing through Genoa on his way from Paris to Palestine, travelling on an American passport. He told a reporter, 'no more letter bombs would be sent, because the system had become too well known,' but 'we are now going to work with other systems.'[21] This Associated Press correspondent met Kam by chance in Genoa's central station. They had met five months earlier when Kam came to a Genoa newspaper office to describe his work for the Stern gang.

He told his interviewer that he had left Genoa by way of Venice and Trieste, heading to Athens. He described the mail bomb campaign as a method of reprisal against Britain's Palestinian policy. He went on to offer a detailed description of the envelopes made of 'manila-type paper . . . the large type used for official communications'. Each held 190 grams of explosive, enough to kill. However, Scotland Yard was doubtful about the amount of explosives. Although no one had been seriously injured or killed, the bombs were lethal. Tests by experts demonstrated that the contents of the letter bombs could blow a hole in a steel plate.

In his interview Kam expressed contempt for the British, telling the journalist that

> the English believe the Stern Gang was composed of only 200 men . . . We let them believe it. But we have our men throughout Europe and throughout the world. We are an important fighting force, and we will fight the British everywhere in Europe as well as in Palestine . . . We mean to bring down the Union Jack.[22]

Although none had been reported to have exploded, Kam seemed fairly certain that four had exploded on opening. He closed by declaring that the Stern gang, 'aided by God', would fight until Britain, prostrate with war, was knocked out.

Ten days after the mail bomb campaign began, a number of Jews were arrested in large scale police raids in Belgium. For the time being they were held for questioning about suspected smuggling of gelignite sticks and material for letter bombs. The police raids took place during the day at a popular Brussels restaurant and combed out likely hideouts. Among the suspects rounded up that day was the French woman 'Elizabeth Lazarus' and her companion Yaacov Eliav.[23]

Although it has never been substantiated, according to President Harry S. Truman he might have been targeted by the same letter bombers in the early summer of 1947. Margaret Truman-Daniel claimed that Lehi had sent some letter bombs to her father but they were intercepted and disarmed by the FBI. Years later Eliav denied this in his autobiography.[24] However, her description of several cream-coloured envelopes measuring about 8 × 6 inches arriving at the White House addressed to the president and members of his staff must be given some credence since it was an apt description of the mail bombs: inside them were smaller envelopes marked 'Private and Confidential'. The second envelope contained a bomb consisting of powdered gelignite, a pencil battery and a detonator rigged to explode when the envelope was opened. Each of the bombs was capable of killing whoever opened it.[25]

Scotland Yard's Special Investigation Branch suggested that 'despite their size' these bombs were 'extremely dangerous' and 'constitute a new move by sympathizers of Palestine terrorists'.[26] Although Scotland Yard quickly deduced that any of the packages could cause serious harm, no casualties were reported.

The FBI and the Palestinian Letter Bomb Campaign

As Lehi conducted its quixotic letter bomb campaign against the British Empire, in June 1947 America's FBI entered the fray, helping to investigate the explosive contents of these weaponized devices in its technical laboratory in Washington, DC. In a folder sent to the FBI, there was information describing an 'infernal machine generally referred to as the "letter bomb" which had been forwarded to various public officials in London from Italy'.[27] The folder contained photos of the letter bomb, a diagram showing how the envelopes containing letter bombs were to be opened and copies of a two-page report summarizing the make-up of the bomb.[28]

FBI analysts described the letter bombs as being from 2 to 4 ounces each containing nitroglycerine explosive made up of '19% nitroglycerin; 11% nitro body; 65% ammonium nitrate; 1.3% nitrocotton; 2.3% woodmeal and 1.2% volatile matter'. The 2-ounce bombs also contained about 0.5–1 ounce of a green powder consisting of 'ammonium nitrate 87%; di-nitro-naphthalene 11% and a green dye. This is described as being as powerful as picric acid.'[29] At the time this folder was sent to the FBI, samples of these bombs had not been distributed to other police agencies and, in fact, 'a sample of this bomb has not even been made available to the Metropolitan Police College, which is located at Hendon on the outskirts of London for study purposes.'[30]

At this time all the original letter bombs were being retained in London since they might be required as evidence at a future date. The American embassy legal attaché, J. A. Cimperman, was provided with a portion of one of the bombs consisting of 'a cardboard back, one battery and the wire spring contact arm'. He reminded the lab that he had promised his London contacts that the FBI would keep this information strictly confidential.

Besides this segment of the infernal machine Cimperman was given three batteries which contained 1–1.4 volts pressure. These were believed to be of American origin and were similar to what might be used in a 'walkie-talkie' radio. The FBI was tasked with determining if the batteries were of American origin and, once this was established, determine how these would be distributed by the manufacturer to foreign bombers.[31]

In one FBI document there was a thorough description of the 'so-called letter bombs' sent from Italy to prominent individuals in England:

They consist of an outer envelope, roughly nine inches by six and one half inches, enclosing an inner envelope (marked

Private and Confidential) in which is contained a piece of cardboard folded over and wrapped around with sheets of carbon paper and ordinary paper. Enclosed within the cardboard are two one ounce slabs of gelignite, three small batteries, and in all cases but one, a small packet of green powdery material enclosed in cellophane. This green material has not been identified. On one side of the bomb the wiring is connected with three small studs. The circuit is interrupted between the second and third stud. The second stud has a piece of loose spring wire attached, and the circuit would be completed on opening the envelope, when the spring wire would make contact with the third stud. We have not yet received a final report on the bomb . . . It is thought probable that the Stern terrorist organization was responsible for the dispatch of the bombs.

The Layout of the Letter Bomb

a)   Batteries.
b)   Terminals of wiring.
c)   Terminals of wiring.
d)   Terminals of wiring.
e)   Spring-wire contact arm.
f)   Cellophane packet containing gelignite – and in some cases another greenish explosive – together with two No. 8 detonators.

The bomb is inserted in the inner envelope in such a way that, when the inner spring-wire contact arm springs forward, it makes contact with terminal (b) and completes the circuit to fire the charge.[32]

The outer envelope was typed on and had the name and address of the intended recipient together with stamps and a postmark. Upon opening the outer envelope there was an inner envelope bearing the words:

Private and Confidential, together with the name and address of recipient. The gross weight of inner envelope was about 8 oz. The bombs contained in the inner envelope consisted of two pieces of white cardboard about 7½ inches long, about 6 inches wide and separated from one another by a space of 0.3 inches to 0.4 inches, and paper was pasted over the edges. Each bomb was encased in five blank sheets of writing-pad paper, having one sheet of carbon paper between these five sheets of paper. Each cardboard bomb was tightly encased in the paper and formed a close fit in the inner envelope. On slitting open the inner envelope at the top and releasing the five sheets of paper, the bomb was fired by a spring which was held in the firing position by the paper encasing the two sheets of carboard.[33]

Each bomb consisted of three small batteries of the fountain pen type, each battery having a voltage of 1–1.4 volts. The batteries were connected in series by soldering. In some cases the bottom battery was soldered at right angles to the second battery, and in other cases the three batteries were in line horizontally and soldered together.

The Farran Affair

There was one last spate of letter bombs before the end of the British mandate in May 1948. One deadly bombing incident can be traced to an incident that took place almost a year earlier in Palestine. Members of the Lehi group were often in their early teens. One of their main tasks was to post-up and glue Lehi-related posters and announcements on walls in public places. One of these young men was sixteen-year-old Alexander Rubowitz from Jerusalem. He was doing just that on the night of 6 May 1947 when he was captured in action by a British special squad. These special army units were composed of soldiers and officers who wore plain clothes and used 'unconventional anti-terrorism activities against underground Jewish groups'. The group that took Rubowitz into custody was led by Major Roy Farran. Rubowitz was forced into their vehicle and was never seen again. However, in the night-time melee Farran dropped his hat. Eventually he was charged, went to trial and was acquitted, and the next day he left Palestine for good. In October 1947 posters were posted in Palestine warning that 'Captain Farran's time will come. We shall go after him to the end of the world.' Around the same time several threatening letters were sent to his family home just outside Wolverhampton. He told reporters, 'I'm not a bit scared of them.'[34]

Lehi was confident that the young man had been tortured and murdered, and once they found Major Farran's hat on the scene he became a target.[35] Having passed a death sentence on him, Lehi agents followed him to England to a small village where he lived with his parents and two younger brothers. It was decided to use a book-sized bomb. During this period Roy Farran had published his bestselling memoir, *Winged Danger*, so it was common for fans to send him copies to sign; therefore, it wouldn't seem unusual. One of the members went to Foyles bookshop and purchased a popular version of Shakespeare. This volume was selected because it was large and heavy enough to accommodate 30–50 grams of explosives without arousing attention. Moreover, since it was a common volume it would be difficult to trace to a particular bookshop.[36] The book bomb was sent to the address almost a year to the date of the kidnapping, arriving on 4 May 1948. The address on the parcel said R. Farran. Rex, Roy's younger brother, opened it at 8:10 a.m. and it exploded, 'eviscerating his pelvis and groin and peppering his face and body with deadly shrapnel'. Before he died at the hospital two hours later, his younger brother Keith claimed his final words were 'Am I brave enough for a Farran?'[37]

By the time police arrived there was little left of the package except indications that it had been sent from the East End of London. This immediately fuelled suspicions that it was the Stern gang or some other Jewish extremists. Roy, the target, had no doubt. He later said he had been careful opening packages since he arrived home and had warned family members. The bomb had been constructed by Yaacov Heruti, a twenty-year-old operative sent to

London the year before with the intent to assassinate two other targets in 1947 including Sir Evelyn Barker, whose bomb failed to detonate. Farran was a late addition to the hit list. Meanwhile, the head of the Crime Investigations Division called in all senior officers from Scotland Yard to coordinate what was said to be 'the greatest hunt for Jewish terrorists ever held in Britain'.[38] Lehi made a point of sending Farran two crudely printed postcards. One said, 'It's your turn to mourn,' and the other was 'simply a drawing of two staring eyes' to remind Roy that Lehi was watching him.[39] He would live a peripatetic life, ending up in Canada where he died of natural causes in 2006.

8

The 1950s: An Iron Curtain Descends

After the end of the Second World War, most people hoped that they could now reap the rewards implicit in a world without war and fascism. However, geopolitically those peace dividends were lost in the transition from a hot war to a cold one. The gradual descending of the Iron Curtain and the proliferation of new political conflicts in Europe and Asia augured a new age of murder by mail. In the United States and elsewhere letter bombs were still go-to weapons to solve grudges, extort, terrorize and kill adversaries near and far.

The Metaphysician

In almost every year of the 1950s letter bomb attacks were recorded, beginning in 1950 when a small, grey-haired, 75-year-old ex-convict, who had served fifteen years in federal and state prisons on charges of counterfeiting and larceny, made headlines. One newspaper article described Frank B. Kucyn as a 'self-styled metaphysician'.[1] It was not long after he got out that he made the transition to mail bomber. A postal official became suspicious when he walked into a post office to mail a parcel. What caught her attention was his sartorial choices: he was wearing a short-sleeved shirt and gloves. Once she received permission to open the package she found three smaller boxes. Each contained a 'cheap table model cigarette lighter, filled with a tea cup of explosive powder' plus a detonating device to set off the gunpowder when the lighter was lit. The wicks were actually fuses.[2] The three packages were prepared for air mailing in one package. One was addressed to his stepson, another to his stepdaughter and a third to his stepson-in-law. Each included a note to a Los Angeles man requesting him to forward the three smaller parcels.

The following month his motive was revealed. All three recipients of the parcels had played an active part in opposing him in a Texas court civil suit. At the centre of the conflict was his attempt to establish ownership of a 100-acre farm near the town of Marshall which had been owned by his former wife. Authorities also found a fourth cigarette lighter bomb similar to the other three. It too contained cotton-packing with black specks. Officers located the business where Kucyn bought the lighters and got a statement from the sales assistant.[3] Kucyn was indicted on two counts for sending 'unmailable explosive' matter through the mail.[4]

A Tale of Two Germanies

During the first half of the 1950s, mail bombs were used in incidents pitting the East German Stasi against democratic West Germany and other perceived enemies in the West. West German police arrested two people on 30 November 1951 in their hunt for the mail bomb plot that killed a newspaper editor in Bremen and a girl in Eystrup, putting the country into a state of terror. The male and female suspects were seen in a car outside the Eystrup Post Office on 29 November when one of the packages exploded.[5]

In one of the more bizarre German mail-bomb plots, American popular culture trumped ideological terrorism as motivation. On 12 December a 24-year-old German man claimed he was influenced by 'American gangster stories when he unleashed his mail bomb plot' that killed two and injured twelve in north Germany. Federal and local police were involved in what was called 'Germany's greatest post-war man-hunt'. Erich von Halacz confessed after three hours of questioning. He admitted he mailed three bombs in a plot to extort money from the families of victims. Authorities said the man told them 'he intended to follow up the "mail-order" bombs with letters threatening death to other members of the families of victims unless they paid him $1,200 each.'[6]

On 28 March 1952 a weaponized letter was sent to the West German chancellor Adenauer. It was intercepted by two boys who turned the package over to police saying it had been given to them by a stranger to mail.[7] It exploded at a Munich police station, killing a demolition expert and injuring four others. The blast was powerful enough to shatter a basement room. The bomb expert, Karl Reichert, lost both hands and suffered head and leg injuries. The injured included two reporters and two police officers watching him open the box.[8] Police eventually arrested a 28-year-old suspect for this attempt. Less than a week later mail bombs were sent to prominent West German officials. One of the leaders of the neo-Nazi Socialist Reich Party, Count Wolf Westarp, actually took a stand against this plot despite the fact that the government was trying to outlaw the party. Westarp commented in a telephone interview, in a thinly veiled threat, that his party would 'accept measures of force' if it had no other means of opposition to the present German government (an obvious threat of action in case the party was outlawed).[9]

In March 1955 an attempt to kill one of West Berlin's leading anti-communists with a mail bomb came up short but still managed to wound two Germans. It exploded as it was being opened in the personnel offices of the giant Schuckert electric plant. The parcel was about 4 × 6 inches and addressed to Carl-Hubert Schwennicke, a director of Siemens and chair of the Free Democratic Party. He was attending a meeting of the city parliament at the time but was convinced the bomb was sent from communist East Berlin.[10] Several months later a communist agent of the East German secret police was being sought for the attempted assassination of Premier Johannes Hoffman by mail bomb, which, postal authorities had intercepted.[11]

In the summer of 1955 a bomb wrapped in a mail parcel killed a Slovak anti-communist refugee leader who had served in the military during Nazi occupation. Matus Cernak, fifty years old, was instantly killed as he unwrapped the parcel in a suburban Schwabing post office. The blast also killed an elderly woman bystander and injured thirteen others, wrecking the delivery room in the process. The area was a well-known artists' colony and a rallying place for refugees from behind the Iron Curtain.[12] West German police figured the assassins 'scored a bulls eye'. Taking a page from the East German Stasi playbook, they probably closely monitored Cernak's habits, including personally calling for mail parcels and opening them in the post office. He had formerly served as cultural minister of Slovakia under Premier Josip Broz Tito between 1939 and 1945 and had been chairman of the National Council of Slovakia, an organization of anti-Red Slovak immigrants in West Germany.[13]

The following year, on 21 January, Willy Kressmann, a West Berlin district mayor, received a weaponized device. He accused the East German government, explaining that he was targeted because he was one of West Berlin's most outspoken anti-communists. The only information on the device was that the bomb was 'fashioned around a beer bottle' and mailed to his home. He turned it over to police and they exploded it.[14]

An Unbelievable Plot

On 23 January 1952 Donald Robert Rankin, 27, of Indiana was arrested for sending explosives through the mail in what police called an 'unbelievable' plot to kill a man in Ohio. Postal inspectors claimed he sent fifteen sticks of dynamite to James McCray, 27, of Bowling Green, Ohio. The device was designed to explode when the package lid was lifted. In December of the previous year someone had tried to kill McCray, shooting him in the shoulder. The assailant was never identified. From here the bomb plot became even more Byzantine. The target of the death plot received a letter on 7 January 1952 from Cheyenne, Wyoming, purportedly signed by an agent from the FBI. The writer said that he had a lead on the suspect that shot him (McCray) and was sending him a package containing photographs of the suspect. McCray smelled a rat and took the letter and package to the county attorney's office, where the dynamite was discovered in the box. The parcel had been traced to Rankin in Denver on the 'basis of an "almost unbelievable motive"', which the Denver postal inspector would not disclose yet. He only said, 'it was [among] the most unbelievable stories I have heard.'[15]

Rankin had an excellent military record during the Second World War and in Korea. Once arrested he admitted to sending the mail bomb. The decorated Second World War paratrooper told police he was plotting a third attempt when arrested by postal inspectors. Rankin said he first tried to shoot McCray but hit him in the arm. He then mailed the booby-trapped package labelled 'from the FBI'. He denied it was due to jealousy over learning that McCray was a former college sweetheart of Rankin's wife. He said he planned to stalk him with a high-powered rifle with a telescopic sight and shoot from 550 yards. He claimed he was hired to kill him for a fellow named 'Al'.[16] Yes indeed, it did sound like an unbelievable story.

The 1950s saw other letter bomb investigations in the Americas. On 21 May 1953 Mexican authorities charged a Mexico City businessman with homicide, assault and attempted fraud in an airmail bombing which killed three on 9 May. Police said Alfredo Del Valle insured himself for $75,000 and planned to time bomb a plane to kill a friend travelling under his name. Fortunately for the friend the bomb package was rerouted and exploded in Mazatlán airport.[17] That same year two Alexandria, Virginia, mailboxes were demolished by explosions. Detectives investigating the origin of a home-made bomb found in the chimney of a new house two weeks previously said two fifteen-year-old boys admitted to two other mailbox bombs but not the chimney bomb. They had created mail bombs from gunpowder taken from bullets and dropped them in mailboxes as a prank. Since they were minors they were charged with manufacturing and possessing explosives and released to their parents.[18]

Several months later what authorities referred to as a 'screwball contraption' almost killed a 68-year-old Boston woman. The device was supposed to be set off by the back flash of an exploding pistol in the box. When she opened the package the gun did go off but shot her through the arm and failed to detonate the larger charge. Police were able to deduce that the package had been addressed to the daughter of the victim by a rejected suitor. When they showed the bomber that samples of paper from the package and ink from the address matched the sample of paper and ink taken from his room, he confessed and was sentenced to eight years in prison.

The following year a crude home-made bomb exploded in a sack of mail at the main New Orleans post office. It had been placed in a shoebox and wrapped in brown paper and twine. Once it arrived in a mail sack from Chicago it exploded when opened, slightly injuring two employees.[19]

The destruction of an aeroplane over Longmont, Colorado, in 1955 and other bomb scares that plagued the nation led the federal criminal justice system to become involved.

Mail bombings had become such a nuisance and threat to life and the postal system that on 26 August 1957 the United States Senate passed a bill decreeing the death penalty for murder by mail. It decreed penalties of death or life for sending mail bombs, poisons and other forbidden materials that resulted in death. The bill also doubled the penalty from ten to twenty years behind bars for sending matter through the mail with the intent to kill, or injure in cases where death does not result.[20]

More Geopolitical Conflict

On 24 May 1953 the Irish Republican Army (IRA) announced it was back with a letter bomb blast in Belfast's main post office. The Belfast bomb was only detected when it exploded prematurely. No injuries were reported. A police search turned up six weaponized parcels addressed to leading personages in Northern Ireland. They were located among sorted mail and in a subsequent search of city post boxes. Each device contained a 'quantity of magnesium and other chemicals with acid in a rubber tube as a fuse'.[21] Another similar mail bomb exploded in County Down. It was believed that the charge had been placed by IRA sympathizers protesting against plans for the coronation of Queen Elizabeth II on 2 June. All the bombs had been mailed in the Belfast district.[22] Police described the bombs as not meant to inflict personal injury. In any case police remained cautious until the Queen's visit to Ulster on 2–4 July. At the same time a number of suspects were kept under surveillance with some detained during the coronation period.

Foreshadowing the Israeli-Egyptian Conflict

In 1956 several letter bomb incidents in the Middle East were har-bingers for the letter bomb campaign in the 1960s that pitted Israel against German scientists working in Egypt, with murder by mail playing a significant role. In the 1950s Mustafa Hafez and Salah Mustafa ran squads of Palestinian infiltrators on bloody raids into Israel. Bomb expert and explosives officer Natan Rotberg worked on a variety of devices in preparation for a letter bomb campaign against the terrorists. He told Institute for Intelligence and Special Operations (Mossad) agents that if they were able to deliver a thick book to Hafez, he could do the rest. Rotberg recounted,

> I cut out the book's insides and poured in three hundred grams of my stuff . . . A detonator is twenty grams – if it explodes in your hand, you will end up without any fingers. So three hundred grams that explodes in a person's face will kill him for sure.[23]

The subsequent plan went perfectly. On 11 July 1956 Hafez was handed a package at the Egyptian military intelligence headquar-ters in Gaza. An eyewitness recalled, 'When he pulled the book out of the package a piece of paper fell out.' Hafez reached down to pick it up and it exploded, killing him.[24] The Egyptian news services reported that he was killed as he performed his duties as com-mander of the 'fedayeen' (militant guerrillas considered freedom fighters by Palestinian people and terrorists by Israelis).

On 14 July the Egyptian military attaché in Amman, Jordan, Salah Musafa, was gravely wounded by a parcel-post bomb blamed on Israeli agents.[25] Three doctors were flown in from Egypt to oper-ate on his severe injuries as he entered the Egyptian embassy. His wounds were mortal having severed both arms and injured his legs and lower abdomen. He died within the week.[26]

The Arab world immediately called the bombing typical of past Israeli army intelligence campaigns against the British. One Cairo newspaper suggested that 'underground war between Egypt and

Israel already has started.' The bomb had been mailed from the Jordan-Israeli Truce Commission offices in divided Jerusalem.[27]

The EOKA and the Da-Riff Case

Except for the IRA and an occasional Indian nationalist, Scotland Yard's Special Branch was never really required to involve itself in international terrorism. The brief Irgun campaign in the previous chapter was among the first times Special Branch had to deal with international groups. However, the Palestinian campaign was a harbinger of things to come. In April 1955 the National Organization of Cypriot Fighters (EOKA) began a campaign to secure union with Greece, and there were other indications that other groups planned to bring grief to London.

One example was the activities of a young student born Gordon Henry, who had converted to Islam in 1954 and changed his name to Konrad Da-Riff. On 6 November 1957 police found nearly two hundred detonators and sticks of dynamite in a shed in Park Road, Kingston upon Thames, to the southwest of London. The explosives were wrapped in newspaper. Just legible on one corner was the name 'Henry' written in pencil. This clue was followed up by a police appeal to newsagents to report any newspaper customers named Henry. A local newsagent identified the paper as one delivered on rounds to a Middle East student who had since gone abroad. Da-Riff had previously come under investigation in Autumn 1956 when he left to fight in Egypt during the Anglo-French-Israeli invasion. He was routinely added to the Branch's Port Watch list. The matter stayed there until 24 January 1957 when Da-Riff flew into Heathrow Airport. Once intercepted he was questioned about the dynamite found at Park Road. He explained that he had been walking the previous summer and came across a store hut near a quarry. He recognized it stored explosives and returned three weeks later, broke in and carried the explosives back to his lodgings. He admitted to being a zealous supporter of Egyptian president Nasser and had studied the Arabic language in Syria. Da-Riff pleaded guilty and was sentenced to seven years in prison for theft and the possession of explosives. This case, according to one history of the Special Branch, 'was the first sign of Arab militancy on the streets of London'.[28]

The Da-Riff case was linked to EOKA, as EOKA planned to send letter bombs to relatives of British servicemen fighting in Cyprus. The plot was cracked thanks to a tragedy. A man was picked at random from the telephone book and sent a bomb that blinded him. The innocent victim was said to be a quiet church-going family man without enemies. Evidence of gelignite and a hearing aid battery were found in the remnants of the bomb. Henry was arrested on his return to the UK from Egypt. He confessed he was a supporter of Arab anti-colonialism and to sending the deadly parcel to test the bomb apparatus. He also confessed that other targets were to be Prime Minister Harold Macmillan, Sir Anthony Eden and others. At the time EOKA was fighting to unite the British colony of Cyprus with Greece. Da-Riff aka Henry had also drawn up a lengthy list of relatives of servicemen to send bombs to. His confession revealed ties between EOKA and anti-British Arab groups and even IRA sympathizers in Britain.[29]

1957

The year 1957 was a particularly busy time for postal bombers in the United States and elsewhere. On 17 May the wife of the prefect of France's Bas-Rhin department and former governor of Algiers was killed in Bas-Rhin when she unwrapped a package addressed to her husband. It was designed to detonate when the lid on a cigar box was lifted. It exploded in her face.[30]

In October a mail bomb was sent to 'a pretty air hostess'. It exploded in her flat in Slough, England. Enquiries were made in the many places she travelled as a hostess for British European Airways. It was mailed in London. When it arrived the postal worker tossed it up to the window of her flat and a male friend caught it and passed it to her. As she opened it a battery-operated detonator set off the bomb – 'a bottle shaped metal cylinder packed with lead shot', which seriously injured her face.[31]

American postal inspectors were kept on their toes in November beginning with their arrest of Charlie Lee Maynard, 28, for mailing a 'homemade dynamite bomb' to a Kentucky judge the previous September. The judge picked up the parcel at the post office and took it to his office. However, the attempt failed thanks to the presence of a deputy sheriff who was in his office when he brought in the mail. He became suspicious and advised against opening it for several reasons. First off, the top of the box bore a comic convalescence card, 'It's Time to Blow Right Outa Here'. He then noticed a string that went through a small hole on the inside. The string was meant to trigger the bomb. With a practised hand the peace officer pried the lid a fraction and could clearly see dynamite. Further investigation found Maynard had cut the stick in half and set both halves with a detonator in a box and mailed it to the judge. As in many of these revenge-oriented mail bomb cases the plot was over what would seem to outsiders to be a rather minor reason. In this case the judge had fined him $200 in a case several months earlier. Authorities found matching bomb parts at Maynard's house.[32]

Just before Thanksgiving a ticking carton was addressed to President Dwight Eisenhower in Augusta, Georgia. Evidence led to the arrest of a man in Pennsylvania, who was committed to a mental institution. Detectives picked him up after postal authorities intercepted the package and handed it over to Secret Service agents. The parcel was described as a box measuring 10 × 10 inches. It consisted of 'a maze of wires, batteries and a clock but contained no explosives'. Doctors found the hardware clerk who sent it to be mentally ill. As it turned out the man had been under investigation for some time as a result of threatening letters he mailed to the president, the first lady, Minnesota senator Hubert Humphrey and two judges. The letters were all signed with a bloody thumbprint.[33]

1959

As the 1950s came to a close, mail bombs rarely made the news outside of the United States. Several cases in 1959 piqued the public's attention. Authorities in San Diego wondered who would want to blow up 'pretty Mrs. Kathryn Morris, 33'. Authorities recognized that whoever did had 'a definite knowledge of explosives and with a strong reason to kill her'. A brother of a man arrested in the case believed Morris knew who killed a Nevada gambler. However, this proved to be a red herring. San Diego police chief Joe O'Connor said there are usually only two possible motives for such an assault – 'money, or love turned to hate – and she doesn't have any money'. She had been separated from her husband and, in fact, had been the target of two previous bombs. The first arrived on 4 November 1959 but exploded outside the apartment. The second bomb came at Christmas in 1959 but wasn't delivered because she had moved.[34] As it turned out it blew up outside a four-family apartment house, injuring a two-year-old in El Cajon, California.

She had been dating several men during her separation and one of her escorts at the time seemed like a good lead. Nathan Silver, a pharmacist, appeared to be the only suspect capable of making a bomb in a box. He had rented a workshop in a San Diego garage. When authorities obtained a search warrant they found wire, powder-covered work gloves, a pistol, tranquillizers and sleeping pills. He was initially arrested for narcotics possession. The next day the spurned lover was charged with attempted murder. Lab results confirmed what authorities suspected and he was sentenced to a long prison stint.[35]

Another California case captured headlines in 1959. In Salinas a carrier postal worker was charged with mailing a bomb to his neighbour. He attempted suicide when he was announced as a suspect. John S. Bates, 33, eventually confessed to mailing the bomb although it did not explode when the neighbour lifted the lid of the parcel. He was seemingly motivated by having been accused by the neighbour of having made advances to her son.

During the 1950s the motivations and tactics of mail bombers varied little from previous years. An increasing number of mail bomb attacks were motivated by geopolitical conflicts such as in the case of EOKA, the IRA and Middle East actors. However, one case in 1959 did bring attention to another form of murder by mail that did not entail explosives but rested on the culinary skills of poisoners, usually women. Mrs Letha Belia Overton, wife of a Baptist Sunday school superintendent in Florida, used the mail to send poisoned candy to thirty students in the class. She confessed to having put arsenic in home-made chocolate fudge 'to spite the Baptists who had neglected her socially'. Twenty-one students ate the candy. Their lives were saved because Letha 'overdid her job'. She had added such a large dose to the candy the students were instantly nauseated and vomited up the poison before it reached their stomachs. She was committed to an insane asylum. In a similar case in April 1958, James E. Gaither sent poisoned candy to his estranged wife in Los Angeles. Four family members wasted no time getting into the peanut clusters. As in the previous account they fell violently ill within half an hour. Gaither admitted to adding rat poison to the sweets and the only reason they lived is because they only ingested small bites.

9

The 1960s: International Conflict and Personal Vendettas

I n the 1960s murder by mail increased dramatically compared to the prior decade as more countries reported incidents. At the beginning of the 1960s the targets of infernal machines ran the gamut from ex-Nazi scientists working in Egypt to a Belgian teacher who supported the leftist Algerian forces, as weaponized mail was used for political and personal grievances. On 27 March 1960 a history teacher in Bressoux, Belgium, known for his 'left-wing sympathies' and often visited by Algerians, died from injuries received after opening a parcel bomb.[1] Later, in the autumn, a potentially lethal bomb addressed to Vice President Richard Nixon was discovered by a South Dakota postal employee, leading post offices in the nation's capital to realert its branches throughout the country to examine more closely any packages addressed to presidential candidates and their running mates. The parcel in question measured 2 × 6 inches and was wrapped with string connected to a triggering device. A note on the package to Nixon said, 'Pull string to open'. The parcel contained an 'artillery simulator with liquid aluminum as its main explosive'. The postmaster said the device was typically used in military training exercises and was 'capable of maiming a person 25 feet away'.[2]

Between 1962 and 1965 Israeli agents targeted German scientists working on an Egyptian missile project and Venezuelan police discovered that communist terrorists had adopted the new strategy of airmailing bombs to police at war with Red guerrillas in the Falcón province.[3] That same year a Front de Libération du Québec (FLQ) terrorist in Montreal was sentenced to four years in prison for sending a mailbox bomb. Meanwhile, on the other side of the world

Communist China was accusing Nationalist Chinese agents of continued use of postal facilities to mail bombs from Hong Kong to the mainland.[4]

Egyptian Missile Programme (1962–5)

On the morning of 2 July 1962 Egypt caught Israel and the wider world by surprise, announcing it had successfully launched four surface-to-air missiles. Two were the new *Al Zafir* (victory) type with a range of 175 miles and the other two of the *Al Qahir* (conqueror) design, with a range of 350 miles. Ten days later ten of each type were on display draped with the Egyptian flag and paraded through the streets of Cairo to the Nile river. President Nasser boasted that his rockets were capable of destroying any target south of Beirut.[5] An Egyptian radio broadcast delivered in Hebrew from Egypt was even more explicit, announcing, 'These missiles are intended to open the gates of freedom for the Arabs, to retake the homeland that was stolen as part of imperialist and Zionist plots.'[6]

The Israeli intelligence community, including Mossad, was caught completely off-guard. Subsequent investigation revealed that Egypt had recruited a group of German engineers who had formerly worked on the Nazi missile project and were now developing missiles in Egypt.[7] These were not just any scientists but had been some of the most senior engineers of the Nazi regime just seventeen years earlier. They had worked at the research base on the Peenemünde peninsula on the Baltic coast where the Germans developed their most advanced weapons, including the v-1 flying bombs and the v-2 ballistic missile.[8]

Information leaked out that Egyptian president Nasser considered arming missiles with weapons of mass destruction such as biological, chemical and radiological warheads. Israel tried to stop the programme through traditional diplomatic channels first, unsuccessfully attempting to convince the Federal Republic of Germany to help halt the project. After the diplomatic approach failed, alternatives were considered. Initially the plan was to either kidnap or kill the engineers. Intelligence was revved into high gear until the head of Unit 188 (a branch of the Israeli Defense Forces) reached the conclusion that the best way to stop the scientists would be to use letter bombs.[9]

The bomb expert Natan Rotberg was directed to start preparing the devices. He began working with a 'new type of explosive: thin, flexible Datasheet'. These were 'sheets of explosive materials developed for civilian purposes. Utilization required fusing two pieces of steel when they went off,' allowing him to make 'compact charges'. Rotberg later said that it was necessary to create a system that could be disarmed and was safe 'during all the shuffling that a letter goes through in the mail system, and then go off at the right time'. These letter bombs were like no other. The letter bombs operated in such a way that the bomb 'was armed not when it was opened, which would make the whole thing very explosive, but only when the contents were drawn out'.[10]

The first target selected for elimination was Alois Brunner, an escaped Nazi war criminal who had been a deputy of Adolf Eichmann and a concentration camp commandant in France. Unit 188 tracked him down to his roost in Damascus where he was training Syrian secret police interrogation and torture units in return for protection. Once they found him on 13 September 1962, Rotberg the bomb-maker said, 'We sent him a little gift.' As soon as Brunner opened it he suffered severe facial injuries and lost his left eye, but he survived.[11]

Encouraged by the Damascus attack, the Israelis decided to use this tactic against the German rocket builders. Not all of the intelligence officers supported this. One Mossad operative objected, saying, 'I oppose any action that I don't control. The mailman can open the envelope, a child can open the envelope. Who does things like that?'[12] Not surprisingly his objections were ignored.

One of the first challenges to launching the bomb campaign was the fact that the scientists in Egypt did not receive their mail directly. Egyptian intelligence collected all of the mail in Cairo. Israeli agents overcame this by breaking into the EgyptAir office at night and placing the weaponized envelopes into the mailbags.

One of the prime targets among the scientists was Dr Wolfgang Pilz, the German director of Factory 333 – a complex of buildings where the German scientists worked on the missile programme for the Egyptians in Cairo. The Israeli agents had been apprised that Pilz was divorcing his wife so he could marry his secretary, Hannelore Wende. When the letter arrived the secretary thought it might be from a lawyer in Hamburg. The planners did not count on her opening it before passing it on to Pilz. On 27 November she did the unexpected. The blast blew off her fingers, blinded her in one eye and damaged the other while blowing some of her teeth out of her gums. Once the authorities heard about this they located the other mail bombs with X-ray devices and had them defused.[13] It was hoped these violent attacks would frighten the scientists and their families enough to go back to Germany, but they were reluctant to leave their cushy, well-paid jobs.

The following day a gift-wrapped parcel sent from a lawyer's office in Hamburg to Cairo killed the Egyptian scientist Michael Khouri and five Egyptian engineers standing nearby. The package was actually addressed to its intended target, General Kamal Azzar, an Egyptian army coordinator collaborating with the German scientists.[14] In 1964–5 Israeli intelligence agents in Israel began sending letter bombs again. On 26 September 1964 two postal workers were injured by an explosive device placed in a letter mailed to a German aircraft specialist working in Cairo. It occurred at a post office in the suburb of Maadi where the German scientists and technicians lived, still helping develop jet fighter planes. The Cairo newspaper *Al Ahram* reported that 'it was part of an Israeli terrorist campaign against the German scientists.' Moreover, Egyptian intelligence was confronting a new wave of weaponized mail that targeted Germans.[15]

A German mechanic working on jet engines in Egypt received a large envelope from the Bank of Egypt. Thinking it was just an advertisement he flipped it onto the back seat of his car. Looking at it a week later he noticed that the glue on the envelope had melted and he could see a tiny wire inside it, piquing his curiosity and alerting him to his deadly cargo. Just two days earlier a similar envelope had been addressed to another German expert but had exploded in the post office. The week before a secretary was 'blinded for life when a package she was opening up exploded in her face'. This tragic episode convinced the Israelis to use targeted killing only sparingly or as a last resort. After this series of attacks it was decided that all letters addressed to the German experts would hereafter be turned over to the Egyptian army bomb squad.[16]

Despite the targets on their backs German experts continued to come to Egypt to help President Gamal Abdel Nasser build rockets and jet planes. Nasser claimed that Russian and American experts were unwilling to help and that he had begun bringing in the Germans almost five years previously. He was careful to note that 'These Germans are not Nazis. That is just Zionist propaganda.' By 1965 close to six hundred Germans were helping Egypt develop rockets and jet fighter planes. Twenty of the workers were closely guarded. Fifteen of the top scientists were working in the desert under Dr Wolfgang Pilz. Despite spending a small fortune on this programme, by 1965 they had only made one single-stage rocket with a slightly longer range and developed a simple guidance system. The rocket experts were housed in special apartment buildings manned by guards, but the scientists and their families were allowed to move around freely. One German said he was there only for the money but 'I resent what these Israeli secret agents are doing to us . . . The Israelis won't get away with it forever.'[17] This campaign against the German scientists working for Egypt had the desired effect of thwarting the German scientists' work for President Abdel Nasser's military ambitions, forcing them to leave Egypt altogether by 1965.[18]

In January 1965 the Palestinian terrorist group known as Fatah launched its first attack inside Israel. This was a different enemy, one that Israeli intelligence had to learn to fight clandestinely. It took almost eight months to come up with a plan to counter the Palestinian threat, including targeting the Palestine Liberation Organization (PLO) leader Yasser Arafat.[19] The decision was made to bring back the letter bomb. Mail bombs were soon posted to Fatah officials in Lebanon and Syria. They used a by then well-known ruse of making sure the letters appeared to be from individuals familiar to the targets. To make the subterfuge more authentic the Israeli operatives mailed them from inside Lebanon. This time it would be a woman who would go to Beirut and mail the letters there. Since she was the daughter of a Jewish father and a gentile mother from South Africa and held a British passport, all bases were covered to protect her identity.

Israeli leaders were sceptical after what happened in Egypt. None of the targets had been eliminated. Mossad chief Meir Amit assured them that they were putting more explosives in the letter bombs to resolve that; nonetheless, letter bombs failed to eliminate any targets. They just caused injuries. Most were discovered and neutralized.[20]

Front de Libération du Québec: 1963

While the Israelis were hunting down the German scientists in 1963 a wave of mailbox bombings by French Canadian Quebec separatists terrorized a Montreal suburb, blowing off the arm of an army demolition expert as he tried to dismantle a bomb. One unexploded bomb was discovered in a mailbox outside a high school. Targets included Westmount, an English-speaking stronghold in French Canadian Quebec.[21] Pierre Schneider, 19, admitted to the Westmount operation, adding that he pleaded 'guilty to loving Quebec and cooperation with others who wanted to free it from colonialism'. He testified that he made three mail drops of bombs in mailboxes himself. Another teenage member admitted making the ten bombs in the Westmount case and depositing five of them in mailboxes.[22] In December Mario Bachand was sentenced to four years in prison for the mailbox explosion that severely injured Major Walter Leja during FLQ terrorism the previous spring. He was also given three years for planting a mail bomb in a mailbox and six months for other bombing-related offences.

Revenge Seekers

While the letter bomb was most prominently used in political and ideological conflicts in the 1960s it was still one of the weapons of choice for revenge seekers and score-settlers. In January 1962 authorities were searching for a suspect in California who sent a mail bomb to a woman in Eckert, Colorado. It exploded when Mrs Mildred Tandy, who operated a general store, opened it. She lost both hands and suffered severe burns on her face, arms and upper body. The bomb consisted of a small box of powder, a flashlight battery detonator and a spring trigger that tripped to explode when she cut string on the package. Fortunately for inspectors the postmark was not destroyed.[23] The letter bomb had been postmarked California.[24]

Later that month David W. Wion, who was described as having a way with women, sat in a Sacramento jail accused of sending the mail bomb to Mrs Tandy. Postal inspectors said he was a suspect from the start once they learned Wion had sent a threatening letter to her a month earlier and she had obtained a restraining order against him to prevent him from molesting or interfering with her. She was recently divorced from a local judge, mostly because of her adulterous relationship with Wion. She said he was the logical suspect because they had been in a relationship for more than two years. She broke up with the bomber when she moved to Colorado to open a general store in Eckert. This was not Wion's first rodeo. He had pleaded guilty to sending a defamatory postcard to his ex-wife five years earlier. He was placed on probation. Earlier in their relationship the now-rejected paramour had filed a $50,000 personal injury lawsuit against both Tandys, claiming he was hurt in a fall in their garage on their ranch. He also had other felonies.

The year after the Tandy case, in one of the more bizarre letter bomb schemes, one that garnered much attention in the United States, an army captain in Vietnam sent his wife his version of a Dear John letter which, unfortunately for both parties involved, exploded in the San Francisco International Mail Center on 18 March 1963, injuring two. It would take another month to sort out all the particulars of the case. Army captain Alvin Klein mailed his wife, Vyrna (or Mickey), a 'Communist Viet Cong booby trap inside a birthday present'. Klein had some type of long-distance disagreement with his wife based on his suspicions about her fidelity while he was away. Although the profiles of letter bombers vary widely Klein was described as an 'introvert – grimly serious and dedicated to his army career. He was deeply religious and tried to help other Jewish soldiers.' Others described him as 'methodical, hard-working and conscientious in his efforts to do a good job'. After the device exploded and injured two postal clerks, a description of the infernal device was provided by the bomber. He admitted wrapping the bomb in a 'blue cashmere and angora' coat he sent as a present. Klein explained to postal inspectors that 'when he wrapped the coat in the package, he had a "last-minute impulse" to put in the "souvenir" explosive device because it would be something nice to have.' His impulse brought him to court on federal charges on 19 April 1963 for sending an explosive device through the mail with the intent to cause bodily harm.[25]

From the very beginning his wife didn't believe he had done it, even after he admitted his guilt. Klein was a member of a u.s. military advisory mission to Vietnam. He had been in the country for one year as a food technologist developing combat rations for South Vietnamese soldiers. He had been married for three years and had been awaiting orders to go to France when he was sent to Vietnam. His wife shared with inspectors a letter from her husband in which he wrote, 'I expect a couple of postal inspectors will be by to see you about a bomb they say I mailed to you. I wouldn't do a thing to hurt a hair on your head.' The bomb exploded with 'window shattering force'. But postal inspectors were able to piece together the package and come up with some initials and a portion of the return address, a trail that led to Captain Klein.[26]

In late 1963 three high school students in Michigan were arrested after admitting that they mailed a home-made bomb to their English teacher. It was addressed to him at school and when he opened it, it burst into flames and he tossed it away. Police quoted one of the sophomores as saying, 'We didn't want to hurt him, we just wanted to shake him up.' Two of the boys had been doing poorly in his class while the third was described as a brilliant student who had agreed to make the bomb.[27]

In the second half of the 1960s murder by mail continued to make headlines. In December 1965, for example, after a five-week investigation of William Hugo Greiff, the 59-year-old farmer was arrested for mailing a bomb to u.s. attorney Frank Freeman in Spokane, Washington. Handwriting analysis of the label was the deciding factor. Greiff, it turned out, was familiar with the use of dynamite for clearing stumps and rocks. The bomb had arrived at Freeman's residence on 30 October and was opened a couple of days later. Its contents included dynamite and blasting caps but it failed to detonate. The target was convinced that the only reason it did not go off was his care in opening it. As it turns out Freeman had presented a government case against Greiff's son, who was charged with failing to report for military induction. Grieff was convicted and sentenced to a year in prison.[28]

The following year saw mail bomb plots in a variety of locations, ranging from Canada to Italy. A case in 1966 was especially perplexing. In Italy a time bomb with a note attached arrived at the post office in Catanzaro. The letter was signed with a skull symbol. The note went on to complain about the glacial mail service. Likewise, 'the bomb's clockwork also was slow' and it failed to explode. It was then dismantled.[29] Just days after this episode, in another case the acting assistant British high commissioner in Aden, Robin Thorne, was seriously injured as he opened an airmail package, losing several fingers and requiring abdominal surgery.[30]

That same year a Florida man, 25-year-old Josip Kucko, was charged with posting a mail bomb to a bridegroom in Titusville, Florida. He was arrested weeks later by postal inspectors at his home near Orlando. He was a Yugoslavian immigrant who had come to the United States in 1961. He was charged with mailing a bomb in a 1-pound box of candy to Kenneth Porter, 20, who received it hours before his wedding to a Titusville girl. The prosecution maintained that Kucko was jealous of Porter because he had previously dated his fiancée. Kucko purchased the box of candy and asked the drugstore clerk to address it and mail it to Porter. But, as in most other cases, the letter bomb was rendered defective due to 'rough mail handling'.[31]

As the very active year moved to its conclusion a mail bomb tore off the hands of a prison guard and severely injured his son in

British Columbia. The victim was a guard at the BC federal penitentiary. He happened to find the parcel when he came home from work just before Christmas 1966. The bomb had gone through the postal system. His young son was standing next to him as he unwrapped the 2-pound parcel, which sent shrapnel into both. The boy lost sight in one eye but later recovered.[32]

The next year saw a number of international bombing cases. On 23 February a Russian bus driver was charged for the murder by mail of his ex-wife so that he wouldn't have to make alimony payments. Ivan Borovkov, 28, was assisted by his new wife and his girlfriend in rigging a bomb inside a small suitcase. They mailed it to his former wife along with an attached key. When she inserted the key in the keyhole it exploded, killing her. Once apprehended, all the mail bomber could muster as an excuse was that he did it 'out of a burning desire to escape alimony payment'.[33]

In October 1967 in Brisbane, Australia, Mrs Tracey Phillips, 23, had both of her hands amputated in a hospital after a mail bomb exploded in her bedroom. She also suffered a fractured jaw and lacerations to the face and body. The bomb was concealed in a box about 6 inches long, 4 inches wide and 21 inches deep and was wrapped in brown paper. The bomb was posted in Melbourne. She was at home with her husband, a tattooist, and her five-month-old child when she triggered the bomb upon opening the box. It was powerful enough to blow off the front section of her home. The baby was also seriously hurt, suffering injuries to his eyes, a fractured forehead and other wounds. Police said that the original address on the package was to her husband's tattoo shop, which he had closed the week before.[34] Further investigation suggested that the device had been sent by a gang member who nursed a grudge against the tattooist.[35]

Days after the Australia bomb, a 44-year-old man in Michigan was arrested and charged with the mail bomb murder of a sandwich shop owner in the town of Marshall. This was a case where handwriting evidence played a key role in solving the crime. Enoch D. Chism was arrested after the state police crime lab linked the bomb sent to the sandwich shop owner to another package containing a

bottle of pills mailed to the victim back in May. The package had
been mailed to Mrs Nola Puyear, 56. The pills were labelled as tranquillizers but contained a form of lye. The handwriting analysis
indicated that the same person had sent both. The bomb was also in
a plain wrapped package. It exploded in her arms as she opened it at
her premises and she was killed instantly. Chism had been convicted
of arson the previous year for setting fire to a home owned by his
brother but was sentenced to only two years' probation and a fine.[36]

At the end of 1967 New York City police were investigating the
possibility that a 'mad bomber' with a grudge against the communist
regime in Cuba may have set off several bombs that exploded in
postal buildings. One exploded in a midtown Manhattan post
office, injuring eight employees and damaging hundreds of packages. This parcel was detonated when a postal clerk tossed it into a
receiving bin filled with medical supplies going to Cuba. It was
inside a 'shoebox size parcel marked "medicine"'. Although there
was suspicion that the two were linked there was no evidence to
substantiate it.[37]

That same month a bomb contained in a parcel post package
exploded in the basement of an Elizabeth, New Jersey, post office on
4 December, causing a flash fire that injured six people. Preliminary
investigation determined that the device 'contained liquid because
the explosion triggered flames'. One of the injured workers
remembered the bomb box was 'about the size of a fruit cake'.[38]

At the beginning of 1968 a bomb disguised as a Christmas
whisky package was sent to the peace advocate David Dellinger of
the National Committee to End the War in Vietnam. He received
the package at his home in New Hampshire. After partially opening
it he noticed wires that seemed out of place. He took it outside and
called the police. A postal inspector told him that if he had opened
it normally or if a heavy weight had been placed on it, it would have
exploded. The device contained a bottle of gasoline, a detonation
cap and a hand grenade wired to a battery.[39] Just a week later a
parcel bomb blew up in a Havana ministry courtyard as it was being
unloaded from a mail truck, injuring five. At the time, the Cuban
government was considering a new policy of 'definitive measures

with regard to parcels coming from the United States'. The bomb was being carried in a mailbag labelled 'United States mail' and had recently arrived by ship from Canada.[40]

Several months later in Petaluma, California, former bank executive Albert A. Ricci drowned. He was linked to a package bomb that had killed a government physicist, Samuel Hammons Jr, in Ohio the previous month. The FBI traced the bomb parcel to 53-year-old Ricci. The coroner ruled out an inquest after the drowning having considered the bomb death of 42-year-old Hammons a closed case. Like so many other domestic cases in the 1960s this one revolved around a love triangle. The coroner commented that 'The bomb, a childish and poorly designed one, was an unnecessary attempt' by the bomber to 'remove a supposed rival in an extramarital affair'. Ricci was described as exhibiting 'paranoid behaviour bordering on the psychotic' in the weeks leading to his drowning. The victim of the bombing died while being operated on, four hours after opening the package in his home kitchen.[41]

The end of the 1960s was a particularly active time for mail bombers. In 1969 alone weaponized bombs exploded in the United States, Vietnam, Tanzania and Canada. On 2 January 1969 it was reported that a dynamite bomb was placed in a mailbox in Ottawa and detonated on New Year's Eve. No one was injured but the device shattered windows on the first five floors of a nine-storey building and tore a 5-foot crater in the street. Authorities were confident the bomb was tied to the Quebec separatist campaign that was marked by bombings in Montreal.[42] The following month a package bomb killed the guerrilla leader Eduardo Mondlane in Tanzania. The parcel had been sent from West Germany and exploded as he was unwrapping it, killing him instantly.[43]

The Vietnam War was heating up in 1969 when mail bombs exploded in a Saigon post office, killing four. The 'two plastic bombs, wrapped for mailing' ripped through the crowded room of Saigon's main post office on 8 May. This incident followed three bombings in the city the night before, which wounded fifteen persons including two Americans. Police confirmed that the bombers left two other bombs in the post office but they did not detonate. The suspects ran out of the building before the explosions and made their getaway on motor scooters. They cleverly planted each bomb at 'opposite ends of the cavernous post office lobby'. The biggest bomb contained about 15 pounds of plastic explosives, the smaller one only 2 pounds. A woman and a South Vietnamese army officer were killed instantly.[44]

In the United States bombs were exploding in home mail deliveries and at colleges. As February ended bombs exploded at two of the Claremont Colleges near Los Angeles, injuring one employee and causing minimal damage to the building. A twenty-year-old woman was injured when she picked up a parcel in the mail at the administration building. It blew up, seriously injuring her right hand and burning her face.[45]

A long-standing mail bomb case was being played out in a Cleveland court room in April in the mail bomb trial of Orville Stifel II, 22, of Groesbeck. He was accused of murder by mail in the death of Daniel Ronec, 23, a Cleveland school teacher, on 8 July 1968. The prosecution maintained he was motivated by jealousy over his former girlfriend jilting him for the victim. The results of atomic analysis of the bomb, a process known as neutron activation analysis, showed the materials of the bomb to have come from the same manufacturer and same production batch as similar materials found after the killing in the laboratory where the bomber worked. A postal bomb expert told the jury that the bomb 'was a sophisticated one, requiring great know-how'.[46] Police said the bomb was made up of two batteries, dynamite and part of a transistor radio that 'cost about $2 to make'. The package containing the bomb was only about 2 inches in diameter and weighed half a pound. Furthermore the analyst said the bomb was probably made of plastic explosive, not gunpowder or dynamite. The fragments of cardboard, red plastic tape and gummed labels used in or on the mail bomb were microscopically identical to material used in the lab where Stifel worked.

Stifel hardly seemed like he had the makings of a mail bomber. Popular in high school, his contemporaries regarded him as intelligent and fun. He was the envy of his classmates. He graduated from Ohio University in 1968. However, all these notions were put to rest after he killed the fiancé of his former girlfriend. Stifel went out with Cheryl Jones for about a year until she broke up with him while he was still at university. In high school he was considered good at science; he even built an amplifier at home. His former girlfriend had another take on her erstwhile suitor. She told inspectors that he had previously threatened to shoot her and her fiancé, Ronec, who was later killed by the package bomb. Stifel had a high IQ and was employed at Procter & Gamble as a laboratory technician. Investigators found 3 pounds of black gunpowder, 2 pounds of pistol powder, a toy radio, one large firecracker and a roll of copper wire in a search of his apartment. Even more revealing, they found copies of the local newspaper that had stories about the bomb killing of Ronec.[47]

As the verdict in the case neared, the prosecution seemed to have an airtight case with '16 alleged' points of evidence. Also presented were letters containing obscenities written to the girlfriend by Stifel in 1966. But he never communicated with her after Ronec's death. Stifel was found guilty on 2 May and sentenced to life in prison.[48]

That same year a similar mail bomb case took place in Washington state. Arnold Maxwell Harris was accused of the murder-by-mail deaths of Ralph Burdick and his fourteen-month-old child. It also seriously injured Harris's estranged wife, who had had the child with Burdick. In July Harris went on trial for the killings as three co-workers testified that he was at work the day the bomb was mailed from Oregon. Harris worked some 70 miles away at a sawmill.[49]

The 1960s demonstrated the growing popularity of murder by mail among a growing cast of actors. While personal disputes and salacious love triangles seemed to dominate the headlines it seemed that this tactic was increasingly becoming part of the terrorism and counter-terrorism arsenals. No matter the perpetrator, the motive and the objective, letter bombs continued to take the lives of bystanders rather than targets, continued to be duds and continued to evoke fear whenever they made the news.

10

The 1970s: Mail Bombs Go Global

n the 1970s Vienna, Rhodesia, Malta, the United Kingdom and the United States were among the countries victimized by letter bombs. Right-wing groups in Britain sent one to a left-wing bookshop and to the communist-affiliated newspaper the *Morning Star*. In the United States the American Nazi party was targeted in Arlington, Virginia, and it was in the late 1970s that the Unabomber began his prolific bombing spree that did not end until his capture in 1996. Meanwhile, murder by mail permeated the Israeli-Palestinian conflict.

Since the 1940s, Palestinian and Jewish terrorists have used everything from improvised explosive devices (IEDs) to mail bombs against each other in their conflict over territory and sovereignty. There was a slight lull in their use in the late 1940s but from the 1950s into the 1970s letter bomb activity increased, with bombings also taking place outside the territory.

The PFLP-GC

Ahmed Jibril founded the Popular Front for the Liberation of Palestine-General Command (PFLP-GC) after splitting from the Popular Front for the Liberation of Palestine (PFLP) in 1968. His biographer dubbed him the 'father of techno-terrorism'. Samuel M. Katz credits Jibril as the first to bomb instead of hijack planes, the first to launch commando raids directly on civilians, the first to attack by hang-glider and the first to use letter bombs and other specialized weapons of terror.[1] Some of these accolades might be warranted but one of these attributions is clearly incorrect. As the previous chapters have shown, he was definitely not the first to use letter bombs.

Early PFLP-GC mail-bomb sorties began in February 1970 when operatives mailed a few booby-trapped letter bombs from Yugoslavia and Frankfurt to addresses in Israel. But they were intercepted before delivery. In a December 1971 attack the group used a parcel bomb to target Jordan's United Nations Mission in Geneva, injuring three civilians. That same month the PFLP-GC tried again to inflict 'a postal reign of terror' as operatives in Belgrade and Vienna posted approximately fifteen letter bombs to prominent Israeli businessmen and establishments.[2] In some cases explosive-laden packages detonated in transit or while being sorted by postal workers.[3]

Jibril turned to letter bombs after early terrorist operations against Israel faced several setbacks and he began searching for a new mode of operation. For this he looked to the skies and the air-mail carried on modern aircraft. For inspiration he looked no further than the downing of Swissair Flight 330 on 21 February 1970. The flight left Zurich bound for Tel Aviv. Seven minutes after take-off an explosion in the rear compartment forced the flight to return to the airport. But just 15 miles before landing it crashed, killing all 47 on board, including 15 Israelis. Subsequent investigation confirmed the crew's suspicions shared with ground control when the 'remains of an explosive device which used an altimeter mechanism' was found in the wreckage. That same day an Austrian Airlines jet suffered an inflight explosion upon take-off from Frankfurt. The plane landed safely and it was discovered that the blast was also caused by an altimeter trigger and the package was destined for Israel.[4] To say Jibril was intrigued by this act would be an understatement. He was even more impressed by the possibilities of bringing sophisticated explosive devices onto jet airliners disguised as airmail.

There was another reason for adopting this strategy. Israel's airport security was second to none. Jibril had a decision to make. He did not want to sacrifice men in gunfights with airline security and was aware that security forces were well-mobilized and prepared to fight back. To bypass the traditional terrorist playbook Jibril's expert bomb-maker, Marwan Kreeshat, developed a new device that could destroy an aircraft mid-air without revealing a link to a group or state sponsor. Kreeshat felt confident of success as long as the plan followed three criteria: (1) the device should have a fail-safe timer that would explode while flying over a body of water; (2) it should be smuggled aboard without diplomatic pouches or foreign assistance; and (3) it should be reliable so that when it exploded en route to Israel it left the victims and possessions at the bottom of the sea, leaving no clues. Once the barometric altimeter devices were ready to go they were packaged in ordinary brown paper airmail packages and allegedly mailed from a post office in Frankfurt, hoping airmail packages would be placed without a security check on the EL AL flight.[5] Jibril was convinced that 'terror by mail' bombs disguised as airmail was a model of simplicity.

Black September

In 1971 the Black September Organization (BSO) emerged as a splinter group from the Palestine Liberation Organization (PLO) Al Fatah group. According to his biographer, its chief of operations was Ali Hassan Salameh. Salameh is regarded as the chief director of the September 1972 Munich Olympics massacre of eleven Israeli athletes. After the BSO's creation, like Jibril's PFLP-GC, it also experimented with weaponized mail against Israel and the West. Indeed, for a short time, this tactic became BSO's signature method of attack.[6]

In 1972 alone the BSO was responsible for 67 letter bomb attacks in September, 11 in October and 79 in November. That same year the BSO mailed letter bombs to recipients in the United Kingdom (one killed), Israel (two wounded), the USA (two injured) and India (one killed). Between 1972 and 1987 the BSO sent dozens of letter bombs to targets in Europe. The most targeted were Israeli firms, attacked 52 times, Israeli embassies, 44 times, and randomly selected Israeli civilians, 41 times. In addition there were eleven attacks on Israelis who worked in United Nations missions, eleven at government entities and four at non-government organizations. Adhering to the strategy of mailing the devices from regions outside the Middle East, mail bombs were sent from the Netherlands, India, Malaysia, Israel and the United Kingdom to countries that included Canada, the usa, Cambodia, Zimbabwe and Congo.[7]

bso operatives mailed more than fifty letter bombs from the Netherlands in 1972. Of these, three packages weighing 8 ounces each were intercepted in Geneva before being delivered to the Israeli diplomatic mission there. In other letter bomb attacks five envelopes were mailed to the Israeli embassy in Vienna, Austria. Each one resembled typical air mail envelopes in style and colour.[8]

In September 1972 bso sent eight weaponized letters addressed to the Israeli embassy in London. One killed Dr Ami Shacori, the agricultural attaché at the embassy, making him the first casualty of the letter bomb war. In the following days, some fifty letter bombs that had been posted from Amsterdam and sent to Israelis were intercepted.[9] Soon after, a second set of letter bombs posted in Malaysia started to arrive, as did a batch posted in India. In late October the Israelis retaliated with a series of letters posted in Belgrade and destined for the desks of Palestinian resistance officials in Lebanon, Egypt, Libya and Algeria.

The bomb that killed Shacori was delivered in a 'thick buff-covered envelope measuring six by three'. When he opened it most of the blast was 'funneled downwards towards his desk so that he escaped the initial explosion, but by the worst possible piece of luck, he was killed by a splinter from his shattered desk'. Similar to other bombs mailed to Israelis and Zionist sympathizers around the world, the device was set off by a mouse-trap-style mechanism in which 'A spring attached to a detonator is folded back when it is put into the envelope and is held in position by the pressure of the closed envelope. When the envelope is opened, the pressure is released, and the spring strikes the detonator head.' Another method of fusing a bomb letter was to use an incendiary adhesive that sparks when the envelope is opened.[10]

Parcel bombs are more efficient because they contain more explosives and give less evidence of their contents. In terms of the Israeli–Black September conflict of 1972 a batch of gaily wrapped

Christmas parcels looking like boxes of chocolates were sent to Israelis; the parcels were found to contain a lethal dose of 8 ounces of explosives. Conversely, the Israelis were considered experts in the use of letter and parcel bombs. A spokesperson for the PFLP could agree with this assessment. Bassam Abu Sharif bore gruesome scars on his face after opening a box of booby-trapped chocolates in Beirut in 1972.[11]

A new spin on murder by mail became known in October 1972 when a Dutch Jew received a letter posted in Karlsruhe, West Germany. He was suspicious and passed the letter to the police, who found it was not a letter bomb but a 'poison gas bomb'. It contained 40 grams of cyanide in powder form. In a chemical reaction with oxygen in the air it would have produced cyanide gas.[12] That same month an American mail clerk had both his hands mangled when an envelope he was handling exploded. He was routinely stamping mail when he tried to seal an open flap on the envelope containing explosives. He said it 'sounded like a cherry bomb'. The bomb was described as about the size of a ballpoint pen, with two metal springs attached in a percussion cap. The orange envelope, 10 inches long and 4 inches wide, was addressed to a national officer of the Women's Zionist Organization of America (Hadassah) and post-marked in Malaysia. A similar letter bomb from Malaysia failed to explode when received by Hadassah the previous week. Between September and October 1972 letter bombs sent from Amsterdam and Malaysia by the BSO continued to show up in cities around the world.[13]

On 11 November 1972 Scotland Yard announced a worldwide probe into the rising letter bomb menace. In India postal authorities were taking extra security measures at post offices throughout the country. British police found and detonated the eighteenth letter bomb mailed to Jewish targets on 11 November. One had already exploded and seriously injured the Jewish director of a diamond brokerage house, injuring his face, stomach, thighs and hands as he opened it. Indian police had warned Interpol that letter bombs were en route but the information somehow never reached Scotland Yard. Three days after the warning a wave of letters arrived from

India. One had exploded in the Mumbai Central Post Office, gravely injuring a worker. Nonetheless the Yard insisted it never received the communication. One Jewish jeweller received one that did not explode but contained a note with the words, 'Black September Group – Revenge'.[14]

The popularity of murder by mail did not die with the Palestinian-Israeli letter bomb war. In 1973 parcel bombs exploded in Vienna at two apartment houses, a police station and a youth corrections centre, injuring two. A fifth was defused. No motive could be discerned, and an arrest warrant was put out for a seventeen-year-old student.[15] The following year saw letter bomb explosions in Northern Ireland and the United States. On 18 June a thirty-year-old police officer was killed by a parcel bomb he had picked up in an alley in Lurgan, Northern Ireland. On 5 December a bomb wrapped in a plain brown package exploded before dawn at a United Parcel Service Center in Pittsburgh, killing one worker and injuring eight others. The package with wires protruding from it had been taken off a conveyor belt because its address did not match its zip code. A driver opened it hoping to find an invoice with the correct information and it blew up in his face, killing him.[16] Letter bombs continued to be lethal and unpredictable.

Shane Paul O'Doherty, IRA Letter-Bomb Maker

On 10 September the IRA bomber Shane Paul O'Doherty, alias S. P., was sentenced to twenty years in jail for masterminding a letter and parcel bomb campaign against prominent people in England. The vessels for his devices were hollowed-out paperback books. His first batch of bombs was received in London on 21 August 1973. All had been rigged in thin paperback books of a music series published by the BBC, including Bach cantatas, Beethoven sonatas and guides to the work of other noted composers. The bombs contained 2–3 ounces of explosives and were constructed with

> a small battery operating an electrical circuit from two metal foil contacts linked with a detonator. The contacts

were kept apart by the pressure from the envelope keeping the book closed and sprung together when the book was removed from its wrapping.[17]

He had the habit of starting the hollowing-out process at page four of each book. His prints were found on a preceding page. It took months for Scotland Yard to collect enough scraps to fit together to get nine full prints and a partial print of his right little finger. After his arrest the procedure of combining multiple prints to get a full fingerprint sample was adopted as standard practice.

On 24 August 1973 the first book bomb injuries occurred at London's Stock Exchange, leaving one employee with facial and hand injuries. A day later two security officers were injured, one losing a hand. On 27 August a secretary at the British embassy in Washington, DC, had her left hand blown off. There was a lull of three weeks before another round of letter bombs ensued. This letter bomb campaign continued into January 1974 with two attacks, including a Bible bomb sent to Gerard William Tickle, Roman Catholic Bishop of the Forces in the UK. The wrapping on the package had 'Presentation Copy' printed on it. The bishop tore it open but fortunately the bomb was the proverbial dud. The following week an Old Bailey judge sustained hand, arm and facial injuries after he opened a letter in Kent, England; several others followed before O'Doherty was arrested in Belfast.[18]

In 1976 O'Doherty was found guilty of sending twenty letter bombs, two parcel bombs and two time-operated bombs. He was tracked down by handwriting experts and by the fingerprints left at his bomb factory. Police seized a book containing two hundred names and addresses of potential targets. One of the more interesting aspects of the case was that O'Doherty had received £300 from British taxpayers when he claimed compensation for minor injuries he suffered in a Londonderry car explosion. His signature on the application form put police on his trail.

Kimball Post Office Explosion

It is not uncommon for letter bombers to escape identification and apprehension – take the 13 May 1976 case when an explosion inside the Kimball Post Office in Kimball, Minnesota, killed the assistant postmaster Ivend Holen. After tens of thousands of investigation hours the bombing remains unsolved to this day. It is believed that Holen was sorting mail early in the morning when he came across a heavy bag of booklets destined for a local school. His 'innocuous toss of the mailbag' apparently triggered the device, which exploded with such force it threw the postal employee across the floor and through the steel door at the back of the post office. He suffered massive injuries to his face, hands and legs. His clothes were still on fire when his body was dragged from the post office building. One foot and part of a leg had been severed from his body. He died in an ambulance on the way to the hospital.[19] By the next day investigators had determined the ingredients of the bomb, which included 'a tackle box, putty, orange electrical wire, and a small but powerful 12-volt battery'. The battery was considered 'somewhat rare due to its relative size and power'. Investigators pronounced it 'similar in size to a lantern battery, but at 12 volts was much more powerful than a 6-volt battery that would be more consistent with the battery's physical size'.[20] Eventually investigators had found enough components to reconstruct the bomb.

Most agreed that Holen was not the target. It was designed to explode when opened. 'Well constructed' and containing a lowgrade explosive, 'possible smokeless powder … authorities were convinced someone with experience in making bombs was responsible.' If their hunch was correct the intended target probably lived on a rural mail route and authorities were looking for anyone motivated by revenge or a love triangle, family or business dispute. One investigator commented that 'Eight out of ten mail bombings can eventually be traced to a love triangle.' In subsequent analyses it was determined that a commonly used military explosive, Composite c-4, was used but it was not substantiated or confirmed.[21] That the bomber used a metal tackle box for mailing the bomb suggested the sender sought to use a rigid container to keep bomb contents stable during impact in handling.

Whatever explosive material was used was most likely 'molded into a block by mixing material with a plastic binder, producing a malleable, formable material that would fit easily into the fishing tackle box'. In the 1970s c-4 was commonly used during the Vietnam War. A typical brick of c-4 was 11 inches long, 2 inches wide and 1.5 inches high. One or two of these together (also known as a Claymore mine) would easily fit in the tackle box. c-4 is very stable and resistant to physical shock, only detonated by a combination of heat and electric shockwave fired from a power source such as a battery.

Mail Bomb Extortion

In June 1976 eight mail bombs in manila envelopes arrived at homes and offices of various companies in the United States. Most were postmarked in Texarkana, Texas, or Atlanta, Texas. One of the bombs detonated in the Manhattan brokerage office of Merrill Lynch, Pierce, Fenner & Smith, Inc., injuring four women employees. This case would not be solved until 1981 when two Texas men were arrested for masterminding the five-year-old B. A. Fox mail bomb extortion case.[22] Federal authorities arrested them on charges of conspiring to extort money from businesses by poisoning products and threatening to kill officials. About two dozen envelopes supposedly containing disease-infected ticks were sent to other firms.

The plot began around 16 October 1975 when General Foods Inc., in White Plains, New York, received an extortion letter signed 'B. A. Fox' demanding that $10 million be deposited into a Mexican bank account; otherwise General Foods' products sold in markets would be poisoned. Similar extortion letters were sent to other companies. Letter bombs turned up in the mail throughout the United States in the autumn of 1975 described as follow-ups to extortion demands addressed to about two hundred leading business executives.

By 1976 the extortion letters contained bombs and ticks. According to the FBI sums demanded in earlier letters totalled millions of dollars with the 'threat of terrorist tactics unless these demands were met'. By 15 June at least sixteen packets containing low-grade explosive devices had been discovered. Only one device exploded, slightly injuring the aforementioned four women at a brokerage house in Manhattan. In Houston the wife of the president of Exxon Pipeline Company opened one 10 × 13 inch envelope. Her son sitting next to her 'took it and fingered it for a while' but miraculously it did not explode. Weaponized mail also popped up in Wilmington, Delaware, Columbus, Ohio, Chicago and Minneapolis and elsewhere. Of the 200 targeted, 140 had been in the agricultural commodity field and the Federal Department of Agriculture. Another group of demands involved executives of oil, finance and insurance companies – none of the recipients complied.

During the 1970s the U.S. Postal Inspection Service had a lot of success preventing such mailings. Earlier in 1976 sixteen mailings led to eleven arrests and six convictions. The year before there were thirteen mailings of letter bombs leading to ten arrests. In comparison in 1974 there were eleven incidents resulting in nine arrests.[23]

Except for their use by the South African police, murder by mail was rare in Africa. However, on 22 January 1977 Jason Moyo, director of 'Rhodesia's black nationalist movements', was killed by a parcel bomb in his office in Lusaka, Zambia. He was a key aide to the Zimbabwe African People's Union leader, Joshua Nkomo. Four others were injured. His office reported it had been sent 'from a foreign country by agents of the Rhodesian racists and fascist'. This took place as Rhodesian prime minister Ian Smith discussed new proposals for transition to Black rule.[24]

Target American Nazi Party

The 1970s ended with a string of mail bombings. On 4 June 1979 a powerful bomb was discovered at the main post office in Arlington,

Virginia. It was contained in a cigar-sized box and addressed to the local American Nazi Party. The bomb was disarmed before it reached its destination and was just one of at least five mail bombs sent to individuals with Nazi party connections. One bomb expert said that if it had exploded it would have killed anyone within 10 feet. The package was disguised in a manila envelope and addressed to Matt Koehl, the commander of the National Socialist White People's Party, the racist and antisemitic group that was the successor to the American Nazi Party founded by George Lincoln Rockwell (assassinated in 1967). It was just one of five lethal bombs sent by an anti-Nazi group to offices of the National Socialist White People's Party in Cicero, Illinois, and Arlington, Virginia, and to a former Nazi ss officer in Paterson, New Jersey, as well as officers of the Nationalist Party in Chicago and the American Nazi Party in Lincoln, Nebraska. None of the bombs detonated.

One caller to the Associated Press claimed that the bomb 'was a warning' and more were on the way.[25] Each bomb contained similar explosives and detonators. Several were accompanied by messages used as subterfuge ending in 'Heil Hitler and White Power'. The group claiming responsibility for the bomb threats called itself the International Committee against Nazism.[26]

In an unrelated British case, several days later, nine-year-old twin boys approached the postman in the drive of their home. He was conducting his mail drops by bike. The mail was inside a pouch on the bicycle. He propped the bicycle on a wall near the house where it tipped over, and the mailbag exploded. The bike was destroyed and mail debris was blown 60 feet away. The letter bomb was the fifth to go off in 24 hours, injuring five people. Three went off in a Birmingham sorting office and another at Hockley several miles away. The postman and the twins narrowly escaped serious injury. Police believed the bomb was meant for a High Court judge nearby who had sentenced an IRA bomber back in 1975.[27]

Mail bombs continued to appear through the autumn. On 22 September police announced that all international inquiries into letter-bomb terrorism would be centralized and coordinated in London. One police official noted that 'letter bombs and other current forms of terrorism were an international political problem.' Meanwhile, officials were addressing stories that X-raying mail might set off explosive devices in envelopes. A spokesman told the press that

> Letter bombs are pretty safe as long as you don't tear them open. You can handle them, even throw them on the floor or on a desk, and they won't explode. They certainly don't go off when they are X-rayed.[28]

In late 1979 people in Britain were warned to beware of 'thick Christmas letters posted in Belgium' after two exploded on 18 December. It was believed that an IRA cell was operating out of Western Europe (Germany, Belgium, Netherlands). Investigators theorized that these were sent by the IRA, who had resorted to Christmas letter bombs in the past against prominent British citizens to drive them out of Northern Ireland.[29] Scotland Yard experts asserted that the unit was made up of Provos, members of the IRA's extremist Provisional wing. The Provisional IRA command in Dublin claimed responsibility for the Brussels-mailed bombs that began turning up in Britain the previous week. Nine were found in Britain and two were intercepted in Brussels. No one was injured. The explosives were small charges mailed in book-sized envelopes. Experts who examined the defused bombs said they had all the trademarks of Shane Paul O'Doherty, the top Provo bomb-maker who was currently serving a twenty-year sentence for the previously mentioned 1973 mail bomb campaign. Indeed, he was believed to have trained the makers of the recent spate of bombs.[30]

11
The 1980s: We Are All, I'm Afraid, Vulnerable

A s if to put an exclamation point at the end of the decade, the IRA mailed out eight package bombs from Belgium around Christmas 1979 targeting some of the top industrialists in Britain and members of the Royal Family. No one was injured. But the 1980s started out with a grim assessment of the state of murder by mail. Authorities suggested that this latest attack stemmed from the recent arrest of several dozen IRA suspects. On New Year's Day 1980 an editorial reported, 'There is no more devilish device in the hands of terrorists today than the mail bomb.'[1] Speaking at the memorial service for his uncle Lord Mountbatten, who had been assassinated by the IRA the previous August, Prince Charles called them 'subhumans'.

In the first month of the 1980s mail sorters in London's central sorting office detected an incendiary device addressed to Prime Minister Margaret Thatcher's residence at 10 Downing Street. Security had been tight since the recent mail bomb campaign by the IRA. However, police experts said this device was 'not the type used by the IRA's Provisional wing in previous letter bomb campaigns'.[2] Moreover, while it could have caused death or significant injury it was mailed to the address and not specifically to the prime minister. Just one day later a large explosion damaged a Royal Air Force Base just outside west London. That same day the self-described Socialist Republican League claimed to have sent the London mail bomb.

Letter bombs were ubiquitous during the 1980s, with reports coming of attacks in one corner of the world or another. More often than not, the bomb proved to be either a hoax tool of a terrorist or extortionist – and when they did explode there were rarely fatalities. However, there were victims who suffered serious injuries.

On 17 July 1980, Manhattan Beach secretary Patricia Wilkerson was killed by a package bomb that exploded in the office of Prowest Computer Corp. Robert S. Manning, a 'Los Angeles born Jewish militant' and member of the Jewish Defense League (JDL), was indicted for the attack but fled to Israel for sanctuary. He and his wife, who both held dual Israeli-u.s. citizenship, were indicted eight years later in 1988 when their fingerprints were retrieved from the box that contained the bomb and a letter. Despite an extradition treaty between the United States and Israel no one had been extra-dited from there since 1967.[3] It took until August 1988 to unravel the true motive behind the attack. As it turned out it had nothing to do with extremist politics. The Mannings had been involved with a former JDL member, William Ross, a Los Angeles area real estate dealer. Manning was charged with sending a mail bomb to another secretary at the firm, Brenda Adams, who had sued Ross over the sale of a house. Unfortunately for Wilkerson, she became an innocent victim when she opened the disguised device.[4]

In the autumn of 1980 a bomb addressed to Jason Himelstein, a former partner at Pacific Associates Inc. in Arizona, was received by one of its employees, Starlene Grimes. She called the former part-ner at home just as the bomb went off in the office. She was grievously injured by the letter bomb, losing three fingers on her left hand, the tips of four fingers on her right hand and suffering damage to her right eye from splinters sprayed by the wooden jewellery box containing the bomb. Seven others were injured, and one later died. Two were severely injured, including Debbie Barkley, a recently married receptionist, who was nearly blinded in the blast, suffering serious facial, eye and torso injuries. Plastic surgeons told her she was looking at five years to repair the damage. Police remarked that it was 'a fairly simple device that could have been constructed by anyone with a textbook'.[5] It would later be revealed that the bomb consisted of two dynamite sticks crammed into a jewellery box. Debbie was relieved that just six months later surgeons gave her back her vision in her remaining eye, thanks to a corneal transplant.

But six months later authorities were no closer to finding out who sent the device.

Barkley recounted that when the parcel arrived at the office she thought it was a Halloween gift sent to Himelstein because on the side of the package was scrawled 'trix or treat'. Like other survivors of mail bomb attacks she had an epiphany in the months following the attack: 'It's amazing how a life can be changed or shattered in one second.' Six months later she was taking classes at Arizona State University and trying to cope with her new normal.[6]

The following year saw continued attacks with infernal machines. In February 1982 a mail bomb loaded with glass and constructed to explode in the recipient's face was sent to British Member of Parliament Jill Knight at the House of Commons. She was well known for her anti-IRA statements. Like most mail bombs there were no casualties but there were fears that the recent death of IRA hunger-striker Bobby Sands might spark a new mail bomb campaign. Initially, law enforcement had little doubt that this attack was linked to the IRA.[7] Hidden in a large envelope, the device was discovered by a mail sorter before it could reach its destination. This was the first letter bomb from the terrorist group since its last wave of attacks in December 1979 when eight were mailed from Brussels to top officials in England.[8]

Following the latest attack prominent Britons were warned to watch out for suspicious packages after a mail sorter discovered the third letter bomb in 24 hours, including one addressed to Prince Charles. Scotland Yard dismantled the bombs, describing them as 'brown padded envelopes and all apparently from the same source'. They also noted that the bombs were crudely constructed, 'unlike the work of the IRA'. The bomb, sent indeed by the IRA from Belgium to Charles, was the 'first ever sent to a member of the royal family' and was 'designed to maim rather than kill'.[9] There was no real pattern in targeting Charles, the PM, the MP and Roy Hattersley, a senior opposition Labour Party legislator, who noted that they shared 'no common thread'.

Meanwhile, on the other side of the pond New York City police checking 76 bomb threats found four bombs. Two pipe bombs were found on 18 May 1981 in mail sent to the U.S. Mission to the United Nations and to the Consulate of Honduras. Both buildings were evacuated. The bombs did not explode. Police described the devices as very sophisticated and similar to three bombs planted at Kennedy Airport the previous weekend. A Puerto Rican terrorist group calling itself the Puerto Rican Armed Resistance Movement, an offshoot of the better-known Armed Forces of National Liberation (FALN), claimed credit for the devices in telephone calls and written messages distributed at the Grand Central Railroad terminal and in rubbish bins all over Manhattan. The message warned the United States and Latin American nations to stop supporting El Salvador's 'fascist, dictatorial government'. It also claimed responsibility for the Kennedy Airport bombs which killed one employee.[10]

The following year saw four mail bombs sent to Hawaiian residents in early March. The first two exploded on 4 March, one on Maui and the other at the Schofield Barracks. The Maui device was described as a 'household power-loss alarm' sent to a thirty-year-old man. The other bomb was a lamp sent to a soldier. No serious injuries were reported. Towards the end of the month, a 31-year-old man was hospitalized with shrapnel wounds in his arms and chest after trying out a pair of electric hair clippers he received in the mail three weeks earlier (he did not order them). The fourth bomb was another power-loss alarm received by a sixty-year-old Honolulu man in early March. He opened the parcel but did not try out the alarm since he did not order it. It was turned over to postal inspectors at the end of the month. In late May the mail bombs were traced to a typewriter at the University of Hawaii Manoa campus.[11]

On 7 May 1982, Mrs Joan D. Kipp, a Brooklyn community leader, noticed a package on her doorstep. It contained 'a hollowed out cookbook that held three .22-caliber bullets rigged to a six volt battery and gunpowder'. When she opened the book it triggered the device, sending two of the bullets into her chest. She died several hours later in hospital. Inside the flap of the cookbook jacket was a note addressed to her husband, warning him, 'Dear Howard, You're Next.' It also threatened other family members. Postal Service bomb specialist Dan Mihalko reported that extra postage had been put on the parcel to make sure it got to its destination. It had been post-marked in Staten Island.[12] Neighbours and friends were at a loss as to who could have perpetrated this act – that is, until three months later, when her 28-year-old son, Craig Kipp, was arrested and charged with the fatal bombing. He had worked for his father Howard at a marine engineering business until October 1981 and had been unemployed since. All the postal inspector Mihalko could muster at this point was that 'there is a deep resentment' between the parents and son.[13]

A Prominent Victim

Letter bombs in the modern era targeted luminaries as well as everyday people. While some were heads of state and industry the bombs rarely made it past the sorting room. Most of those injured or killed by bombs were individuals embroiled in petty squabbles or with revenge on their minds. However, figures in the public eye have also been targeted for their political views, usually in a well-planned assassination. Such was the case of the prominent white South African oppositionist author Heloise Ruth First. A child of Latvian Jewish immigrants who were founding members of the Communist Party of South Africa, Ruth, as she was better known, became politically active as she grew up. She was married to Joseph Slovo, a senior leader in the banned South African Communist Party and a leading strategist for the outlawed African National Congress seeking to overthrow South Africa's apartheid government. In 1956 she and her husband as well as Nelson Mandela were among more than one hundred anti-apartheid activists on trial for treason.[14] They were all acquitted but immediately faced 'new banning orders' necessitating flight to another country until the current state of emergency was lifted in 1960. She left South Africa for good in 1964.[15]

On 17 August 1982 Ruth was killed while in exile in Mozambique's capital of Maputo. A booby-trapped package blew up in her hands at the Centre for African Studies at the Eduardo Mondlane University. Three others were wounded in the explosion. One security official opined that the bomb 'resembled others' used by the South African secret service. It is impossible to overlook the unfortunate coincidence that Ruth was killed at Eduardo Mondlane University, named after the Mozambican liberation leader who was also killed by a letter bomb in Tanzania in 1969.[16]

'Dynamite Is an Old Mountain Tradition'

On 5 September 1982 Jack Daniel from Lexington, Kentucky, lost both legs and two fingers in a mail bombing at his home. The device was a '30-inch long cylindrical parcel believed loaded with up to five pounds of high explosive'. In addition Daniel suffered serious burns and damage to his left ear and spent 87 days in the hospital undergoing seven surgeries.[17] Almost a year later a machine shop owner and former coal operator from Salyersville named Robert Barnett was indicted for the attack. The motivation according to the prosecution was the huge monetary loss he suffered in a 1974 business deal with the victim. Moreover, he had filed an unsuccessful lawsuit against Daniel years earlier. During his first trial the jury was 'hopelessly deadlocked'.

The trial was notable for a defence strategy that portrayed the trial as a difference between 'mountain' people and those from the 'flat country' (the federal prosecutor was from Lexington, Kentucky, a more rural area). The defence 'made light of the prosecution' claim that Barnett was a licensed blaster with access to dynamite, commenting, 'Dynamite is an old mountain tradition and anyone can get it.' Furthermore, said the defence, 'There were 3,200 state residents with the same blasting licenses.' The defence got even more bizarre after pointing out that a German Shepherd sniffer dog was of German extraction and saying that perhaps 'he's a master dog,' referring to Hitler and Nazism. He added that the dog could even have been East German and 'may have been influenced by communism'. Handwriting and other evidence were also linked by the prosecution to the crime but much of the rest of the trial consisted of the character assassination of both parties.[18] No matter its results, Daniel would spend the rest of his life in a wheelchair.

In November 1982 the prime minister of the United Kingdom was once again the target of a mail bomb. This time it was a device that contained a 'gunpowder base mix designed to burn rather than explode'. At the time of the explosion Prime Minister Margaret Thatcher was in her ground-floor room. According to a spokesperson for 10 Downing Street, 'At 12:15, a yellow Jiffy bag-type envelope eight inches by four inches ignited whilst it was being opened by an official in his office. He received superficial scorching of his face and hair.' A similar parcel had been sent to Industry Secretary Patrick Jenkin the week before but the suspicious parcel was defused by the bomb squad once it was noticed. The Scottish National Liberation Army (SNLA) claimed responsibility although Scotland Yard revealed that a letter in the package claimed that it was from the Animal Rights Militia. Security was at a loss to explain how the parcel bomb got to No. 10. This event was significant because it was 'the first device which has exploded inside the building'.[19] Days earlier four identical bombs arrived at the Commons. They were sent by a group calling itself the Animal Rights Militia. A spokesperson for the British Union for the Abolition of Vivisection replied that they had never heard of the group. 'They must be some fringe, lunatic organization if they exist at all.'[20]

The following year a mail bomb detonated in the home of a New York school superintendent. Postal authorities remarked that they 'had never seen this type' of mail bomb before. Fortunately for the target, metal pellets released by the blast hit the official's wife without breaking her skin. As usual no one could come up with a suspect in 'sending the deadly paper-wrapped box'. It was noted in newspaper coverage that five people around the country had been killed by mail bombs in 1983. Postal bomb investigator Dan Mihalko remarked, 'You have all kinds of different motives: you have extortion, love triangles, and business disputes.'[21]

The SNLA

In the 1980s the British Isles contended with a new letter bomb threat from a hitherto unknown source. The SNLA, dubbed the

Tartan terrorists, emerged as one of the fringe groups fighting for Scottish independence. It was started in the 1970s by a former soldier with the Argyll and Sutherland Highlanders named Adam Busby. During the 1970s and early 1980s the group stayed under the radar, mostly engaging in 'low-level violence against English "settlers"'. They admitted sending devices to several government officials in the early 1980s. But in 1983 the group made its presence known with 27 letter bomb attacks including targets such as Thatcher and the Princess of Wales. Busby, the former soldier, left for Dublin after the 1983 mail bomb campaign and supposedly offered his services to the IRA. He was rejected and was finally arrested for the campaign in 1997.

In February 1983 the SNLA claimed responsibility for an incendiary parcel bomb that ignited at Glasgow's City Chambers. In a letter claiming credit for the bomb the SNLA made it clear it was 'a protest against the Princess of Wales's first official visit to Scotland' and warned that there would be 'more attacks to follow'. The device went off as mail was being opened in the City Chambers. However, the only damage was minimal burning of the carpet.[22]

Over the next decade investigations revealed that the SNLA was actually a very small group of extremists who adopted an 'ideology of rejection of the British state'. In 1984 it claimed responsibility for a letter bomb sent to Thatcher at the end of November. She was away at a summit when the bomb was intercepted and defused by a bomb squad. In 1986 security officers at the state-owned British Steel Corporation discovered a letter bomb, which was dismantled without incident. The previous week saw the same results when one was sent to the Scottish Secretary at his office in the House of Commons. The group was tied to mail bombings into the 1990s and the twenty-first century.

On 14 February 1984 a mail bomb exploded in the hands of a teacher to whom it was addressed in the central office of Sheepshead Bay High School in Brooklyn. The sixty-year-old teacher suffered burns on his hands, face and abdomen. Two administrators standing nearby when the parcel exploded were slightly injured. The package was described as 'about five and one half by six and one half inches and wrapped in brown paper'. Further investigation revealed the package held three or four M-80 firecrackers rigged to explode when the parcel was opened.[23]

In June a 35-year-old white South African woman, Jeanette Schoon, and her six-year-old daughter, Katryn, were killed by a powerful parcel bomb in Lubango, Angola. They were living in exile like Ruth First and were vocal opponents of racial segregation in South Africa. Both 'were killed instantly'. Seven years earlier the family, including her husband Marius Schoon, had been banned from South Africa under its security laws which meant they were confined to Johannesburg and the government decided who they could speak with. Although no responsibility for the blast was claimed there was little doubt it was the work of the South African security apparatus. The family escaped to neighbouring Botswana, then to Zambia before settling in 'Marxist-ruled' Angola in 1983. They stayed there although the British embassy in Botswana warned them in August 1983 that 'they would be likely targets of South African commandoes.'[24]

As mail bombs continued to inflict carnage it was announced in October 1984 that the Soviet Bloc state of Bulgaria had executed a man for planting a mail bomb that killed three people in a post office earlier in the year. The death sentence for Plamen Antonov Penchev for his deadly bombing was announced on 4 July and carried out in October. No information was available as to the means of execution or his motive.[25]

In the mid-1980s single issue extremist groups adopted murder-by-mail tactics. Anti-abortion groups were among the latest terrorists and criminals to employ mail bombs in the furtherance of their agendas. A concerted violent campaign against abortion included more than forty arson and bomb attacks on abortion facilities in the 1980s. In 1985 four 'anti-personnel parcel bombs' were sent to abortion agencies in the Portland, Oregon, area. One was delivered at the beginning of December to the Portland Feminist Women's Health Center and three others were intercepted by postal inspectors before they left mail facilities. While none of the four exploded, abortion supporters viewed the attacks as 'a serious escalation' which for the first time targeted people and not build-ings. The bomb was described as 'about the size of two shoeboxes, bearing an illegible address'. When it was delivered clients and physicians were in the building. Police asserted that the bomb was capable of not just killing and maiming people but burning down a building.[26]

On 21 August federal postal inspectors began searching for clues in an attempted bombing of an Alamogordo, New Mexico, home. The package bomb had been mailed days earlier but was dis-armed after the homeowner found it in his mailbox. It was 'strong enough to destroy a large room' and was set to explode upon open-ing. The recipient escaped intact by opening the box from the side instead of from the top; otherwise it would have triggered the pipe bomb. Investigators pronounced the device 'the work of a profes-sional. Packed carefully in a cardboard container the size of a cigar box' and 'rigged with a home-made clothespin-like trigger'. It was a

> 4-inch piece of steel plumbing pipe packed with blasting powder. The pipe was about two inches in diameter and was etched with grooves so it would break up into shrapnel when detonated. A filament such as used in light bulbs was inserted in one end to ignite the powder and was connected to a small battery and the trigger. The pipe rested on a piece of plywood for protection.[27]

But a sharp jolt could have caused the pipe to drop and release the trigger. All that was known for certain was that a mail carrier had delivered the parcel. The target had no clue who might have wanted to do him harm.

In late September one hundred letter bombs were sent from Libya to Tunisian journalists working for print media and the coun-try's official radio and television service. They were all defused by security officials. Tunisia had recently broken off diplomatic rela-tions with Libya after two letter bombs exploded and injured two postal workers. Tunisia accused Libya of smuggling the devices in a diplomatic pouch after the Libyan leader, Colonel Muammar

Gaddafi, warned that force might be needed to silence that country's press. Gaddafi was especially angry over Tunisian reportage of Libya's expulsion of 30,000 Tunisian workers.[28]

The following month a package exploded at the u.s. Postal Service (usps) bulk mail centre in Warrendale, Pennsylvania. It exploded while being processed mechanically at the post office. It damaged equipment and scattered debris but no one was injured. Attention was immediately focused on a Florida man who sent the parcel to a woman he had known in school but had not seen in fourteen years.[29]

After over two years of investigating a mail bomb plot at the Saddle Brook Veterans of Foreign Wars (vfw) post in 1982, authorities linked the attempt to a sex scandal at the New York City consulate of El Salvador. After interviewing more than 250 people, using up to forty federal agents and every forensic technique from fibre analysis to hypnosis, usps surmised that a Salvadoran diplomat had been caught having an affair with another consular employee and had tried to use his guerrilla contacts to kill the whistle-blower with a mail bomb. All that kept the plot from coming to fruition was that the address label fell off en route to the whistle-blower and it was sent to the fictitious return address of the vfw instead. The vfw address was utilized to make the package seem more authentic. The bomb was 'packed with about thirty .22-caliber bullets, gasoline, and enough screws and nails to do a number' on anyone nearby when it exploded. However, before anything happened the quartermaster at the vfw noticed suspicious looking wires inside the package and called the Bergen County bomb squad. The particulars of this case were not divulged until May 1985 due in large part to the 'sensitivity of u.s.-Salvadoran relations'.[30]

In May 1986 postal inspectors were tasked with trying to find the origins of two mail bombs found in Oklahoma's Noble and Osage county. Both were postmarked in Oklahoma City. Postal investigators from the very beginning did not see any connection between the two targets. Moreover 'the construction appears to be somewhat different.' One of the bombs addressed to a Ponca City area man was defused with water after the man took it to local authorities. Just the day before, an army bomb squad from Fort Sill detonated an explosive package mailed to the Ponca Indian tribal headquarters in nearby White Eagle. The bomb had actually been sitting in the office for ten days before someone noticed a 'tripping wire around the cigar box-shaped package'. He took a look inside and saw a hand grenade attached to plastic explosives. The bomb had been addressed to a contractor doing maintenance work at buildings managed by the Ponca tribe.[31]

It would take almost six months to solve the twin letter bomb case. In November a federal judge ordered a psychiatric evaluation for a Ponca City man who mailed a bomb to someone that he believed had sexually assaulted his wife. The judge sentenced 51-year-old Ervin Nelson, a local carpenter and handyman, to twenty years in prison. Nelson was originally charged with sending bombs to two men he believed had assaulted his wife. Neither of his targets were charged in connection with the purported assault.

During the late 1980s mail bombs sporadically made the news from Australia and Africa to the Americas. On 19 January 1987 a parcel bomb exploded in a Brisbane, Australia, mail sorting office, destroying the ground floor and injuring six people. There was no immediate claim of responsibility.[32]

Less than a month after the Brisbane blast, a 64-year-old physical anthropologist and former university professor named John Buettner-Janusch was arrested for sending weaponized mail through the postal system to u.s. district court judge Charles Brieant. Buettner-Janusch was the chair of the New York University anthropology department until he was sent to prison in 1980 for running an illicit drug operation in his university laboratory, manufacturing LSD and methaqualone. He was convicted and sentenced to five years in prison. He was released after three years and plotted to have his revenge on the judge who he thought had ruined his life. In 1987, he put his plan into action, anonymously mailing poisoned Valentine's Day chocolates to the home of Brieant. His wife received the package and, assuming they were for her, dived into the sweets, narrowly escaping with her life. Little did she know they contained atropine and sparteine. DNA and fingerprint evidence would later prove it was Buettner-Janusch who sent the package. It later came out that he had also sent similar boxes of poisonous chocolates to former colleagues in the past. He pleaded guilty in 1988 and was sentenced to twenty years in prison. He died of AIDS in 1992.[33]

Just two weeks later a love triangle led a 33-year-old Ohio man to mail a pipe bomb that exploded in the Dallas, Texas, Mail Center. The former Waco resident mailed a 40-pound package concealing a pipe bomb to his former girlfriend there. She had recently remarried and he was 'having a little trouble coping with that'. It was believed that the parcel 'flipped on the conveyor', leading to an explosion, but no one was injured.[34]

In late April 1987 a mail bomb arrived at the office of the Cuban American National Foundation in Miami-Dade County, Florida. It caused panic but it turned out to be just a videotape and was blown up by the bomb squad. The destruction was required after a police dog trained to sniff out substances derived from nitrogen, such as nitroglycerine, reacted positively to the package. What interested the investigators was the fact that the package had the return address of Manuel Antonio Sanchez Perez, a Cuban government official who had defected to Spain three years earlier. A foundation member called Perez and described the package, and he replied, 'it sounded much like the package he received that contained a bomb.'[35]

In Spokane former electrical engineer Gary Lee Tong, 28, pleaded guilty in July to state and federal charges for mailing a bomb to a Hewlett-Packard co-worker. Like so many other revenge bombers he demonstrated mental and psychiatric problems. As a result he was sentenced to a federal facility where treatment was available. He was charged with sending a package bomb that exploded in the face of Katherine 'Kitty' Crowley as she tried to open it on 4 March outside the plant. She suffered first- and second-degree burns over her face, neck and hands and spent ten days in the hospital. In court Tong apologized to his victim. They had met each other several years earlier at work and he became so obsessed with her that he programmed his computer in 1986 to make repeated 'dead air' phone calls to her. He became increasingly frustrated because she would not respond to him. On several occasions he laced drinking water bottles with potentially fatal doses of rat poison and pesticide. Tong admitted to police that he tried to kill her, reasoning, according to psychiatrists, that this was the 'only way of resolving his feelings of hopelessness and paranoia'. In court Tong was described as 'a shy and withdrawn person, who suffered through much of his life from social fears, feelings of inadequacy and chronic depression'. Moreover, while he was not judged insane, he 'was incapable of forming the requisite specific intent required for conviction for attempted first degree murder'.[36]

Later that month Everett Albert Green, 43, a California roofer, was convicted of attempting to mail a bomb to his brother-in-law in Utah. It failed when the intended recipient moved and did not leave a forwarding address. Green had sent a '7-inch square package' designed to explode when opened. However, before it could leave the mail room in Provo a postal worker dropped it on the floor and 'it popped'. The focus on Green stemmed from the fact that he had been mailing threatening letters to his brother-in-law over the previous few years. When he was arrested he was charged and convicted of being a felon in possession of a firearm, possession of a silencer for the M-11, .380 calibre automatic pistol and of a fragmentation grenade, also unregistered.[37]

In November 1987 a man was accused of mailing a bomb that damaged the Irwin, Pennsylvania, post office. He told a neighbour that 'God didn't intend nearby fields [to be] used by a soccer club.' The bomber was one of a group of local residents who opposed the development of soccer fields on nearby farmland. The government's case rested on the notion that 43-year-old William Donnelly was so intent on stopping the transition that he sent a pipe bomb containing more than 2 pounds of gunpowder to the soccer club president. But it exploded in the Irwin Post Office on 23 March 1985 when it was tossed into a mailbag on the floor. The clerk was slightly injured but the office sustained $1,000 worth of damages. Donnelly was a skilled welder and machinist and had access to many bomb-building components. He was linked to several threatening letters sent to local print and television media outlets. He had also planted another bomb near the soccer field itself.[38]

As the 1980s demonstrated, mail bombers have employed their deadly devices for a host of reasons. Some were motivated by extremist political views but they were more likely to use them for personal reasons. The IRA was one of several terrorist groups that sporadically used murder by mail. The IRA remained busy in 1987 sending letter bombs to the homes of Thatcher's press secretary and several senior civil servants. All were defused safely. Scotland Yard regarded the three bombs as 'viable and identical'. The press secretary's wife, a former police officer, remembered opening her mail and finding 'a small black book wrapped in [insulating] tape'. She called the police who defused it. IRA experts noted that the three bombs were delivered the day after member Kevin McKenny was jailed for sixteen years for his role in a 1985 bomb plot. The judge at sentencing expressed the belief that McKenny was also responsible for several other bomb attacks over the past twenty years, including the 1984 Brighton bomb that nearly killed Thatcher in a hotel where the Conservative Party was holding its annual conference. Five were killed and thirty injured.[39]

In September 1987 Vernon Lee Branham, 39, was arrested for manufacturing postal bombs and mailing them with intent to cause harm or death to his former sisters-in-law, one in Utah and the other in Indiana, who he accused of hiding his estranged wife from him. Neither bomb exploded. One bomb was 'a beer can filled with gasoline and connected to a battery' which did not explode when opened. The other contained gunpowder but was safely intercepted and detonated by authorities. By most accounts it was doubtful that either of the bombs would have functioned as intended. He was convicted in September 1988.[40]

Murder by mail continued well into the late 1980s. Connie Weatherby, for example, was killed by a paper-wrapped package bomb after she opened the 'rough wooden box' at her apartment on the afternoon of 24 October 1988. Her visitor was seriously wounded by the blast as well. She had received an out-of-state phone call the night before from someone who told her he was 'going to send her a souvenir'. The visitor had 'unwittingly delivered the package' to the victim – Weatherby had asked the visitor to pick up her mail from the Grants Post Office. Weatherby was expecting it to have a yellow postal slip indicating someone had mailed her a package. The parcel looked like a book about 'two inches thick and 20 inches long'. Weatherby thought it was a gift from a friend for her daughter. A New Mexico State University graduate was arrested for the mail bomb death the following month.[41]

12

From Junkyard Bomber to Unabomber

A dmitted into Harvard at the age of sixteen, Theodore 'Ted' John Kaczynski went on to earn a PhD in mathematics from the University of Michigan before being hired as an assistant professor of mathematics at the age of 25 by the University of California, Berkeley (the youngest hired there at that time). Two years later he resigned abruptly and relocated to a remote cabin in Montana in 1971. Few 'certified geniuses' become serial bombers, let alone serial killers. There have been cases of serial postal bombers but none could hold a candle to Ted Kaczynski, who became the target of 'the most expensive manhunt in American history', ultimately costing the authorities close to $50 million. One of his biographers described him as the most elusive criminal ever encountered by the FBI.[1]

Making him so difficult to catch was the fact that 'he was "not one" but "many bombers".' Through his various incarnations he evaded capture for almost eighteen years. He began as the so-called 'junkyard bomber' or 'recycler bomber', creating infernal devices from abandoned household junk including used lamp cords and screws, fishing wire and scrap wood.[2] His third bombing utilized a simple household barometer, earning him the moniker 'airline bomber'. In between he menaced university professors and those associated with computer and timber businesses. On occasion he left devices that were disguised as road obstacles, waiting for a gullible citizen to remove them to a more out-of-the-way location. He earned the sobriquet 'Good Samaritan Bomber' for this strategy. Later he was labelled the '*New York Times* Bomber' for 'selecting targets from leaders in computer science and genetics recently profiled in the paper'.[3] Finally, the FBI tagged him the Unabomber (university and airline bomber).

Born in Chicago in 1942, Ted was a healthy infant until he re-entered the hospital at nine months suffering from a serious case of hives. Hospital policy limited his mother to once-a-week visits for the month he was there. During this time he was 'not held or com-forted, pinned down with splints, spread eagled naked to a bed'. Restraints kept him from touching ointments or moving compresses on his body. His mother, Wanda, would later recall how she 'saw her child crying, shaking, standing in the crib and [holding] out both arms to her' before she was forced to leave.[4] Beginning with his return home he was on his way to evolving from a socially awkward and unsocial tyke to a pathological loner. His mother said that she noted a 'perceptible personality change' and he 'had developed an institutionalized look'. 'Some experts on infant trauma and his mother traced his aversion to being touched' to his infancy. The birth of his brother David in 1950 'made him even more withdrawn'.[5]

Ted Kaczynski was a mathematical wunderkind long before he relocated to the Montana wilderness in 1971, where he constructed a hermit's dream abode lacking electricity or running water. From his cabin he witnessed at first hand the devastation of the wilder-ness around him, feeding his growing hostility towards the modern industrial world. He resolved to do something about it by sending a series of package bombs through the postal service to universities, airlines and other targets between 25 May 1978 and 24 April 1995 that left three people dead (one in New Jersey, two in California) and close to two dozen wounded, many grievously.

Kaczynski's bombing campaign began on 25 May 1978 when he left a package in a car park near Northwestern University in Chicago. It was stamped and addressed to a professor at the Rensselaer Polytechnic Institute in Troy, New York. However, a good Samaritan found it and probably tried to fit it into a nearby mailbox but gave up when it proved too large and brought it home. She contacted the professor and he sent a messenger to pick it up. It was passed on to campus security since it seemed suspicious. When the officer began to unwrap it the package exploded, causing only minor injuries. This was the first attack by Ted Kaczynski, who specialized in using the postal service to send incendiary devices to preselected targets. He was disappointed with his first device, later telling an interviewer, 'I hoped that a student – preferably in a science and technology field – would pick it up and would be a good citizen and take the package to the post office to be sent to Rensselaer or would open the package himself and blow his hands off or get killed.'[6] The box was later described as a 'shoe-boxed size parcel, wrapped in brown paper'.[7] One of the more peculiar aspects of the bomb package was that it had ten one-dollar Eugene O'Neill stamps on it. However, their symbolism was only known to the bomber. It turned out he had bought his stamps for mail bombs in bulk years before his spree.[8] Serial killer profiler John Douglas surmised that the O'Neill postage 'may have been a symbolic reference to the playwright's support for anarchists'.[9]

Ecoterrorism

Kaczynski's crusade against technology was just the latest incarnation of movements intended to delay technological progress and industrial change. In 1812 the English Luddite movement, named after a fictional Ned Ludd, began in response to independent weavers being put out of business by factory owners who adopted 'a stocking frame and automated power loom'.[10] In response weavers created a guerrilla movement, attacking factories and destroying machines. Several Luddites and the owner of one factory were killed. Parliament had made this a capital crime and three Luddites were hanged. By 1817 the movement had been vanquished.

The Luddites were not an environmental movement per se but, to simplify, they were opposed to new technologies. Nonetheless by the 1970s some ecoterrorists would identify with the group. Unlike the murderous bombing campaign unleashed by the Unabomber, the first radical environmental groups engaged in the destruction of property, not life. In the 1970s and '80s radical environmental groups took up the protection of the earth and seas. Their activities were in part inspired by Edward Abbey's 1975 radical environmentalist book

The Monkey Wrench Gang. Earth First! is considered the first of these radical groups. It lacked any hierarchy and was decentralized. Ted Kaczynski followed a similar script, operating as what criminologists refer to as a lone wolf terrorist.

How much the earlier ecoterrorist groups inspired Kaczynski is unknown but it has been suggested that he might have been influenced by Earth First!'s magazine *Live Wild or Die!* and its 'Eco-Fucker hit list' from which he 'chose at least one of his victims'.[11] On the contrary, criminologist Donald R. Liddick claimed to have received a letter from the imprisoned Unabomber in which he 'disavowed all connection to radical environmentalists'. Nonetheless, he did share their 'desire for the downfall of modern technological civilization'.[12]

Most of the violence attributed to American ecoterrorists took place in western America. However, Ted's victims ranged from New Jersey and Illinois to Utah and California. Following his first Chicago area bombing it appeared to investigators that he had moved his base of operations to California. Half of his bombings occurred in northern California or from devices mailed from that region. By 1993 all of his communications and bombs were sent from the San Francisco Bay area.

A Love Affair with Explosives

Ted had a long-standing interest in explosive devices dating back to his school days. All his early devices were small-scale. For example, one friend remembered him 'blowing up weeds' in a field. Another acquaintance recalled how Ted 'had the know-how of putting together things like batteries, wire leads, potassium nitrate and whatever' – skills that would come in handy in subsequent decades.[13] Moreover, his former friend recalled how they would 'go to the hardware store, use household products and make these things you might call bombs'. On one occasion the erstwhile friend recounted Ted handing 'a girl he had a crush on a letter bomb, a little wad of paper that exploded when you opened it', making a similar noise to that of a firecracker.[14]

Profiling a Serial Bomber

Various criminal profilers took a crack at understanding the Unabomber and his motivations during his bombing campaign, including FBI psychological profilers such as John Douglas. Their earliest assessment contained several clues to the person they were looking for – a loner with an obsessive compulsive personality, with bombs 'representing his longing for power, probably poor, holding a less than marginal job, driven by a keen sense of revenge from real or imaginary grievances'.[15] From the obsessive compulsive side of things, the way he created each bomb clued in investigators that this was no run-of-the-mill mail bomber. He meticulously crafted every bomb component by hand, from wooden boxes to endcaps and pipes, and even made his own chemicals.[16] Moreover, 'Every screw was filed to erase telltale tool marks, every nail was hand-sculpted from wire.'[17] Methodical in his bomb-making, Kaczynski covered his tracks by wearing gloves and vacuuming any trace of hairs, fibre and DNA.

Kaczynski must have studied failed bombers in the past and found out how one mail bomber in 1957 was tripped up when a battery was traced back to him by postal inspectors. It would later turn out that Ted 'stripped the store-bought batteries of their metal coverings so they could not be traced back to him'.[18]

FBI agent John Douglas was brought in after the first two Chicago bombs and the airline bomb. Although he had little experience with mail bombers, Douglas was a seasoned investigator best known for his work with serial killers. And by all accounts Kaczynski was just another type of serial killer – someone who kills at least two individuals with a cooling off period between each killing. Profilers look for patterns, looking for a trail that could lead to their demise. Douglas suggested that since the first two bombings were in the Chicago area he was probably from that area (which he was) since 'people start where they are most comfortable.' Moreover, the university settings suggested that the perpetrator was familiar and comfortable in university settings. A serial bomber's first targets 'are usually most significant' and indeed the link to aeroplanes and college campuses suggested what would follow.

One of the challenges in tracking down the Unabomber was his propensity for altering his modus operandi. His first two bombs were his most amateurish. In some cases he would leave packages in public places just waiting for a good Samaritan to pick them up. At other times he mailed them to individuals. He 'went back and forth between these two techniques as it suited him'. Further stifling the profilers was his ability to move between different jurisdictions across the United States.[19] The subsequent jurisdictional linkage blindness between police departments didn't help the investigation.

It wasn't until his third bombing that authorities suspected a single person was responsible for the mail bombs. For authorities the stakes became much higher after a bomb exploded in the cargo hold of a passenger jet. Demonstrating the potential for mass casualties, on 14 November 1979 a bomb exploded in the mail carrier of an American Airlines jet midway through its flight from Chicago to Washington, DC, leading to an emergency landing at Dulles Airport. Investigators described it as a 'very low yield' bomb 'encased in a juice can container then a wooden box'. This led them to surmise that the bomber was an autodidact, but a sophisticated one, noting that 'he had converted a cheap barometer into an altimeter switch, which meant he understood some fairly complex concepts about airplanes and barometric pressure.'[20] This further lent credence to the notion that this was no run-of-the-mill bomber.

The device was wired and set to ignite at an altitude of 2,000 feet. While the blast filled the plane with smoke (from the burning mailbag) and caused cabin pressure to drop, several passengers suffered only smoke inhalation. Kaczynski wrote in his diary that his 'plan was to blow up an airliner flight' but 'Unfortunately, the plane was not destroyed, bomb too weak.'[21] Unlike the two Northwestern University devices, this bomb gained national attention and ratcheted up the public's fear of flying.

Further investigation led the FBI to detect its similarities to his first two bombs on the Northwestern campus in 1979. An FBI Explosives Unit examiner deduced that the bomb builder had no military experience and was quick to regard the device as crude, relying on 'smokeless powder, a weak explosive available at gun and sporting goods stores'.[22]

Aeroplanes and Mail Bombs

Postal inspectors typically show up whenever there is a major airline crash simply because aeroplanes carry mail.[23] Indeed, u.s. postal facilities can sometimes unknowingly act as 'executioner by proxy' as the service 'forwards and delivers deadly parcels to unsuspecting victims'. With the growth of mail transport by air in the 1950s the u.s. Postal Service (usps) was on the scene for the growing number of aeroplane crashes. Whenever the FBI and other federal authorities were present, so too was the usps, who was tasked with recovering mail, sorting it and getting it to its final destination.

In 1955 a bomb exploded on a plane for the first time in the usa. Investigators discovered that the bomb had been mailed, and signalled the need for the postal service to step up its game. FBI agents arrested Jack Gilbert Graham on 14 November 1955 after linking him to the bomb placed in his mother's luggage on a domestic flight. He had taken out a $37,500 flight insurance policy on his mother, who died along with 43 other passengers. Although not directly connected to mail bombings, the Postal Inspection Service became alarmed at the potential for bombs to be shipped by airmail, and was an important harbinger for the Unabomber's airline mail bomb. In the wake of the 1955 Colorado explosion bomb scares became common. The Graham case focused attention on the need for specific legislation by the government. On 3 September 1957 killing by mail became a federal crime punishable by death. The bill was revised by President Eisenhower to include 'placing deadly substances in the mail. The punishment includes the death penalty of life in prison if death results.'[24]

The Bombing Campaign Continues

Like most serial bombers Kaczynski's bomb-making skills improved with each attack. Each device was essentially a pipe bomb 'with anti-movement or anti-opening firing switches'.[25] He made the transition from using smokeless powders 'to a mixture of ammonium nitrate and aluminum powder and took time to handcraft devices, using wood and metal components'.[26]

His fifth bomb was left in a business classroom on campus at the University of Utah on 8 October 1981, indicating not only that the bomber felt more secure working outside his Chicago comfort zone, but reinforcing the notion that he was comfortable walking around classrooms and lending weight to the probability that he had a college education. His next bomb was sent to a professor at Vanderbilt University and it exploded seconds after his secretary opened it on 5 May 1982. It was mailed from Utah. The bomb was a pipe bomb contained in a wooden box filled with smokeless powder and matchheads. Now relying more on delivering devices by mail, he had figured out that there was a lower risk of exposure compared to personally delivering the bombs. Two months later bomb number seven was sent to the computer science department at UC-Berkeley. Again it was a small metal pipe bomb, leaving a student seriously injured on 2 July 1982. This attack on Berkeley made it increasingly likely that his focus was on academia and that perhaps he had ties to schools and locations he targeted. If there was any doubt it was probably removed three years later, on 15 May 1985, when he sent a second bomb to the Berkeley computer lab. This turned out to be his most powerful thus far, thanks to his new explosive formula mixing ammonia nitrate and aluminium powder. In this case a student picked up the package, suffering serious eye and hand injuries.

A month later his ninth bomb packaged in a wooden case was mailed to the Boeing Company in Auburn, Washington. However, uncharacteristically, it did not detonate. On 15 November 1985 his tenth bomb targeted a professor at his alma mater, the University of Michigan, Ann Arbor. It was mailed to a psychology professor's home with a page taped to the outside informing the recipient that the sender would like him to read the book inside. Both the professor and his assistant suffered powder burns on the arms and legs and shrapnel wounds. Once more he had changed his modus operandi by mailing to the university target's home address. Like other mail bombings it further distanced him from the crime and limited his exposure. According to the profiler Douglas, the suspect might have had obsessive compulsive disorder but was flexible enough to be able to alter his strategies to stay ahead of the investigation.[27]

It was not until his eleventh attack that a bomb fatally injured a recipient. In this case he had shifted his MO once more and gone back to an earlier method of personal delivery.[28] On 11 December 1985 a computer store owner walked out of his back door at his shop in Sacramento, California. He saw 'a block of wood with nails protruding from each end'. As he picked up the device it exploded, tearing through his chest and blowing off his right hand. Kaczynski later wrote in his diary that the victim 'was blown to bits'. This was his most powerful bomb thus far. He jotted down, 'Excellent. Humane way to eliminate somebody. He probably never felt a thing.'[29] The victim died within half an hour. What made the bomb more lethal was that the Unabomber had used 'three pipes of equal length and increasing diameter . . . fitted within each other like Russian matryoshka dolls'.[30] Much more experienced since his first bombs, the bomber 'understood the containment vessel, with more gas pressure built up during ignition, produced a stronger blast' with its lethality ensured by filling it with nails. One account suggests that the victim had actually taken a maths class from Kaczynski. This proved to be his most dangerous device thus far as he had added pieces of metal 'to increase the amount of shrapnel from the blast'. According to one FBI profiler, this indicated that he was willing and ready to kill, and that he was 'growing more confident and dangerous'.[31] Here we see him returning to his earlier MO of personally delivering bombs to his targets.

The Sketch

The famous composite sketch of a hooded bomber suspect was the result of a witness claiming to see a man leave a bag of wood near a computer store in Salt Lake City on 20 February 1987. While it became an indelible image to the public and law enforcement, it never brought authorities any closer to solving the crime. In this case the store owner picked up what looked like 'wooden two by fours with nails sticking out', setting off an explosion that left him with severe facial, arm and hand injuries.[32] After this attack Ted went underground for the next six years, possibly because he realized how close he came to being identified. In any case it was a close call and he returned to the anonymity of mailing devices instead of personally planting them to be discovered in public. John Douglas said this was not surprising because 'bombers are cowardly types who are terrified of being discovered.'[33]

Six years later, on 22 June 1993, the bomber returned with a vengeance having perfected a new type of device with a more powerful explosive mixture. When the geneticist Charles J. Epstein opened a mail package he received at his home in Tiburon, California, it 'blew him across the room', injuring his arm. Just two days later David Gelernter, a Yale University computer science programmer, was severely injured when he opened a mail package. It blew off his right thumb and little finger and badly mangled what fingers remained.[34] FBI profilers recognized that 'the more his MO evolves the more it remains the same.'[35] It appears that he had returned to mailing the devices once again.

The Unabomber did not know it but he was only two bombs away from capture. Both were mail bombs that resulted in fatalities. On 10 December 1994 a public relations executive was instantly killed in his North Caldwell, New Jersey, home when he opened a package. The Unabomber would later report in his diary that the device 'gave a totally satisfactory result'.[36] Less than six months later, on 24 April 1995, Gilbert Murray, president of the California Forestry Association in Sacramento, became his third and final homicide. The recipient had opened the package, which was 'packed with such force' that staff biologist Bob Taylor, who had left the room seconds earlier, was unable to find Murray's body, 'blown to bits'.[37]

The Manifesto

Without anything more than bombs to go on, investigators had hoped his communications with authorities might lead to his capture. Until Ted began communicating with authorities and the media, no one could be certain about motives, ideology or sanity. Investigators often depend on communications from bombers to gain insights and clues. Initially he left no information about his motivations before transitioning to writing and mailing communiqués to the news media. His last communication was a manifesto containing his thoughts, which ultimately led to his capture.

As the fatalities began to mount the FBI recognized that at this point they had to follow a different tack, especially as the bombs became increasingly dangerous. Kaczynski's downfall was put in motion on 24 June 1993 when the *New York Times* received a letter signed by 'an anarchist group calling ourselves FC'.[38] By now the consensus was that there was only one bomber and this letter was an attempt to deflect attention onto some fictitious group. Little did he know that during the examination of the bomb parts from his sixteen previous attacks it was noticed that half of the bombs had been affixed with a metal tag inscribed with the same letters, FC (Kaczynski would later admit it stood for Freedom Club). In June of 1995 the *New York Times*, *Washington Post* and *Penthouse Magazine* received copies of his 35,000-word screed, or essay, which Kaczynski referred to as his manifesto. Titled 'Industrial Society and Its Future', it was dubbed the 'Unabomber Manifesto'.[39]

His communication along with the document told the media recipients that if they published the complete essay he would 'permanently desist from terrorism'. At first they declined to take part but Attorney General Janet Reno convinced them to print it, hoping that someone would recognize the author's style or thoughts. Reno's intuition paid dividends after Kaczynski's brother David (and his wife) recognized startling similarities with a 1971 anti-technology essay

Ted had written. It took his brother months, until February 1996, to overcome his reluctance and alert the FBI about his suspicions. Ted's cabin in Montana was immediately put under surveillance and he was arrested on 3 April 1996. The 10-×-12-foot cabin provided a treasure trove of evidence for investigators, including letters and diaries referring to the bombings, a partially finished bomb and a completed bomb 'packaged and partially addressed'. Investigators also uncovered a list of potential victims and the typewriters used in his communiqués.[40]

The Unabomber trial began in the autumn of 1997. A plea deal was reached in which the prosecution would not seek the death penalty if he pleaded guilty to thirteen federal offences, including three murders, and accepted responsibility for all sixteen bombs between 1978 and 1995. He was sentenced to four consecutive life terms plus thirty years on 4 May. By most accounts the Unabomber's campaign of terror set back the radical environmentalist movement in the years to come.

One of the more interesting features of Ted's psychopathy was his inclination to build 'redundancies [more work than was needed] into his bombs, providing more initiators than required'. The aeroplane bomb, for example, had a backup 'pull-loop switch, whose contacts would touch closing the circuit between the batteries and the initiator when the lid on the box was lifted'. In this case the initiator was made of lamp cord, wooden dowels and filaments in a cigar box bomb, similar to an earlier one at Northwestern University. Once an investigator noticed the parts he said he 'knew it was a serial bomber'.[41] The parts, loop switches and initiators were made in the same fashion as the Northwestern University bomb; both used smokeless powder. Coincidence? Investigators thought not. A postscript to this finding harkened back to Ted's school days. Once a former professor of his at the University of Michigan heard about these redundancies in his bomb construction he 'remembered that when [Ted] solved math problems, he "offered much more proof than was needed"'.[42]

Coda

It has been said that imitation is the greatest form of flattery. Perhaps this found its best expression in the saga of the 'Italian Unabomber' between 1994 and 2005. This unidentified serial bomber planted over thirty bombs during his extended spree. Despite a massive police investigation he was never caught. He was similar to the Unabomber in that he placed small, booby-trapped objects in public places designed to detonate when picked up. However, his bombs were meant to cause injuries but not kill (unlike the Unabomber). Perhaps his best strategy was never communicating with the press or law enforcement. When the American Unabomber published his manifesto it led to his arrest after eighteen years. The bomber dubbed the 'Italian Unabomber' by the international press left no political or economic demands. However, other than the fact that he left his devices in public spaces any other similarities between the two bombers is tenuous at best.

To celebrate the fiftieth anniversary of Ted's class graduation at Harvard, students were sent questionnaires to fill out. Retaining a sense of humour that few were ever privy to, Ted responded to some of the questions, listing his occupation as 'prisoner' and listing under awards 'four life sentences'.

In attempts to begin collecting on the $15 million restitution that was part of his sentence, in 2011 his possessions were sold on an online auction, bringing in close to $200,000. His personal journals brought in over $40,000. His 'iconic sweatshirt and sunglasses depicted in the police sketch' were purchased for $20,000, as was his handwritten copy of his manifesto. He was initially serving his life sentence in the federal maximum security prison in Florence, Colorado, along with several other notorious bombers, including the first World Trade Center bomber Ramzi Yousef. Their row of cells is sometimes referred to as 'bomber's row'. In 2021 he was transferred to a North Carolina prison due to his declining health. After more than 25 years in prison he committed suicide on 10 June 2023, at the age of 81.

13

VANPAC: The Roy Moody Mail Bomb Murders

ail bombers have employed deadly devices against a variety of targets for many reasons. One of the most common is revenge. In some cases, as the case in this chapter shows, bombers might have mixed motivations. In the case of letter bomber Walter Leroy (Roy) Moody Jr, he targeted a judge for what he deemed was an unfair court decision. The FBI dubbed this the VANPAC case. It was one of the best-known murder-by-mail cases of the era, only overshadowed by the Unabomber case that began before Moody's letter bomb campaign. In another case Moody sought to kill a car dealer who repossessed his car. Subsequent investigations into his bombings in 1972 and 1989 offer a detailed portrait of a mail bomber.

The First Bomb (1972)

Roy Moody began his long path to death row in 1972. He had paid the last instalment on a used car he purchased from a man named Tom Downing. However, it bounced and set off a chain of events that would resonate for the next twenty years. The car was repossessed by the dealer on 7 May 1972. Moody was beyond angry and later set out with his wife to deliver a home-made bomb to the Atlanta car dealer. The bomb exploded prematurely in the car, injuring his wife. This set off an investigation by the Bureau of Alcohol, Tobacco, and Firearms (ATF). Little did they know that their investigation in 1972 would lay the groundwork for bringing the lethal bomber to justice eighteen years later for another crime. Moody was charged with the manufacture and possession of unregistered explosives and was sentenced to five years in federal prison in Atlanta. He was paroled out after doing half his time.

ATF agents in 1972 were able to reconstruct the package that detonated in the car. It was a pipe bomb with two small, square, steel plates held to each end by threaded rods about 4–5 inches long. The device was packed with double-base smokeless gunpowder. It was ignited by an ordinary flashlight bulb from which the glass had been removed in order to expose the filament, which grew white hot when wired to a D-cell battery. Also found was a cryptic note that contained threatening message fragments implying a warning. However, the capper for the agents was finding a label addressed to the car dealer, Tom Downing.

Who Was Roy Moody?

Moody was born on 24 March 1935 in Rex, Georgia. The oldest of three children, he was fascinated by machinery as a child. He had four children, including one with a girl next door whom he raped. All detested him and in time none took his name.[1]

Following his release from prison in 1975–6 Moody tried to find his bearings in life. He was middle aged at this point and was intent on going to law school. However, with a felony on his record, unless it was expunged, he could not join the bar. By the end of 1988 he estimated that he had spent close to $15,000 and countless hours of time studying. He would need a court to erase his record. Meanwhile, his goal of becoming a lawyer seemed less and less attainable. In 1988 Moody appealed his 1972 conviction. The Eleventh Circuit Court reviewed the appeal. One of the three judges on the panel was Robert Vance, who denied the appeal. He would become Moody's first victim the following year.

Moody was a classic narcissist and psychopath with what is today referred to as antisocial personality disorder, characterized by lacking empathy for others and inability to show any remorse for his actions. This condition is marked by narcissism, pathological lying, lack of empathy or remorse, impulsive behaviour and absence of guilt in harming others.[2] He exhibited all these hallmarks during his lifetime. One psychologist, Dr Park Dietz, diagnosed Moody as having a 'sociopathic personality based on his behavioral history'. Like many other bombers he was motivated by vengeful feelings. In his interviews with Dietz, Moody displayed a 'burning sense of aggrieved victimization'.[3] Moody was dubbed a 'compulsive litigator'. Psychologists spent much of 1990 looking at 10,000 pages of court documents in state and federal courts – the 'footprints of his litigious life'. His lawsuits ranged from a divorce and custody battle to his efforts to block his siblings from inheriting his mother's estate and the 1972 criminal proceedings. The compulsive litigator was also a compulsive liar. He had even lied about his felony conviction when he registered to vote in 1986.

Back to Bomb-Making (1989)

Moody was obsessed with newspaper accounts related to two scientists in Utah who claimed to have discovered cold fusion. Roy told his wife he wanted to try and replicate the experiment in his home laboratory. He began by looking through old chemistry textbooks. Moody sent his wife Susan on 'arcane missions' to purchase specific supplies for his new madness. He then added a new element to his madness, instructing her to 'move with elaborate secrecy, using disguises and false names and to be sure and park the car out of sight wherever she made purchases'. He encouraged her to travel miles out of her way to buy routine materials such as wire brushes, paper towels and cardboard packing boxes. Used to bossing his partners around, both in business and in marriage, Moody ordered Susan to give him every original shopping list so he could destroy it once she returned home. She obeyed his every command.[4]

It would have become clear to a more discerning partner that Roy was not working on a 'chemical project', particularly after he began ordering chemicals delivered to an abandoned business in the form of two 5-pound canisters of a drying agent. His obsessive work in his laboratory required a neverending supply of odd and ordinary items, including kitchen scales, Clorox bleach, distilled water, rat poison and baking soda.[5]

'Roy, we aren't making bombs here, are we?'

In the autumn of 1989 Roy told a friend that he needed some welding done in order to make parts for a boat engine he was working on. He collected the materials from a marina repair shop – nuts, bolts, threaded rods and a piece of 2-inch pipe about a yard long. Moody directed his friend to cut the pipe to a specific length. Moody had him do it several times until he had the requisite number of 6-inch-long pipes. He then directed him to weld flat plates of metal, cut from scraps on the shop floor, onto the ends of the pipes. Each plate was drilled with several holes giving access to the interior of the capped pipes. His friend then looked at Moody and matter-of-factly asked him, 'Roy, we aren't making bombs here, are we?' He assured the welder that they were not.[6] After the welding was finished Moody had one last favour to ask. He requested that he cut several lengths of threaded rods, each slightly longer than the pipes with the welded plates. After this was done, he asked his friend to go to Atlanta and pick up a large quantity of gunpowder and he would come for it later. By now the welder was sure Roy was building bombs and told Roy he would not pick up the gunpowder.

In December of 1989 several pipe bombs were mailed to locations in the southeast. Two exploded, killing both their recipients. The first bomb killed federal appeals court judge Robert S. Vance and seriously wounded his wife when he opened the package in his house in Birmingham, Alabama. The second parcel took the life of Robert E. Robinson, a prominent civil rights lawyer and National Association for the Advancement of Colored People (NAACP) official in Savannah, Georgia. Two other bombs were intercepted and disarmed before reaching their targets at the NAACP office in Jacksonville, Florida, and the Eleventh Circuit Court headquarters in Atlanta, Georgia. The one common link tying the targets together was that all engaged in civil rights issues. Although no one claimed responsibility, from the get-go law enforcement agencies were convinced there was a racial component to the motivation of the bomber (while some suspected drug dealers).

It was a typical Saturday afternoon on 16 December 1989 with Christmas fast approaching. Helen Vance was busy wrapping gifts when a mail carrier interrupted her, delivering two packages to the big house on Shook Hill Road. One was from the in-laws which she was sure contained early Christmas gifts. The other had a return address on it bearing the name of the Eleventh Circuit bench judge Lewis 'Pete' Morgan of Georgia. It was close to 2 p.m. when her husband, Judge Robert 'Bob' Vance, came home through the back door in the kitchen like he always did. Helen bounded downstairs to meet him, picking up the mail and parcels as she went. She sat about 4 feet away from where her husband stood at the kitchen table. He opened the package from the judge first since he recognized the name Morgan on the package, due to their shared interest in horses. He told his wife, 'I guess Pete is sending me more horse magazines' like the year before.[7]

Vance ripped off the plain brown wrapping paper bearing a neatly typed red-and-white label and stamps depicting the American flag flying over Yosemite Park. He then lifted the cardboard lid, unknowingly bringing together inside the box 'two carefully cut slivers of aluminum pie plate', thereby 'completing an electrical circuit powered by flashlight batteries'. Electrical current coursed through it into a detonator rigged from a ballpoint pen barrel loaded with high explosives. The makeshift detonator was jammed through a hole in one of the end caps screwed onto a 5.5-inch steel pipe. The pipe was packed with smokeless powder. Outside, rubber bands held eighty finishing nails in place. The device erupted into 'a furious fireball as the pipe burst into pieces of shrapnel, jagged whirring tearing propellers ripping through the middle of the judge's body, tossing him into a lifeless heap in the corner . . . crumpled, bloody and still'. Though injured, Helen drove to a neighbour's house, bearing cuts over her face, arms and legs. Later at the hospital a cautionary X-ray showed the bomb had sent a nail into her chest, slicing through a lung, lacerating her liver and almost exiting her back. It was the only one of the eighty nails 'traveling at bullet speed of 13,000 miles per hour' to hit her.[8]

The closest anyone could come to a motivation for such an act was the possibility that it was from a drug cartel that Vance had prosecuted. Nonetheless the next day a telex message was sent out to u.s. marshals ordering them to notify all circuit judges, district judges, magistrates, bankruptcy judges and other members of the judicial family to report any packages received via usps, United Parcel Service (ups) or hand delivery, and to turn them over to marshals immediately.

It was not long before another bomb was found wrapped in the same paper and stamps as the one that killed Vance. One investigator saw on the X-ray screen 'the opaque silhouette of a 7-inch pipe, with wires leading to a pair of flashlight batteries'. The box holding this bomb was longer, thicker and deadlier than the one that killed Vance. The pipe was fastened to the box with heavy-gauge aluminium wire. Once the bomb was removed an FBI agent and twenty-year bomb expert said he'd 'never seen a pipe bomb like it, and this guy meant to kill somebody'.[9] The agent observed, 'The pipe itself was ordinary, galvanized steel, at seven inches long and two inches in diameter – nails affixed to the bomb with rubber bands. What stood out was the ends of the bomb,' bookended with 'square metal plates welded on each end of pipe'. This design was distinctive since ordinarily terrorists would 'simply enclose powder in a pipe and screw commercially available caps on each end'.[10]

In this case the bomb-maker went to the trouble of inserting a long-threaded rod through holes drilled in each end plate. The rod thickness measured ⅜ of an inch and ran the length of the bomb, tightly bolted at each end. One agent from the ATF said it was one of the best bombs he had ever seen, crediting its maker as 'a methodical thinker . . . very smart'. The consensus was that the mail bomber had a good grasp of chemistry and physics, especially considering that the bomber had figured out how to 'bolster the bomb at what otherwise would be two weakest points . . . This would delay by milliseconds the bursting of the pipe after detonation, causing a greater buildup of explosive force within and a more powerful blast.'[11]

Robert E. Robinson

A little more than a week after the Vance bombing, civil rights lawyer and NAACP official Robbie Robinson was relaxing in his office in Savannah, Georgia, after another gruelling day at work and just one hour before the annual office Christmas party. Meanwhile, Roy Moody, a bitter failure in all aspects of his life, brooded over his failed marriages and business schemes and an unfair prison sentence.

Like Robinson, Moody worked long hours, mostly in his make-shift laboratory behind locked doors. However, unlike the civil rights lawyer trying to contribute to society the malevolent Moody 'nursed a sense of victimization that engendered plans for retaliation'.[12] His family members always wondered what he was up to behind closed doors. When his wife, young enough to be his daughter, had the temerity to ask, he took advantage of her naivety and lack of schooling and told her he was working on nuclear fusion. If she did venture into his inner sanctum she would have found the strange assortment of materials with which he worked, including pipes, nails, torch batteries, ordinary household tinfoil and a 4-pound container of smokeless gunpowder. Moody was prone to conspiracy and secrecy with a healthy dose of paranoia thrown in. Indicative of his penchant for secrecy, he purchased the gunpowder from a gun shop 'while dressed in a comical disguise of a curly wig and plastic glasses'.[13]

As he waited for his Christmas party in Savannah, the civil rights lawyer Robinson glanced at his mail stacking up and a package captured his attention – perhaps a Christmas gift or some legal documents. He picked up the shoebox-sized parcel bearing a priority mail sticker and a red-and-white pasted-on label neatly typed with a return address from Rev. John E. Jackson. Robinson was unfamiliar with this name but opened it anyway. When he lifted the flap of the box the bomb inside exploded as designed, taking both of his hands in the blast. Three hours later he died in surgery.[14]

Following the two deadly letter bombings two more bombs were intercepted and disarmed before they reached their targets.

A screening device in Atlanta detected a bomb inside a package that arrived by mail over the weekend. It was addressed to the clerk's office of the Eleventh Circuit Court headquarters in Atlanta, just blocks away from Vance's office. It had the return address of an attorney who practised in a nearby building. As half a dozen men watched the package on the conveyor belt, they were horrified when it fell off the end of the belt 3 feet onto the floor, but it did not explode. It was later revealed that even if they were all wearing protective gear it would have killed them all.

The same day another bomb turned up at the NAACP field office in Jacksonville, Florida. The shoebox-sized package was addressed to the long-standing chapter executive. She never got around to opening it. Once she heard about the Robinson case, she alerted the sheriff's office. While defusing the bomb investigators found a cryptic note threatening the NAACP. The letter proved a gold mine of forensic information and was the bomber's first major mistake since he left two identifiable fingerprints on the paper.

VANPAC Case

More than one hundred FBI agents as well as investigators from the ATF and other law enforcement agencies were assigned to the bombing case that was referred to as the Vance Package Bomb Task Force (VANPAC).[15] Investigators focused on the unusual design of the 1989 bombs. One agent assigned to the case of the 1972 bomb, which used a similar design to the 1989 mail bomb, soon shifted his focus onto Roy Moody. Once investigators identified the components of all four bombs and fragments they were sure it was the same bomber. As ATF and FBI investigators gathered to discuss the case they passed around sketches of the bomb on 19 December 1989. Coincidentally ATF agent Lloyd J. Erwin, the principal witness at Moody's 1972 trial for another bombing, chimed in, informing his colleagues that the similarities between Moody's 1972 bomb and the 1989 bombs were so evident that he 'might as well have put his signature on them'.[16] Erwin recognized eleven 'technical similarities' between the mail bombs. The ATF conducted a computerized database 'signature search for 10,000 bombs and found that none bore such a striking resemblance to Moody's bombs'.[17] The head of the FBI explosives lab in Washington, DC, described the parts of all four bombs as 'carbon copies' with technicians finding nearly 1,000 similarities between the 1972 and 1989 bombs.[18]

As the ATF expanded its investigation of Moody they discovered a storage space he had been renting since the 1970s. Inside an old trunk was a hotchpotch of terrorist paraphernalia including the *Anarchist Cookbook* and inventive recipes for making various booby traps. Sorting through the materials, an agent noticed a device that resembled the 1972 bomb. Others recognized it as being more sophisticated than the 1972 contraption but less so than the 1989 bomb. 'It was as it were, the missing link in the evolution of the bombs.'[19]

Trial

While the FBI and ATF continued its investigation into the 1989 bombings, they were informed that Moody had coached and bribed witnesses for his 1988 appeal. These acts became a part of a second line of investigation and prosecution as they tied him to the killing of Judge Vance. In November 1990 Moody was indicted for murder. Due to so much pre-trial publicity a change of venue moved the Georgia trial to Minnesota. Against the advice of his attorneys he took the stand in his own defence and tried to shift blame onto the Ku Klux Klan. All psychopaths try and control the narrative and he would not have missed his opportunity to be the centre of activity one last time. He claimed to have been in Florida when the bombs were mailed in Georgia. Prosecutors argued that his failure to have the 1972 case overturned led him to commit the bombings. Burnishing this claim was a court-authorized electronic bug with which the FBI intercepted a conversation in his cell while he was awaiting trial for obstruction charges related to his first offence. He was recorded saying to himself, 'Kill those damned judges . . . I shouldn't have done it, idiot.' After a three-week trial he was sentenced to seven life terms plus four hundred years with no chance of parole.

He next faced an indictment in Alabama on state murder charges for the mail bombing in Birmingham of Vance. After more than four years of delays the case went to trial in October 1996. The following month the jury found him guilty and he was sentenced to die in the electric chair on 13 February 1997 at the Holman Correctional Facility in Alabama. However, he was not executed until 18 April 2018, when he was 83 years old. He has the distinction of being the oldest inmate executed in the United States in the modern era (post-Furman period).[20]

14

The 1990s: Mayhem by Mail Is Now a Fact of Life

No year in the 1990s went by without reports of mail bombs in some corner of the world. There was no easy profile of a bomber or their target. One thing that did not change was that letter bombs were more likely to injure than to kill and, in even more cases, they were intercepted by authorities, especially in serial bombing cases. Technologically the mail bombs of the 1990s had not progressed much beyond the devices sent in the previous two decades. Targets ranged from evangelical leaders in the United States to hunters in Great Britain.

One long-running serial bombing campaign ended at a Montana cabin in 1997, eighteen years after the first package bombing by the Unabomber, Ted Kaczynski. Meanwhile the Viennese Unabomber Franz Fuchs terrorized the Austrian environs between 1993 and 1996 with a similar campaign of terror.

Letter bombs ushered in 1990 as Scotland Yard's anti-terrorist squad warned of a new IRA letter bomb offensive after two devices addressed to senior army officers at Aldershot were defused. Investigators suggested that these bombs were 'a new slim type which is more difficult to detect'. They were sent in Jiffy bags by mail and were discovered through routine X-ray checks and then detonated. This was considered the IRA's first letter bomb campaign since 1987 when six devices, all falsely franked with an Ulster University mark, were mailed to civil servants. Security officials believed that the IRA was now using 'more sophisticated' packages, not only slimmer bombs, but a variety of postal addresses. According to one reporter:

A letter bomb can be made by spreading a little of the Czech plastic explosive Semtex between thin pieces of cardboard, one glued to the front of the letter and the other to the flap at the back. The action of opening the letter and separating the cards triggers an explosion.[1]

Several months later a package bomb addressed to Rev. Pat Robertson exploded in the Christian Broadcasting Network's mail room in Virginia Beach, Virginia, injuring a guard, who suffered shrapnel wounds to his left leg. Robertson said it was a crude device that, if it had been more sophisticated, could have killed the guard. Robertson opined that it could be related to recent attacks, including one with a mail bomb that exploded at the home of Rev. John Osteen of Houston, injuring his daughter. Moreover, 'This could be part of a pattern of attacks against evangelical Christians,' said Robertson.[2]

Federal investigators found many similarities between both bombs but were hesitant to conclude they were connected. However, both were sent from Bladen County, North Carolina. The first bomb exploded in the 10,000-member inter-denominational church in Houston in January 1990.

In June two letter bombs – one addressed to new Welsh Secretary David Hunt – were removed from the Palace of Westminster by anti-terrorist squad officers. The other bomb was addressed to the Tory MP for Pembroke, likely by the Welsh organization Sons of Glyndŵr. Police were investigating a series of similar infernal machines. No one had claimed responsibility but the best theory was that Welsh extremists sent them. Two bombs were handed to police unopened and were described as buff-coloured, 10-×-7-inch packages sealed on three sides with masking tape and with stencilled addresses.[3]

Meanwhile, in 1990 the anti-apartheid priest Michael Lapsley was sent a letter bomb by a South African government's 'death squad', the Civil Cooperation Bureau. It was hidden inside two religious magazines. He lost both hands and his sight in one eye and was seriously burned. The attack 'opened up new avenues for his work and earned him the trust of black South Africans who otherwise might have been leery of a white outsider'.[4]

Iran and Turkey: Political Motivations

After the overthrow of the regime of Shah Reza Pahlavi in 1979 Iran's leaders adopted various tactics to liquidate opponents of the new Islamic state. Beginning in the early 1990s the Iranian government began using letter bombs. According to the Swedish public service television broadcast company (svt), the Iranian regime ordered the targeting of regime dissidents abroad with mail bombs. These efforts led to the killing of close to sixty targets.[5] Many of the attacks were directed at Kurdish dissidents, including one on 6 September 1990 which killed Efat Ghazi, a Kurdish refugee from Iran, then living in Västerås, Sweden. She was a former member of the Kurdistan Workers' Party (pkk) and later the Independence Party of Kurdistan. While the bomb was addressed to her husband she was the one to open the parcel. She died three hours later.[6] That same year the Kurdish politician Karim Mohammedzadeh, who had sought asylum in Sweden beginning in 1988, was seriously injured when he opened a package in his flat. He lost both hands and died from his injuries two years later. It has never been proven that the Iranian government was responsible but his Kurdish politician friends felt certain it was.[7]

By the early 2000s the Iranian regime had abandoned the use of letter bombs as Western law enforcement intelligence units became much more capable at thwarting these attacks. For example, French law enforcement arrested an Iranian diplomat for a plot targeting Iranian opposition figures in 2018. The diplomat gave a package containing 1.1 pounds of explosives and a detonator to two accomplices. The officers intervened before the remote-control transmitter could be used to detonate the bomb.[8]

The Iranian mail bomb campaign did not match up to the lethality of the Turkish letter bomb campaigns in the 1990s and into the twenty-first century. Unfortunately Turkish records do not specify the type of bombs used in these attacks. By some accounts mail-delivered bombs made their first appearance in Turkey as early as the 1970s. By official accounts Turkish package bombings began in the late 1970s. No one was ever officially charged but the prime suspects were Turkish intelligence agents who had instigated clashes between far right and far left groups. These clashes were used as justification for government oppression of extremists from both sides.[9] In one of these cases four packages were mailed from Ankara to Adıyaman, Adana, Kahramanmaraş and Malatya provinces on 7 April 1978. Of these the first three failed to explode. However, the Malatya bomb was successful, killing the province's municipality mayor, a man aligned to right-wing and nationalistic ideology.[10] In this incident the package had arrived while the mayor was out of town. When he returned two weeks later he saw that the package was posted by a friend of his. Thinking he had mailed him some packets of cigarettes he took the package home, and it exploded as he opened it, killing not just the mayor but his two grandchildren and their mother.[11]

By the 1990s Turkish intelligence officials began using weaponized package bombs. According to one terrorism expert, terrorist groups in Turkey between the 1970s and the early 2000s lacked the capacity to construct sophisticated letter and package bombs. During the Cold War, according to this terrorism expert, foreign intelligence officials operating in Turkey taught the country's intelligence officials how to construct them. These Turkish officials then infiltrated left-wing and nationalistic groups and taught them how to make postal bombs. These letter bombs used a variety of explosives including A4, a military-grade explosive commonly used in grenades, as well as C-4, a common variety of the plastic explosive family known as Composition C, and RDX, an explosive that can be used alone or in combination with other ingredients to make plastic explosives. These are all high-yield chemical explosives. Some of the attacks that used RDX-based explosives were committed by foreign agents.[12]

In October of 1990 a Turkish university professor was killed by a package device. In this case Bahriye Üçok was notified that she had received a parcel at a cargo company. The package looked fairly innocuous: tied with rope, with one corner of the parcel torn, revealing two books covered by a letter. Her daughter brought it home and it detonated as soon as her mother opened it on the front lawn. Speculation as to who perpetrated the action included allegations that it was from a jihadist group. A subsequent investigation was unable to determine its origins.[13]

As the 1990s ended mail bombs in Turkey continued to claim victims. In 1999 the Turkish journalist Ahmet Taner Kışlalı was targeted with RDX explosives. Similar to tactics used by the American Unabomber the package was left on the windscreen of his car and detonated when he picked it up.[14] Well into the next century infernal devices would plague the country. In May 2015 Islamic State of Iraq and Syria (ISIS) sent a package to a target; it appeared to be a simple flowerpot but was actually filled with explosives. It detonated, injuring six people.[15] In Turkey package bombs have been used for non-ideological purposes as well. In 2016, for example, an office in Istanbul was targeted by a bomber posing as a courier who left a package bomb at the business. He was arrested when police linked him to his fingerprints on the box. He later confessed that he intended to kill his father. However, he wounded six civilians in the office building instead.

Targeting the English Royal Family

On 19 July 1990 a letter bomb 'came within an ace of penetrating' the security of Princess Diana. The 'lethal magnesium-packed letter' was uncovered by one of her staff minutes before it would have been handed to her at her Kensington Palace home. One Palace insider said, 'There is no question that at the very least it was an attempt to disfigure or blind the Princess.' The letter bomb was opened by a royal butler or secretary but did not explode. Palace protocol allowed only letters from known sources to be handed unopened to members of the Royal Family. Bomb squad officers weighed in with the opinion that it was not a professional bomb-maker since the chemical magnesium is 'particularly volatile in powder form, shavings or in thin sheets and burns with a brilliant light and intense heat'.

An expert on the substance said, 'an ignition device would have been needed to trigger the bomb.'[16]

The Ultimate Dysfunctional Family

Over the next few years letter bomb attacks were less frequent or, at least, less reported. In 1991 Alaska and Cuba reported mail bomb outrages. In September a package arrived for George Kerr at his home in Alaska. His father, David Kerr, opened it and was blown to pieces and his stepmother injured. The house was destroyed, windows and walls blown out and a hole blasted in the ceiling. The explosion tore the clothes off the stepmother and shattered her eardrums and all the bones in her face, pummelling her body with splinters of wood and metal. Her husband lost his right hand and forearm and was wounded in his right side. The postal investigator reported that 'His face was pretty mutilated, his eyes were gone' and 'there were flash burn marks all over his body.'[17] He died soon afterwards.

The bombers were caught and went on trial in early 1995. Alaska residents Craig Gustafson and Peggy Gustafson-Barnett were tried for constructing the deadly device. They claimed another person, Raymond D. Cheely, had long plotted revenge against the couple after they helped convict him and his accomplice in a 1990 shooting case. Prosecutors said that George Kerr was targeted since he was the only witness to the highway shooting and went to the police.[18] At the 1995 trial for the Kerr bombers – the Gustafson siblings – Cheely's attorney deemed the attack 'a family affair ... They are the ultimate dysfunctional family to say the least.'[19]

In March 1995 a letter bomb exploded in the office of the Cuban leftist weekly newspaper *Cambio*, killing a 21-year-old journalist. The explosion blew out windows on the upper floor of the two-storey building, showering glass across the street. Melissa Alfaro was killed when she opened the letter. The editor blamed paramilitary groups. *Cambio* was branded as a mouthpiece for the pro-Cuban Túpac Amaru Revolutionary Movement, a guerrilla group that began in 1984. In June the previous year a letter bomb had killed an airport official in a store opposite the *Cambio* office, the victim of a botched attack. Also in March 1995 a letter bomb had wounded a lawyer affiliated with defending victims of human rights abuses.[20]

In 1993 murder by mail moved back into international headlines. That year, a self-styled SNLA commander named Andrew McIntosh was jailed for twelve years for engineering a terrorist campaign that included planting mortar bombs at oil company offices and sending letter bombs to political targets.[21] A Scottish official noted that 'They are a very, very small group of fanatics. This type of device is typical of their work; it is very crude but could seriously injure someone.'[22]

Later that year, two men sent mail bombs that killed five people within ninety minutes in northern New York. Both pleaded guilty in February 1995 with one testifying against the other for a reduced sentence in a federal penitentiary. Michael Stevens was described as the mastermind behind the plot against his girlfriend's family during the 1993 holiday season. The 'dynamite and metal fragment bombs' killed two people in a Rochester townhouse, another two at an armoured car depot, and blasted a 2-foot crater in the hardwood kitchen floor of one victim.[23] The 54-year-old Stevens directed the plot against his 31-year-old girlfriend's family because he thought they were trying to break up their relationship. Moreover, he was worried about losing his two-year-old son if they broke up. Those killed included her mother at her home, her sister and her boyfriend in the townhouse and her stepfather and one of his co-workers at the armoured car depot. Two of the bombs failed to detonate or were intercepted by the police. The suspects were quickly rounded up and admitted buying explosives in Kentucky and driving them to Rochester in a car owned by Stevens. At trial it was revealed that Earl H. Figley, the accomplice, built prototype bombs by installing wires, batteries and a switch inside plastic toolboxes at his mother's house in Rochester then stored them elsewhere. The two men then sent one package through the U.S. mail service, four through a private delivery firm and dispatched another via a Rochester taxi company.

That same month letter bombs injured targets in Germany and Colombia. One letter bomb in the form of a radio exploded in

Hanover, Germany, after members of a Yugoslav family unpacked it and turned it on. Five were injured. One victim lost one hand and fingers from the other hand. His 23-year-old wife and 11-year-old daughter were badly hurt and two younger children hospitalized.[24] Meanwhile, the late drug lord Pablo Escobar's brother was seriously injured by a letter bomb in his jail cell. Roberto Escobar suffered wounds to an eye, the chest, face and hand when the letter bomb blew up at the Itagui Jail just outside Medellìn.[25]

The year 1993 continued to shape up to be one of the busiest years of letter bomb attacks in recent memory. In July a Venezuelan Supreme Court employee opened a manila envelope addressed to the court magistrates. The c-4 explosives inside the parcel blew off his left hand. The following month two former police officers were held in connection with the Supreme Court bombing and two other unexploded letter bombs sent to the homes of the court's president and vice president.[26]

As the year neared its conclusion another letter bomb was sent to a Staffordshire animal company by animal rights activists. Police officials warned all animal breeders and animal product dealers in the area to be on guard for devices sent in the mail. The most recent incident followed a similar one the week before. Police revealed that five people had been injured after two letter bombs exploded and that a total of thirteen had been received by firms in England. No faction claimed responsibility but the Animal Liberation Front suggested it could be the work of a fanatical animal rights splinter group calling itself The Justice Department.[27]

Franz Fuchs: The Austrian Unabomber (1993–6)

The eighteen-year mail bomb spree of Ted Kaczynski that ended with his capture in 1996 popularized the term 'Unabomber' for serial mail bombers. However, in 1993, on the other side of the Atlantic a mysterious wave of letter bombs in Austria, including an attack on a popular Vienna mayor, shattered the stillness of the bucolic alpine country. The spate of letter bombs began on 3 December when an infernal device was sent to the pastor, August Janisch, in the southern Austrian town of Hartberg. He was targeted for his charitable acts of taking in refugees. He survived with serious hand and facial injuries. That same day Silvana Meixner, a popular television show host, survived a mail bomb. These were just the first steps of the increasingly violent terrorist campaign of a far-right extremist named Franz Fuchs, which lasted until 1996. Fuchs, 48, was described as 'an intelligent loner' and 'a reclusive engineer' who lived with his parents in a small town in southern Austria. He was easily recognizable for his Hitler-style moustache.

Police were confident after the first two attacks that they were looking for one or more far right-wing extremists driven by anger over the thousands of refugees seeking shelter in Austria from the violence and poverty of post-communist Eastern Europe. The first two devices were part of a series of ten letter bombs that rattled Austria over a four-day period. All had the same size and thickness and common postage.[28] Only four of the packages exploded; the rest were discovered and defused.

On 16 October 1995 a new spate of bombings began with a letter bomb seriously injuring a prominent refugee activist and a foreign-born doctor. Syrian born Dr Mahmoud Abou-Roumie was wounded in his left hand in Stronsdorf, where he had lived since 1979. Another bomb injured an activist whose project to integrate 145 refugee families with the 55,000 residents of Poysdorf earned him an award in 1994 from the UN Commissioner for Refugees. Maria Loly suffered injuries to both hands and her face when she opened a letter at the post office. She had recently received a letter that threatened to set houses on fire and proclaimed, 'Death to the Bosnian'. Indeed, most of the refugees in her project were from former Yugoslavia. Several days later Helmut Zilk, the mayor of Vienna and a well-known supporter of integrating foreigners, was seriously injured. Zilk was a prominent champion of minority rights and was instrumental in opening Vienna's first post-war Jewish museum. He barely survived the blast and ended up losing his left hand during surgery. The next day Fuchs sent a letter bomb to a Vienna law office, injuring a secretary. The next six devices were intercepted before they could reach their Austrian targets.

His string of non-lethal bombings ended on 5 February 1995 when he set off a bomb that killed five Romani people. Unlike the others this one was *not* sent by mail. The recent bombings brought the number of injuries in Austrian letter box attacks to 21.[29] His final bomb was sent in December 1996, targeting the mother-in-law of Caspar Einem, the Austrian interior affairs minister. She was not harmed. On 1 October 1997 Franz Fuchs was arrested in the case that continued to draw comparisons to the American Unabomber attacks. His letter bombs had killed at least four and injured eleven since 1993. He was arrested after police stopped his car as they hunted a sex predator. As soon as he was pulled over an explosion ripped through his car, tearing off both his hands and injuring two police officers. A search of his home 130 miles from Vienna turned up bomb-making materials linking him to the bombing spree between 1993 and 1996.

Similar to the American Unabomber, in both cases police sought what they thought would be an intelligent loner with extreme political views and an apparent grudge against modern society. During the search of Fuchs's home police found pipe bombs, a booby trap packed with explosives and nails, computer equipment and other materials.[30]

As for his motivation, was it political or personal? His brother had said that he had quit his science studies because he could not afford university. He then spent five years in Germany with a woman from former Yugoslavia who eventually disappeared with his life savings. But most of his victims were minorities or immigration advocates, such as Mayor Zilk. He had set off a bomb to kill himself but it exploded in his hands. He was absent for most of his 1999 trial because he was prone to courtroom outbursts, launching into nationalistic anti-foreigner racist tirades. He was diagnosed with 'schizoid, paranoiac, obsessive and narcissistic' tendencies. In March 1999 he was convicted on multiple counts of murder and attempted murder and was sentenced to an institution for 'mentally abnormal offenders'. In one of his more memorable tirades he yelled himself hoarse, telling the court:

Long live the German people. Foreigners? No thank you.
Minority Privileges? No thank you. Pure blooded communist rule? No thank you. Our living spaces swallowed up by
foreigners? No thank you. Anti-German propaganda? No
thank you. Zionist persecution of German people? No
thank you.[31]

As a postscript, Theo Kelz lost both hands when he tried to
defuse one of the bombs. In March 2000 Austrian surgeons sewed
new hands onto the police bomb disposal expert. At the time it was
only the second operation of its kind. Kelz has lived with artificial
limbs since the injuries. This operation took place just one month
after the Austrian Unabomber committed suicide in his cell.[32]

The year 1994 was marked by mail bomb attacks in Colorado,
New York and Scotland. A mail bomb explosion killed a man and
seriously injured his wife in April in Colorado Springs. She had
picked up the package at the post office earlier in the day and it
exploded as she opened it in her driveway. A neighbour told reporters that he saw the victim 'fly through the air and land on the
ground'. At the time she was on a moped and it blew her almost
7 feet away. Bomb fragments were found two blocks away. The
woman sustained serious head injuries and a broken arm.[33]

Perhaps the most publicized mail bomb attack of 1994 was that
of a 75-year-old woman who ended up in a New York hospital in a
critical condition with shrapnel wounds to the stomach. Investigators from the beginning suspected that the bomb had been meant
for 61-year-old Richard McGarrell of Barnegat Township since the
envelope had been addressed to R. M. McGarrell. However, it was
mistakenly sent to the home of his sister. Authorities eventually
linked the attack to a feud over family inheritance. The device went
off when Alice Caswell, a widow who lived alone, opened it.
Subsequently it was found that a similar device had been sent to
another relative in another state but it did not explode. The bomb
that injured Caswell was packed 'in a 9-inch by 7-inch envelope' and
addressed to her brother, a retired customs inspector, who had once
lived at his sister's house and still used it as a mailing address.

Investigators observed it was put together with some skill. It 'contained bullets of black gunpowder and pellets and was triggered by a cap'.[34]

In June 1994 a Bedworth man in the UK was charged in the wake of seven letter bomb discoveries that authorities linked to animal rights activists. Staff members suffered injuries in three of the attacks at firms connected with the animal industry. One woman was hurt at a chicken breeding company in Scotland when she opened the envelope. She survived after treatment for her wounds and shock in hospital. Another was opened at a pig breeding firm in Oxfordshire, injuring a staff member. The third took place in Kent at a ferry company that accepted livestock deliveries. Some addresses received more than one letter bomb.[35]

The Mardi Gra Bombings (1994–8)

Another serial letter bomb case between December 1994 and March 1998 involved the British extortionist and bomber Edgar Eugene Pearce and his older brother, both in their sixties. The three-year terror and extortion campaign was waged in the vicinity of London. It apparently all stemmed from a dispute with Barclays bank. They targeted six different branches with home-made bombs. The bombs were all addressed to the managers and hidden in video tape boxes disguised with Christmas wrapping paper. Inside each one was 'a shotgun cartridge linked to a spring and a simple mechanism to fire the cartridge as the box was opened'. The first two detonated in branches in the morning, causing slight burns to the faces and hands of employees. The other four were quickly defused. The bomber left only one clue – an image from the Quentin Tarantino cult movie *Reservoir Dogs* on the cover of the boxes with the words 'Welcome to the Mardi Gra Experience' superimposed on top.[36] By most accounts the 's' was deliberately left off the word Gra(s). All of the devices had the same omission. Investigators deduced that 'the presumed reference to the pre-Lenten Mardi Gras festival may be a red herring', a game the bomber was playing with the police and the press.

On 28 April 1998 the two elderly retired brothers, Ronald Russell Pearce, 66, and Edgar Eugene Pearce, 60, were arrested in connection with the bombings after a surveillance operation netted them at a cashpoint machine. Arrested in a sting operation, they were wearing false beards and wigs. Police raided their home in Chiswick, west London, and found a bomb factory with two newly constructed devices in trademark Mardi Gra style. They were accused of sending bombs around London, mainly to Barclays banks and Sainsbury's supermarkets. They had started on 6 December 1994 with $1 million blackmail threats to the bank and later Sainsbury's. The final attack was on 17 March 1998. In total there were believed to be 34 bomb attacks, but no deaths.[37] In the investigation, Scotland Yard was helped by criminal psychologists and the FBI's Behavioral Science Unit, who suggested that the bomber was likely over 48 years of age, above average intelligence and lived alone.[38] This summed up the brothers precisely. By July the brothers faced new charges but most of the onus for the attacks was directed at the younger brother Edgar.[39]

Over the next few years mail bombs became a fixture in media stories from Great Britain to Asia. On 16 May 1995 a letter bomb detonated in the office of Tokyo governor Yukio Aoshima. An aide lost his left hand and right thumb when he opened the 'notebook-sized envelope'.[40] The blast occurred shortly after the arrest of Shoko Asahara, the leader of the Aum Shinrikyo cult suspected to be behind the 20 March sarin gas attack on the Tokyo subway system that killed twelve and injured thousands. Cult member Naoko Kikuchi was finally arrested for the attack in 2012. He was also indicted for helping ex-members acquire the ingredients for making the parcel bomb sent to a Tokyo metropolitan government office that seriously injured a secretary. Kikuchi had been on the run for seventeen years, having been on the wanted list for her participation in the sarin gas attack.[41]

In the summer of 1995, in England, a letter bomb campaign targeted 'the heart of Cheshire's hunting community'. Members reported receiving incendiary devices disguised as letters. The most serious attack occurred in Huxley, where a bomb exploded in the home of a 38-year-old man, who suffered burns on his arms when he opened what he thought was a greetings card. His son was also present and suffered eye injuries. Police had been on the lookout for mail bombs and defused several similar devices. Each letter was sent to individuals closely tied with the Cheshire Hunt. Police quickly began investigating animal rights extremists.[42]

On 2 March 1996 a Lawrence, Kansas, man was arrested for trying to kill his ex-wife with a mail bomb. The pipe bomb did not go off at its destination and there were no injuries. A local police chief said it 'did not appear that the bomb was made by an expert' but could have killed anyone nearby if it exploded. It was rigged to explode when the box was opened. 'Anytime you have black powder and butane fuel and other ingredients it could explode.' The bomb also contained ball bearings similar to those used in shotgun shells.[43]

In September the Icelandic singer Björk was sent a letter bomb charged with explosives and sulphuric acid by fan Ricardo Lopez. The bomb never made it to her home, having been randomly intercepted by the London police. Lopez then committed suicide. He was a Uruguayan-American pest control worker based in Hollywood, Florida. He was an obsessed fan who became angry over her relationship with another musician.[44]

As the 1996 Christmas holiday beckoned, police in upstate New York pursued leads after a ten-year-old girl was injured by a package bomb. On Christmas Eve Jordan Reardon of Clifton Park suffered burns and cuts over 27 per cent of her body after a package she was opening exploded in her family's kitchen. The parcel had been brought inside from the mailbox. Police were soon investigating a worker from the same company as Jordan's mother. A search of the suspect's father's house uncovered 30 pounds of gunpowder and equipment for handling explosives. A second check found a live pipe bomb. Meanwhile investigators looked into other recent parcel bombings including one involving a lawyer in Santa Cruz, California, hoping to find a connection.[45]

From an international perspective 1997 was an especially busy year for postal inspectors and law enforcement. That year the eighteen-year mail bomb campaign of the Unabomber, Ted

Kaczynski, went to trial after his arrest following a tip-off the previous year in Montana. Kaczynski had killed 3 people and wounded 23. But mail bombs continued to make the news around the world in 1997. The year began with a letter bomb scare in Great Britain where several sports stars were warned to be on guard against a neo-Nazi letter bomb campaign. The campaign was organized from Denmark and was targeting 'high profile people in mixed race marriages'. Members of the right-wing group were alleged to have sent three letter bombs from Sweden to London. This was just the latest example of neo-Nazis resorting to mail bombs against left-wing politicians.[46]

A Jailed Cleric

Eight booby-trapped letter bombs surfaced in early January 1997, apparently from followers of an Egyptian cleric jailed in the United States for conspiring to commit acts of terror against America. Three of the bombs were sent to a federal prison in Leavenworth, Kansas, addressed to the parole officer – two on 2 January and a third on 3 January – and five others were intercepted on their way to the Washington office of the Arabic newspaper *Al-Hayat*.[47] All the bombs bore postmarks from Alexandria, Egypt. It did not take long to determine that three followers of Sheik Omar Abdel-Rahman, the radical Muslim cleric convicted with nine others of conspiring to bomb the United Nations headquarters and other New York City landmarks, were inmates at Leavenworth. Meanwhile, the FBI's legal attaché in Cairo was collaborating with Egyptian authorities to find the bombers.[48]

Investigators suspected that the letter bombs sent to Leavenworth and Washington were armed with Semtex, a plastic explosive preferred by terrorists around the world. One expert said 'an orange color on the explosive material and a distinctive odor' prompted authorities to suspect Semtex. FBI agent Buck Revell noted that 'It is very powerful, and it can be put into thin sheets. It is very malleable, and you can put it into different shapes and so forth.' All of the bombs being studied were defused and were in

5.5-×-6.5-inch envelopes with computer-labelled addresses. They were designed to explode when opened.[49]

Target *Al-Hayat*

On 13 January 1997 two postal clerks were injured when one of four letter bombs addressed to *Al-Hayat* in London exploded, the latest attack in a campaign of terror against the paper owned by a Saudi prince. The London explosion occurred in the morning. The letter containing the bomb was opened by a mail clerk who was accustomed to passing an electric security wand over suspicious packages. Later that same day two more letter bombs sent to the paper were located and defused at the United Nations headquarters in New York. That night two more were found as workers continued to search incoming mail. The New York Police Department (NYPD) Bomb Squad defused them all. The newspaper has a circulation of about 200,000 and is owned by Prince Khaled bin Sultan, the former deputy defence minister for Saudi Arabia's military. In recent weeks the newspaper had received bombs in its offices around the world including two at its Riyadh headquarters in the first week of the month. Similar to the booby-trapped cards sent to Washington, DC, and Leavenworth prison, the envelopes were all created to look like greetings cards and contained paper-thin sheets of Semtex, a plastic explosive favoured by Middle-Eastern terrorist groups. Each bomb was to be triggered by what one official described as a 'sophisticated detonator', rigged to explode when the envelopes were opened. The bombs sent to London and the United States showed enough similarities to suggest they came from the same source as the Leavenworth and Washington, DC, bombs sent from Egypt. New York authorities nearly short-circuited their investigation after firing a water cannon on one of the envelopes. The water smudged some of the ink on the postmark and a magnifying glass was needed to discover its similarity to other envelopes dated 21 December from Egypt.[50]

Murder by mail reached Asia in April 1997 when a parcel bomb killed the eldest daughter of a high-ranking military officer,

Lieutenant-General Tin Oo, in Burma. Burma's military government had been on top security alert since December the previous year when two bombs exploded at a Buddhist temple killing five and wounding seventeen. The government cast blame on the Karen National Union guerrilla group, although they denied it. Lieutenant-General Tin Oo had a well-earned reputation as a hardliner and could often be heard exhorting his troops and citizens to 'annihilate' anyone who opposed the government.[51]

A growing concern about mail bombs in 1996 led the u.s. Postal Service to implement 'the extraordinary step of prohibiting customers from depositing any stamped package weighing 16 ounces or more in collection boxes'. The edict had a dramatic effect on all international parcels and mail to military units overseas that weighed 16 ounces or more. Now, these parcels would have to be presented in person and the sender would be required to complete a Customs declaration stating the parcel's contents. These changes were, in part, a response to the 17 July crash of the Trans World Airlines Flight 800 off Long Island. Postal officials refused to say whether the 23,000 pounds of mail aboard the flight were screened for explosives. Nonetheless safety experts have long acknowledged that mail and cargo placed on commercial aircraft pose a serious terrorist threat. This latest move by the Postal Service seemed more directed at preventing use of mail by individuals such as the Unabomber. The Unabomber was said to have used particular stamps when he mailed his bombs, placing excessive postage on the parcels to ensure they were delivered. One of the bombs went off on an American Airlines flight, forcing it to make an emergency landing at Dulles Airport in 1979.[52]

The Australian Experience

Australia experienced its first twentieth-century letter bomb attack in 1975 when one exploded at the office of the Queensland premier, Sir Joh Bjelke-Petersen. Over the next 25 years there were sporadic letter bomb attacks. The only letter bomb death came at the Adelaide office of the National Crime Authority. The blast killed

Detective Sergeant Geoffrey Bowen and seriously injured a lawyer. Like many letter bomb attacks the first one remained a mystery and injured two mail room workers. One of the more bizarre Australian attacks took place in 1981 when a Melbourne woman lost an arm to a device then gave birth to a baby girl ninety minutes later. Three years later an east Sydney restaurateur had fingers blown off one hand and massive facial and head injuries.

On 2 December 1998 Australia experienced the worst letter bomb campaign in its history, when 23 letter bombs were sent to tax office employees. A 43-year-old suspect mailed the letter bombs to tax officials, offices and homes across Australia. Twenty-one were eventually found at the Canberra mail centre, only discovered after a parcel bomb exploded there at 12.25 a.m., injuring two. Police evacuated the centre and the surrounding area and Australia Post staff started checking more than one million pieces of mail. By 9 a.m. the other twenty devices were found and all mail into and out of Canberra was stopped. Following a nationwide alert and the search of mail exchanges across the country police revealed that a similar device had been addressed to the Sydney residence of an employee of the Human Rights and Equal Opportunities Commission.

Another bomb was found in a mailbox in Richmond, Melbourne, targeting a former federal sex discrimination commissioner. The bomb was detonated by police, who proceeded to check if it was linked to her former employment. Like those discovered in Canberra, the white package measured just over 4 × 4 inches and was 1 inch thick. It was designed to go off when opened and seemed to have originated in Canberra, as with the other packages.[53]

All 17,000 employees were warned not to open packages. At 4:30 p.m. that day it was announced that 23 bombs had been found and there were probably more out there, and that each device was capable of maiming or killing someone.[54] Police believed that since most of the bombs were sent to Australian Taxation Office personnel it was reasonable to assume the bomber may have had a feud with the tax office. Moreover the police also suspected that the bombing campaign could have been triggered by an internal complaint over an issue such as 'sexual harassment or the collection of family maintenance'.[55] The design of one of the bombs was identified as one probably 'learnt on the Internet'.[56] As one observer put it, 'There's nothing like this in Australian history. Letter bombs are usually sent in ones, twos and threes. This is by far the biggest one we have ever seen.'[57] Compared to the rest of world, according to one official, letter bombs were 'rarely used' in Australia.

In 1999 it was estimated that mail bombs exploded an average of sixteen times a year in the United States. Individuals were often maimed and injured but in most cases the bombs failed to go off or reach their final destinations. Between 1992 and 1997, according to the u.s. Postal Service, 105 bombs were mailed and only 36 exploded, taking 3 lives, injuring 36, with 49 arrested for their involvement. During that same period another nineteen were injured from bombs not mailed but left at post offices and letter boxes. More than 2,190 'such bombs were planted, resulting in 1,905 explosions'.[58] Nonetheless, statistically speaking, the mail service is relatively safe. According to the u.s. Postal Service the chance of opening a mail bomb is more than 10 billion to one, less than the chance of being struck by lightning (1 in 3.4 million).

There is no one profile of a bomber or a victim that will lessen the chance of receiving a letter bomb. Victims and perpetrators come from all walks of life, with a range of motivations. In 1995, for example, targets included a federal judge, business associates of bombers, spouses and lovers. The following year the targets were similar. In 1997, however, motivations included personal disputes and terrorist ideologies. One postal expert suggested that 'Most tend to be white males in the 30–50 age group.' He also speculated that females were less likely because they were probably less familiar with the tools required for making explosive devices. Nonetheless the expert conceded that it was easy to make one. 'You can find out on a web site how to make a bomb. Before the Internet people could just go to the library.'[59]

15

The MAGA bomber: Cesar Sayoc Jr's War on the Democratic Party

On Monday, 22 October 2018, a former male stripper living 'a scattered and bizarre life in South Florida' retweeted a post saying, 'The world is waking up to the horrors of George Soros.'[1] That same day a crudely made parcel bomb appeared at the billionaire liberal activist's Westchester County estate. This would be the beginning of five days of terror directed at the familiar faces of the American Democratic establishment. The following day Bill and Hillary Clinton received one of the devices in the mail, and in short order more bombs were found at the homes of prominent critics of President Donald J. Trump, including those of California senator (later vice president) Kamala Harris, New Jersey senator Cory Booker, former CIA director John O. Brennan and others. Other devices were sent to former vice president Joe Biden Jr, California representative Maxine Waters, former attorney general Eric H. Holder, Democratic donor Tom Steyer and James R. Clapper, former director of national intelligence. These targets represented a virtual who's who of Trump's enemies.

No serial mail bomber could match the profile of 57-year-old Cesar Sayoc Jr. Variously described as a 'nobody' and a 'weirdo', he was regarded as an outcast by individuals who crossed paths with him on social media or in person. But by the time he was arrested for his mail bomb spree he was 'bankrupt, foreclosed upon, estranged from his family – was suddenly something else: famous'.[2]

Like many mail bombers Sayoc's life was marked by mental instability and professional failure as he flitted from one job to another, none for very long as he sank further and further into a dangerous fantasy world. As he moved into middle age he clung to his glory years as a stripper. He posted pictures of himself bare chested and flexing his muscles around the same time he was arrested in 2002 for possessing steroids with the intent to distribute. He was now too old for his former line of work and was relegated to offstage jobs at Tootsie's and the Pure Platinum strip clubs where he worked the door and monitored champagne rooms. Although his dream was to open his own strip club in the midwest that he would call Cesar's Palace Royale, it was just one more figment of the fantasy world he inhabited.

Somehow, despite working mostly ephemeral jobs, he was able to buy a house in Fort Lauderdale. However, by 2009 his house had been foreclosed and he was forced to move in with his parents in their Aventura condominium. Three years later he filed for bankruptcy and transitioned to living out of a van.

Sayoc claimed Native American heritage and drove around with a sticker on his van that read 'Native Americans for Trump'. Although he claimed Seminole origins there are no tribal records to support this but this did not stop him from claiming in a 2014 federal lawsuit deposition that he had Native American, Italian and Filipino roots. All accounts assert he was born in Brooklyn, New York, to a Filipino father and a mother of Italian descent. He grew up in Florida and attended North Miami Beach High School. Those who knew the young Sayoc suggest his behavioural quirks might have been triggered by his father's desertion of the family and return to the Philippines. Sayoc would contend with abandonment issues, lack of self-worth and mental health problems throughout his life. Never able to quite get his act together, he remained 'inarticulate' and 'immature' late into middle age. Anyone who crossed paths with him had a Sayoc story to tell. He was not one to keep his opinions to himself. To one person he 'proclaimed his love for Hitler and ethnic cleansing'. He even warned his lesbian boss 'she would burn in hell'.[3]

No matter what, he was intent on showing the world he was a 'somebody' rather than a 'nobody'. He used a number of aliases, perhaps trying to distance himself from his reality, using names such as Cesar Altieri and Cesar Randazzo. An observer suggested it was just Sayoc trying to find a new identity; indeed, his ultimate conversion to a political cause perhaps was the result of his many failures in searching for an identity. He made his political beliefs well known long before he began his mail bomb campaign. Sayoc apparently found his *raison d'être* at a Trump rally sometime in 2016, embarking on his plot to terrorize critics of then-President Donald J. Trump. He expressed his fealty to Trump in almost every way possible, from wearing the red MAGA (Trump's slogan 'Make America Great Again') baseball cap to attending raucous Trump rallies. His social media postings testified to his obsession, filled with pro-Trump stories, photos of himself and conspiracy theories. In fact, 'His Twitter timeline was a greatest hits collection of right-wing conspiracy theories.' By the time he was arrested and convicted in 2019 he recognized that Trump rallies 'became like a new found drug'.[4]

At the time of his arrest he was still living in his 'large older-model camper style' van. Journalists and local residents dubbed it the 'MAGAmobile'. It was hard to miss, often parked near a Hollywood, Florida, funeral home.[5] Indeed, it was unmistakable, festooned with bright signs attacking Trump critics and plastered with Trump and conspiracy theories. Somehow he managed to support himself delivering pizza on the graveyard shift and working as a floor manager at a strip club. Despite his sorry state he claimed to have been a Chippendales dancer, champion bodybuilder, a professional wrestler, a popular DJ and a veterinary medicine student who once played soccer for AC Milan in the Italian League. He would boast to anyone who would listen that he owned a strip club, the Cesar's Palace Royale, which of course 'only existed in his mind'.[6]

Like many modern domestic terrorists he was an avid user of social media, posting all kinds of threats online. On Twitter he posted photos of rifle scope crosshairs over the faces of Hillary Clinton, former president Obama and film-maker Michael Moore. Another post stated 'CNN sucks' with an 'image of Trump standing on a tank in front of fireworks and an American flag'. Thanks to his social media presence investigators were privy to a trove of clues including the same spelling errors on his online posts as on his mailings to targets. Perhaps his lawyer summed up his client best when he said, 'This is not a criminal mastermind by any stretch of the imagination.'[7]

He was distinct from most serial bombers mainly for the fact that his bombs were not built to harm anyone. He would later say that the devices were 'intended to look like pipe bombs' but he did not intend for them to detonate, although he admitted there was a risk of some of them exploding under extraordinary conditions. He ultimately sent sixteen devices to thirteen people. At his trial in March 2019 a federal judge in New York declared that 'For five days in October 2018, Cesar Sayoc rained terror across the country, sending high ranking officials and former leaders explosives through the mail.'[8]

On the night of Sayoc's arrest, just four days after the first bombing, he was sleeping inside his van, outside an auto-parts shop near Fort Lauderdale, 'that stank of dirty laundry, delivering pizzas on the graveyard shift and working as a "floorman" inside a smoky dimly lit gentleman's club'. He regularly showered on the beach or at local gyms, with some observers remembering him as a 'well groomed, cologne wearing dependable pizza delivery man'.[9] It did not take investigators long to track their suspect down. Sayoc left a trail of clues that led them to him just days after his bombing campaign began. Lab technicians had linked his fingerprints to several of the mail bombs. Moreover DNA linked him to ten of the mail bombs. At the same time investigators searching his social media found the same spelling errors in his rants that were found on the parcel addresses of his targets (that is, 'Hilary' Clinton; Debbie Wasserman 'Shultz'). Cyber investigators examining his laptop and other devices also found that he had searched for 'hilary [sic] Clinton hime [sic] address', 'address for Barack Obama' and 'john [sic] Brennan wife and kids'.[10]

The 57-year-old Sayoc had amassed a long rap sheet by the time of the bombings, dating back to an arrest for larceny when he was 29 years old. In other incidents he was arrested for grand theft and fraud in south Florida and for domestic violence when he assaulted an elderly relative (the charge was later withdrawn). In a harbinger of his future bomb campaign, in 2002, sixteen years earlier, he pleaded guilty without trial and was sentenced to probation for a bomb threat in which he promised that Florida Power & Light power company 'will get what they deserve and will be worse than 9/11' for what he considered an outrageous power bill.[11]

Like Ted Kaczynski's Montana cabin, Sayoc's van proved a treasure trove of evidence for the FBI. It was chock full of bomb-making equipment and evidence of his mailing more than a dozen potentially explosive devices from his south Florida 'redoubt' to political targets around the country. The pipe bomb materials were mostly purchased over the counter at local retailers. He used his mother's official address in an Aventura condominium.

Sayoc's lawyers sought a ten-year sentence, explaining that their client was using copious amounts of steroids when he became delusional in his support for President Donald Trump, making him 'ripe for conversion to a political cause because of his constant failure in his search for identity', with Trump filling his paternal void 'like a surrogate father'.

He truly believed wild conspiracy theories he read on the Internet, many of which vilified Democrats and spread rumors that Trump supporters were in danger because of them ... He heard it from the president, a man with whom he felt he had a deep personal connection.

Trump and his allies 'repeatedly pushed back against the idea that his incendiary rhetoric could be linked to extremist violence'.[12] After a package bomb was recovered from a Manhattan postal facility, CNN contributor and former director of national intelligence James R. Clapper noted that 'This is definitely domestic terrorism, no doubt in my mind.'[13]

In October 2018 57-year-old Cesar Sayoc Jr testified in a Manhattan federal courtroom as to how he assembled numerous pipe bombs in his van before sending them to prominent Democrats and Trump critics that autumn. He sent manila envelopes replete with misspelled names and packed with crude explosive materials, most of them passing through the Opa Locka postal facility. Sayoc described the construction of the bombs, consisting of 6 inches of plastic pipe with a small clock battery, wiring and 'energetic material'. Each device was packed with a potentially deadly mix of fireworks, fertilizer, a pool chemical and glass fragments. Once this was done he inserted into each package a photograph of the intended target, marked with a red X over the face.[14] He admitted to creating the bombs so that they looked like pipe bombs and filling them with explosive materials. The judge asked him if the devices were intended to explode. Sayoc said no. He then asked the defendant 'What would prevent the powder from exploding?', and Sayoc admitted he 'was aware of the risk they would explode'. He pleaded guilty on 21 March 2019 for sending pipe bombs to Trump critics and CNN in a series of postal attacks that spread fear of political violence across the United States, although no one was harmed. The best that the former stripper and bodybuilder could come up with as he entered his plea in federal court was that he was 'extremely sorry' and 'never intended for the devices to explode', as he sobbed and apologized for the potential lethality of his plan.[15]

There was more than enough evidence that he sent sixteen devices to intended victims across the country right before the 2018 midterm elections. He read a prepared statement in the courtroom explaining that he had sent out the infernal machines 'to threaten and intimidate people' and with the intent to only injure property. In a handwritten letter filed in the U.S. District Court for the Southern District of New York he told the judge that 'the first thing you here [*sic*] entering Trump rally is we are not going to take it anymore, the forgotten ones, etc.' Sayoc recounted how he met all types of people at the Trump rallies and 'It was fun, it became like a new found drug.' Moreover he wrote that 'Trump's self-help CDs reprogrammed his mind' and detailed the negative reaction he got from the Trump stickers on his car, including having his tires slashed and windows broken.[16]

The ex-body builder then shifted his excuses to his abuse of steroids and hundreds of different vitamins and supplements. Sayoc explained, 'It was the most scared time of my life . . . I lost my head, steroids altered my growing anger. I made a bad choice . . . I lost control of myself and mental state from them.'[17]

Prosecutors described his bombing campaign as a 'domestic terror attack' despite no one being hurt. He pleaded guilty on 65 counts, which included 'using a weapon of mass destruction and interstate transportation of an explosive'.[18] He was looking at a life sentence. In exchange for his guilty plea he was sentenced to twenty years behind bars.

16

The Modern Era

At the onset of the twenty-first century America was still reeling from the Oklahoma City bombing that left 168 dead. Although it took place in 1995 it was still fresh in the minds of domestic terrorism analysts and everyday citizens. Unlike most mail bomb campaigns the death toll was unimaginably high. Except for the eighteen-year spree by the Unabomber, no mail bombing resonated for any length of time. After the 9/11 terrorist attacks in the United States letter bombs seemed rather quaint and rarely made the headlines outside the jurisdictions in which they occurred. But they still appeared throughout the new century. Compared to the 1990s, the early 2000s were relatively quiet in terms of murder by mail.

Tesco Bomb Campaign

Beginning in August 2000 fifty-year-old electrician Robert Edward Dyer, aka 'Sally', began an extortion campaign against the Tesco supermarket chain in Bournemouth, England. When he was captured over six months later he was linked to almost a dozen attacks. His plan was to extort money from Tesco with a mail bomb campaign against its customers. His plan was for the supermarket chain to clandestinely pay him through a cash machine ruse. He said if they didn't comply he would send letter bombs to customers in three areas in Dorset that would get bigger and more dangerous. One retired person was injured when a letter bomb blew up in her face. He would eventually admit to nine counts of extortion and one count of assault between August 2000 and February 2001. He was caught when one of his extortion letters was left in a newsagent's

photocopier. Dyer was perhaps one of the most incompetent mail
bombers in history. He had created deadlines for payments that
'were unusable because he muddled his dates up'. What is more,
three devices never reached their destinations because he used too
few stamps. He signed all of his letters 'Sally'. His numerous errors
typified his pathetic campaign. Once he realized he had left a copy
of his extortion letter in a photocopier and had mailed the letter to
Tesco he tried to set fire to the post box in which he mailed it. The
letter arrived at Tesco 'only partly singed and with the added clue
that detectives knew which [postal] box he used'. One couple
received a parcel and when the husband tried to open it a cassette
inside exploded. Police believed Dyer followed victims home from
the supermarket to get addresses. Investigators determined he lived
with his two teenage daughters in a two-bedroom bungalow. His
wife had died in 1992 from asphyxia – 'a plastic ligature was found
around her neck.' A pathologist said it could have been suicide but
an open verdict was rendered.[1] This of course brings into question
whether he had any culpability in her demise. But this was never
substantiated.

Dyer did take precautions, but not enough to trump his many
mistakes. He wore kitchen gloves to place the envelopes and used
water instead of saliva to put on stamps to avoid DNA evidence.
Police described his extortion demand letters as similar to other
blackmailers, including the Mardi Gra bomber, Edgar Pearce. The
Tesco bomber was sentenced to sixteen years in prison.[2]

The Smiley-Face Bomber: '5 Days of Terror'

Less than a year after the World Trade Center towers were
destroyed, a pipe exploded in a rural mailbox in Eldridge, Iowa, on
3 May 2002. Four rural mail carriers and two postal customers were
injured after six of eighteen bombs placed in rural mailboxes across
the Midwest exploded. Among the victims was Delores Werling,
who was injured by debris when her mailbox in Tipton, Ohio,
exploded, injuring her ears, gashing her face, arms and hands,
knocking out a tooth and ruining her glasses. Hers was one of six

that exploded in eastern Iowa and western Illinois that day. In another explosion a mail carrier was slipping a new telephone book into a mailbox when it set off an explosion, leaving the carrier bleeding and struggling to get out of the vehicle. Some said she was saved because of the thickness of the phone book, which absorbed much of the blast.[3] That same day a young pregnant woman opened her mailbox in Eldridge and noticed a pipe bomb next to the newspaper. It did not detonate, unlike the six that injured carriers and customers that day.[4]

As it turned out eight bombs had been placed in a 'circle seven counties around'. Some of the parcels included a '440-word letter wrapped in a plastic bag that warned of more "attention getters" to come'. Over the next three days ten additional bombs were located in Nebraska, Colorado and Texas, with none detonating. As one journalist put it, 'The pipe bombs added a pit-in-the-stomach fear to an everyday act: going to the mailbox.'[5]

Rural mail residents were advised to leave their mailboxes open and were told how to safely open boxes by 'using a spool of string or fishing line, a treble hook and a secure barrier'.[6] The next day the FBI issued an all-points bulletin looking for Lucas John Helder after being notified by his father. Following an intensive manhunt, the 21-year-old engineering student at the University of Wisconsin-Stout was taken into custody just east of Reno. He was armed with a rifle at his arrest. On 5 June a federal grand jury in the Northern District of Iowa indicted him on two criminal counts: using an explosive device to maliciously destroy property used in interstate commerce and using a firearm (pipe bomb) to commit crimes of violence. Almost a year later he was being held at a federal medical centre in Rochester, Minnesota, still awaiting trial. In 2004 he was declared incompetent to stand trial. It would later be revealed that his purpose in selecting bomb locations was to create a 'large smiley face' when plotted on a map.

In the days following Helder's arrest Philadelphia police found and detonated a mailbox bomb that had a note attached referencing al-Qaeda and containing the phrase 'Free Palestine'. As it turned out, Preston Lit, who had a long history of mental illness, was attempting a copycat bombing inspired by the series of Midwest mailbox bombs earlier in May.

Over the next two years several international cases caught the public's attention for a brief time but, like most other mail bombs over the past 150 years, had little impact beyond the doors of the victims and quickly receded into memory. In early 2004, in England, the leader of the British Labour Party's Euro MPs received a parcel bomb postmarked Bologna. It was at least the seventh package bomb sent to EU politicians over the past two weeks in a campaign of intimidation that reached from Manchester to Frankfurt and Bologna to Brussels. The attacks were attributed to a shadowy group of Italian anarchists.

Gary Titley was in his Manchester office when a parcel burst into flames and made a noise 'like a party popper' before filling his office with smoke and flames. Titley's secretary was opening a padded envelope and 'it began to emit smoke.' She threw it to the ground as it burst into flames. The office manager bravely jumped up and down on it until it went out. The letter bombs appeared to contain a book or video; all bore the same Bologna postmark as the incendiary package sent to the Italian home of the European Commission president on 27 December 2003. A group calling itself the Informal Anarchic Federation claimed responsibility. Its claims seemed spurious to Italian authorities. However, it issued a communiqué claiming that it 'planted bombs to hit at the apparatus of control that is repressive and leading the new democratic show that is the new European order'. During the Christmas break more letter bombs were sent to the European Central Bank's president in Frankfurt and the EU's public prosecutor and police cooperation offices in the Hague. They were defused.[7]

Mail bombers continued to lay low over the next four years before heating up again in 2007. In January a bomber calling himself 'The Bishop' sent several unassembled bombs to financial firms in the United States and was arrested in April. John Patrick Tomkins, aka The Bishop, 42, was a machinist in Dubuque when he sent several threatening letters to investment firms and advisors between 2005 and 2007. In January 2007 he mailed an unassembled bomb package to two financial firms in the United States. He was reportedly motivated by his declining financial situation. He thought attacking financial institutions would lower their share price, increasing the value of his speculative bets against them. He thought wrong. He was arrested on 25 April 2007 and sentenced to 37 years in prison.[8]

Targeting a 'Surveillance Society'

During the first two months of 2007, in England, Miles Cooper, 27, a primary school caretaker from the Cambridge area, sent seven letter bombs over a three-week period to public institutions and private companies that he believed were creating a 'surveillance society'. His bombs injured eight people. It would turn out that he was angry that the police would not delete his father's name from a national database.[9]

Cooper admitted to sending the devices but insisted he did not mean to cause harm. His knowledge of musketry and rudimentary explosives that he gained as a child on his father's farm in Scotland came in handy for constructing letter bombs. He made the bombs by filing down match heads stuffed into a pipe. He launched his first attacks in January. The first two devices were disappointing so he decided to alter the design on subsequent ones, making them 'potentially deadly by filling nail varnish bottles with fireworks powder, knowing the glass would explode on detonation'.

This coordinated series of attacks drew comparisons to the Unabomber (arrested in 1996) except Cooper's targets seemed to be institutions and companies involved in regulating cars and drivers. His crusade stemmed from a growing resentment to what he thought was mounting threats to civil liberties in Great Britain. Like many other bombers and sociopaths Cooper had a challenging time forming social relationships. All he needed to embark on his bombing spree was a trigger, which came in 2003 when authorities decided to hold on to his father's DNA despite him being cleared of the crime he was accused of committing.

Cooper selected his victims with great care. Among them were three forensic scientists who worked for a company involved in DNA research. He also targeted a firm called Vantis, which provided digital speed cameras to the police. While none of his victims were seriously hurt, most 'suffered shock and superficial injury'. One of the targets, a driver and vehicle licensing agency (DVLA) employee, however, suffered post-traumatic stress disorder after opening a bomb. Neighbours described Cooper as weird, a loner who at one time would come out at night and 'arrange candles in the front garden'.[10] He was arrested on 19 February 2007. He was sentenced to an 'indeterminate' sentence but would have to serve a minimum of five years in prison before being even considered for release.

Also in 2007 long-time white supremacist leader Dennis Mahon mailed a large pipe bomb to a Scottsdale, Arizona, Office of Diversity and Dialog, whose director was an outspoken Black advocate of civil rights. It exploded in the office, seriously wounding him and injuring three others. Almost a year later Mahon was convicted of the attack and was sentenced to forty years in prison.[11]

An Aspiring Actor and Model

In August 'an aspiring actor' named Adel Arnaout, 37, was arrested for three mail bombings in Canada. He was a native of Lebanon and had moved to Canada from the United States in 2001. The first two were sent to targets in Toronto and the third to a home in Guelph. The third bomb came in a courier package and contained a 'homemade explosive device'. The recipient was suspicious enough to call the police first. A bomb disposal squad cleared the area before detonating the device, sending debris flying and blowing a hole in his backyard deck sufficient to kill a person. The two bombs delivered to separate Toronto homes were also inside bubble-wrapped courier envelopes but contained 'an explosive petroleum-based fluid'. A security expert at the time correctly opined that 'these things usually happen in clusters ... I'd suspect it is the same person or persons doing this.' If the Guelph bomb was made by the same bombers then they were probably 'refining their technique ... They're learning about this as they go – figuring out how to make better bombs. They'll have noted that only one of their bombs detonated, so they'll have switched to conventional explosives.' Moreover the security expert noted that gasoline bombs were not dependable, 'difficult to set off and relatively easy to detect because of smell of gasoline'.

This is an interesting case study due to the findings and supposition by the Canadian bomb experts, who speculated,

> The bomber may also have fine-tuned the delivery of the explosives . . . The two Toronto bombs were in envelopes with properly addressed courier receipts, leading police to speculate that they might have been delivered by the bomber in person, while the Guelph device was sent through Canada Post. That would limit their exposure in delivering the explosives to their target. Of course, it may be as simple as him not having access to a car . . . so he couldn't have delivered the Guelph bomb himself . . . Every bomb gives the police a better idea who the targets are. It narrows the field of suspects.[12]

Further adding to the intrigue surrounding this case was the fact that after Arnaout's arrest he was charged with eight counts of attempted murder from a plot three years earlier to poison staff at four Toronto modelling agencies. In this case he was charged with injecting chemicals into bottles of water and then having them sent as promotional items to these agencies in June and July 2004. The director of one of the firms reported his suspicions to police in 2004 when he noticed 'a pin prick in one of the free bottles – said it was easy to spot that the water looked cloudy'.[13] Evidence of this previous crime was obtained when authorities searched his living quarters in conjunction with the mail bombs in late August 2007.

In August 2010 Arnaout was found guilty on eleven counts of attempted murder for sending letter bombs and spiked water bottles to a variety of targets that included his lawyer, a judge and two modelling agency owners. In court the defendant was described as 'a self-aggrandizing, narcissistic person who took the wrongs in his own mind and blew them out of proportion'. This profile would be remarkably familiar to anyone studying serial bombers. Arnaout would not go down without saying his piece. He claimed that he never intended to hurt anyone and that he was just on a campaign against the police for not investigating his complaints about other people, including problems with a bullying room-mate and a talent agent who took money but 'did not properly promote him'. However, this plea was ignored, particularly after his typed statements to his victims were read, threatening to 'terrorize them, burn them alive, and strip the flesh from their bones ... Its time for you to die.'[14]

The Anarchists Are Back

A number of letter bomb incidents punctuated the beginning of the 2010s. Late in 2010 suspected Greek terrorists unleashed a two-day campaign of mail bombs targeting embassies in Athens, international organizations and foreign leaders. The attacks began on 1 November when a letter bomb addressed to the Mexican embassy exploded at a delivery service in central Athens injuring a postal worker. Two men in their twenties were arrested shortly after the blast, carrying mail bombs addressed to French leader Nicolas Sarkozy and the Belgian embassy along with handguns and bullets in waist pouches.[15]

On 2 November infernal devices exploded at the Russian and Swiss embassies. Meanwhile German authorities destroyed letter bombs sent to German chancellor Angela Merkel. By the end of the day at least eleven mail bombs had been detected in Athens, one addressed to Sarkozy and others to the embassies of Russia, Germany, Switzerland, Mexico, Chile, the Netherlands and Belgium. Two more were destroyed in controlled explosions at Athens airport, one addressed to the EU's highest court in Luxembourg and the other to Europol in the Netherlands. The campaign was notable for the small size of the devices, which only injured one and caused minimal damage. On 2 November 2010 the Greek government 'took the unprecedented step of suspending international airmail for 48 hours'. It would be an understatement to suggest that the recent spate of parcel bombs targeting Merkel, the Italian premier, Silvio Berlusconi, and Sarkozy, as well as a number of foreign embassies in Greece and across Europe, caused a major security scare.

It was unclear if the mail bomb sent to Germany was delivered by land or air. If sent by air it would highlight the potential limitations of air cargo security that still remained, despite the concern triggered by mail bombs dispatched recently from Yemen (see below). In 2010 transportation officials admitted that there were still 'few, if any security checks on packages transported within the European Union by road or rail'.

The package that arrived at Merkel's office had been sent from Greece by UPS delivery two days earlier and resembled the Athens packages, which looked like books. The package contained a pipe filled with black powder. A terrorism specialist in London said packages that are addressed to embassies and state leaders were not likely to reach their targets but the bombers achieved their aim by generating publicity. 'If they had just left the devices on the streets of Athens it wouldn't have gotten anything like attention.' This was happening close to the Yemeni attempt to get bombs into the United States and suggested that a delivered letter bomb 'has more of a resonance than it would otherwise'.[16]

In late December a mail bomb was defused at the Greek embassy in Rome. It was reportedly sent by anarchists seeking to avenge comrades in Greece. The Italian group Informal Anarchist Federation claimed responsibility for the intercepted letter as well as two that exploded at the Swiss and Chilean embassies in Rome on 23 December, which seriously injured two. Italian police believed the device sent to the Greek embassy was in response to the arrest of Conspiracy of Cells of Fire (CCF) members who claimed responsibility for sending fourteen letter bombs to embassies in Athens in November. The CCF, described as an anarchist-oriented guerrilla group, emerged around 2008 and was soon one of the most prominent terrorist groups in Greece. Italian and Greek police believed that anarchist groups across the EU maintained close ties through the Internet.[17]

The al-Qaeda Bomb Plot

In November 2010 Yemeni special forces launched an offensive searching for the al-Qaeda bomb-maker believed responsible for designing explosives concealed in printer cartridges. The month before, al-Qaeda in Arabian Peninsula (AQAP) attempted to use mail bombs unsuccessfully in international terrorist attacks. The group used delivery services to send two package bombs with plastic explosives to addresses in Chicago. The addresses were locations that had formerly been synagogues but the real intent appears to have been for the bombs to detonate mid-air en route to their destination, blowing up the cargo planes carrying them. However, information from Saudi Arabian intelligence led to their detection beforehand. Both packages were found on planes transiting through Dubai and Britain. The urgent manhunt for Saudi-born immigrant and bomb-maker Ibrahim al-Asiri intensified and was made even more urgent once the plot to blow up aircraft over the United States was discovered.[18] He was considered one of the most lethal strategists for the terror organization and was suspected of building the bomb to hide in the underwear of a Nigerian student dubbed 'the underwear bomber' in an attempt to bring down an airliner in 2009.

In the spring of 2011 the cross-town rivalry of Glasgow's top football clubs was one of the 'oldest, and the most dangerous' in all of sports. One observer called the Rangers–Celtic story 'one of the age-old Protestant and Catholic enmities that are one of the ugliest strains in Scotland's history'.[19] In mid-April it was revealed that four 'crude bombs were sent through the mail' to Celtic's manager and two of the club's leading supporters over a six-week period. Between 1 March and 15 April 2011 Trevor Muirhead and Neil McKenzie allegedly sent parcel bombs to Paul McBride, a lawyer; Neil Lennon, Celtic football club manager; and Trish Godman, a former Labour Party MP. Both men were hard-line Protestant loyalists and anti-Celtic Football Club (and anti-Catholic) extremists. They were arrested in May 2011 and sentenced the following year. All of the devices were intercepted and destroyed without injuries even though they contained flammable liquids and nails.[20]

Before 2011 ended German authorities announced that a suspicious envelope intercepted by Deutsche Bank employees was a letter bomb sent by an Italian anarchist organization to its chief executive, Josef Ackermann, considered 'one of the most powerful and controversial in European banking'. His name became synonymous with 'an industry whose reputation has plummeted since the financial crisis'. The Anarchist Federation had a history of sending letter bombs and claimed responsibility. The year before, a package bomb from the group addressed to Merkel was intercepted in her office's mailroom in the midst of the wave of letter bombs in Greece aimed at foreign embassies and traced to Greek anarchists.[21]

Individualists Tending Toward Savagery (ITS): The Mexican Unabombers

The Unabomber influenced mail bombers across the globe. Typically it was one individual but in one Mexican case it involved an 'eco-anarchist' group called Individualists Tending Toward Savagery (ITS). The self-described 'Mexican Unabombers' was one of the stranger manifestations of the Unabomber paradigm. While Mexican authorities conceded the group was responsible for some violent actions, many of the group's claims remain unsubstantiated. It maintained that its terrorist activities began in 2011 by sending letter bombs to university professors dedicated to teaching nanotechnology and related sciences in Mexico. There is little doubt that its members were inspired by Ted Kaczynski on some level. On 27 April 2011 a package bomb exploded at the Polytechnic University of the Valley of Mexico, seriously injuring an employee. ITS claimed responsibility for the attack and began sending incendiary devices to researchers at other schools although most were either deactivated or did not explode.

In August ITS took responsibility for a package bomb that severely injured a computer scientist at the Monterrey Institute of Technology and Higher Education. Dr Armando Herrera Corral was severely injured by the shoebox-sized parcel bomb. It stated on the outside that it was some type of award. He got a little suspicious when he heard 'something solid [that] jiggled inside'. He decided to confer with a colleague and robotics researcher and asked him to open it for him. He set the box down on his desk to open it. As he did so, a 'twenty centimeter long pipe bomb' exploded. The colleague took the main force of the blast with a piece of metal puncturing one of his lungs. Dr Herrera escaped with minor injuries including a burst eardrum and burns to his legs. The following day ITS claimed responsibility for the blast in a harangue against nanotechnology issued online. This followed the group's claims of responsibility for attacks at other universities in April and May. In 2012 one leading expert on ITS asserted that 'No other developing country has suffered a comparable string of anti-technology attacks.'[22]

Between 2014 and the end of the decade postal bombs continued to injure, take lives, and terrorize people around the world. On 14 February 2014 a series of bombs were sent to seven Armed Forces recruitment offices in the UK. Observers noted that the tactics bore all the hallmarks of Northern Ireland. The following month letter bombs were found at two postal sorting offices weeks after those sent to the army facilities. Meanwhile infernal devices were found in Londonderry addressed to prison officers.[23]

It is rare to hear of crimes occurring in the People's Republic of China, let alone violent cases with multiple casualties. However, in September 2015 news reached the Western world that at least six people had been killed and dozens injured in explosions at fifteen locations in Liucheng County in China's Guangxi Zhuang Autonomous Region. In this case, the explosives were concealed inside express delivery packages.[24]

The following year, Jim Alden of Philadelphia suffered wounds to his face, chest and hands after opening a manila envelope left at his door in the middle of the night. It exploded in his kitchen at 4 a.m.[25] In Germany a package with an explosive mechanism mailed from Greece and addressed to Wolfgang Schäuble, a German government minister, was intercepted. The extremist anarchist group the Conspiracy of Cells of Fire claimed responsibility for the March 2017 action. That same week a weaponized package was sent from

Greece to the offices of the International Monetary Fund (IMF) in Paris. It exploded, injuring an employee, although it had been intended for the IMF director. In an attempt to mislead authorities the name of another prominent German politician was written on the package as the sender. This incident came as the Greek anarchist group claimed responsibility for a failed letter bomb sent to the German finance ministry several days earlier. Both letter bombs were similar in construction. The secretary who opened the envelope was wounded in the face by shrapnel and injured one of her eardrums.

Echoing the anarchist American May Day bomb attacks a century earlier, the Greek group Conspiracy of Cells of Fire warned that the attack 'was part of a concerted campaign by international anarchist groups'. Like most other mail bombs it contained low-grade explosives similar to what you would find in firecrackers. Many Greeks saw this as a manifestation of the country's economic problems and the austerity measures imposed by the IMF and the European Union, both linked to Greece's bail-out programme.[26] As if to put an exclamation mark on the March attacks, a suspected letter bomb exploded inside the car of Greek prime minister Lucas Papademos, injuring him, his driver and another official. The device had been placed inside an envelope and detonated while they were driving to Athens.[27]

Mark Conditt: Terror in Austin

The year 2018 was marked by two serial bombing campaigns. The story of the MAGAbomber Cesar Sayoc was covered earlier. But before that short-lived campaign a more deadly series of devices terrorized the Austin, Texas, and suburban San Antonio areas between 2 and 21 March when 23-year-old Mark Conditt sent six package bombs that killed two and injured five. The terror began on 2 March when 39-year-old Anthony Stephan House was killed after picking up a parcel delivered to his home. Ten days later seventeen-year-old Draylen Mason was killed and his mother injured by a mail bomb; this bomb had been reportedly delivered to the wrong address. Also on 12 March a third device severely injured a 75-year-old man who was visiting his elderly mother.

On 18 March, in a residential neighbourhood, two young men were seriously injured after setting off a tripwire device. Unlike the previous bombs, which were left on doorsteps, this bomb was innocuously left on the side of the road attached to a sign that said 'Caution: Children at Play'. Following this fourth explosion Austin Police warned the public of a serial bomber possessing a 'higher level of sophistication, a higher level of skill' than initially thought. On 20 March, shortly after midnight, a fifth bomb detonated in a package at a FedEx facility in Schertz, Texas, injuring one employee. The package was intended for an Austin address. Later that day a sixth infernal device was intercepted and defused at a separate FedEx facility in southeast Austin. The two packages were conclusively sent by the same person from a FedEx store in Sunset Valley.

Initially investigators detected a potential racial motivation because the bombs targeted a section of Austin that was home to poor, African American and Latino residents. What was unique about this bomber was his changing strategy, which initially confused authorities. The first three devices were not mailed but just placed near the homes of the victims. Two of the first three exploded when they were picked up. The other after being opened. The fourth bomb was set off by a tripwire and the fifth was triggered at a FedEx sorting facility. The sixth was discovered and deactivated at another sorting facility.[28]

On 21 March Conditt blew himself up in his car near Round Rock, Texas, as police closed in. Authorities searching his home found a wealth of bomb-making materials requiring the evacuation of a four-block perimeter. The materials were consistent with those found in other bombs. Meanwhile authorities were unable to produce a motive for his spree. News services reported that 'a key part of the puzzle was the discovery of an "exotic" and foreign battery in each explosive' which helped authorities link the blasts.[29] Authorities were able to trace a large purchase of nails to be used as shrapnel in the devices. Conditt had no criminal record and had left a 25-minute video confessing to the bombings and detailing the devices but his motivation was never explained.

Shortly after the Conditt mail bombs in the spring of 2018 a judge in Manitoba, Canada, found a man guilty of trying to murder his ex-wife and two lawyers with letter bombs. Guido Amsel was arrested and charged after three explosive parcels were sent in July 2015. A lawyer who had represented the ex-wife in a financial dispute lost her right hand when one went off in her office. The judge said the defendant wanted to hurt his wife and lawyers for their alleged roles in a contentious lawsuit he filed over profits from an auto body shop he co-owned with his ex-wife. As if to throw the authorities off his trail, he dropped the lawsuits shortly before he sent the bombs. The explosive compound in this case was contained in a 'hand-held voice recorder that came with a note instructing the prosecutor to press play'. Police safely detonated the other two devices.[30]

Also in 2018 a Swedish citizen, Jermu Michael Salonen, was convicted of sending a letter bomb to a London bitcoin company and threatening letters to parliament members in Stockholm. He had mailed a package holding 'two pipe bomb-like devices' in August 2017. It was sent to the London-based bitcoin company Cryptopay in the care of an accounting firm, and when it was opened did not explode. Police were able to link the bomber to his DNA found on the bomb by British police. He was convicted on twenty accounts of sending threats to legislators in 2017, including one to the prime minister with a white powder that proved harmless. Salonen was sentenced to seven years in prison.[31]

On 5 March 2019 three package bombs were located near transport hubs in the London vicinity, including Heathrow Airport, a mail room at Waterloo Station and the City Aviation House near London City Airport. A fourth device later turned up at the University of Glasgow. The parcels were all similar in description, 'midsize white envelopes with padded manila envelopes inside'. These attacks were followed by another suspect package that arrived on 22 March at a mail sorting centre in Limerick, Ireland. Among the suspected perpetrators was the IRA dissident splinter group, the New Irish Republican Army (NIRA).[32]

Just a week later Scotland Yard issued an alert related to the letter bomb attacks. What concerned authorities the most was that one of the five letter bombs sent by the terror group was still unaccounted for. The NIRA claimed it was sent to an army recruitment office. The devices bore similarities to those sent in the past by dissident extremist groups in Northern Ireland. All the packages were 'A4-sized white postal bags containing yellow jiffy bags' and appeared capable of igniting a small fire when opened. The stamps on the packages appeared to be those issued by the Irish postal service for Valentine's Day 2018, featuring a heart motif and the words 'Love Eire N'.[33]

Russia and the Ukrainian Conflict

Attempts to murder, or at least injure, by mail continued into the 2020s, including a probable campaign against Ukraine by Russian operatives. In November and December 2022 at least six letter bombs were mailed to government buildings in Spain, including to Prime Minister Pedro Sánchez and the u.s. and Ukrainian embassies. The envelope to Sánchez was intercepted by security on 24 November because it appeared to contain 'pyrotechnic materials'. However, one exploded at the Ukrainian embassy, slightly injuring an employee. Another letter bomb was sent to the headquarters of Instalaza, a Spanish firm that manufactured weapons and military equipment, including some used to help Ukrainian forces. The envelopes had been sent from within Spain. The targets of the Spain attacks were either connected to Ukraine or had expressed support for it against Russia.[34] Authorities were confident that the target selection in Spain and Ukraine implicated Russian intelligence.

The following year a 74-year-old man was charged in Spain's national court for sending the aforementioned weaponized mail to the country's prime minister and to the u.s. and Ukrainian embassies in Spain. One person was wounded in the handling of the devices that were sent in November and December 2022.[35] American and European authorities believed that a Russian military intelligence officer directly associated with a white supremacist militant group based in Russia had carried out the attacks. Attention was focused on the Russian Imperial Movement, a radical group that has members and associates across Europe and military-style training centres in St Petersburg. The group has been designated a global terrorist group by the u.s. State Department. American authorities were convinced that the Russian officers who directed the mail bomb campaign were attempting to keep Europe on its toes and off-guard by testing proxy groups in the region in the event Moscow decided to escalate the conflict. The ability to use the Russian Imperial Movement as a proxy force is useful to Russian intelligence because it makes it more difficult to attribute their actions to the Russian government.[36]

In March 2023 a number of news stations received letter bombs in Ecuador. The motivation was understood – to silence journalists. Five of the devices were sent to journalists at radio and television stations. One exploded without causing significant injury. The devices were all the same – an envelope containing a USB memory stick that exploded when inserted into the computer. It was loaded with RDX, a military-grade explosive. Authorities wondered whether the bombs were connected to the fact that Ecuador had recently declared war on the drug gangs, many operating in prisons.[37]

Package Bombs and Terrorists: 1970–2017

Murder by mail is an extremely rare occurrence regardless of method or motivation. From 1983 to 1993 an average of fifteen bombs per year were sent through u.s. Mail and few detonated as planned. During the 2010s an average of sixteen letter bombs appeared among the 170 billion pieces of mail processed in the United States. Postal authorities noted that 'the chances that a piece of mail actually contains a bomb average far less than one in ten billion.'[38]

According to one of the leading terrorism research groups, in the period 1970–2017 'Terrorist attacks involving package bombs were least likely to be successful compared to attacks involving other weapons.' Explosives detonated in only 39 per cent of package bomb attacks worldwide. A major finding of the National Consortium for the Study of Terrorism and Responses to Terrorism (START) that corresponds with non-terrorist-related letter bombs is the fact that 'The vast majority' of these devices are 'non-lethal (88%)'.[39]

Between 1970 and 2017 there were 560 terrorist attacks across the globe involving weaponized mail 'or made to appear as if they were sent in the mail'. More than 50 per cent of package bomb attacks took place in Western Europe compared to 12 per cent in North America. Of the 368 attacks documented for this period they ranged, in descending order, from the United Kingdom (102), Spain (63) and the United States (59) to Italy (43) and Greece (27).[40]

This book has documented hundreds of selected mail bomb cases. Many of the terrorist letter bomb attacks have been covered in chapters covering the past fifty years. The following are the perpetrators of the majority of the attacks: Black September (208) in 1971–2; Basque Fatherland and Freedom (29) in 1987–2006; Irish Republican Army (24) in 1973–90; Informal Anarchist Federation (19) in 2003–13; and Conspiracy of Cells of Fire (19) in 2010–17. Only nine victims perished in these aforementioned bombings, chiming with the fact that non-lethality is a hallmark of 'murder-by-mail'.

Email Bombs

Mail bombs have evolved over the past 150 or so years. Fewer and fewer people use the postal system, preferring the instant gratification of letters by email. However, this has not escaped the eyes of the bad actors of the Internet. One of the latest versions of the mail bomb is the 'email bomb', which began to appear in the 1990s. They are a denial of service (DOS) tactic design to make targeted emails 'unusable or cause network downtime'. Typically a victim's email will be bombarded by 'automated bots' that will subscribe a target's email address to 'multiple lists per second' including newsletters, retail mailing lists and so forth. This type of attack is difficult to defend against and will overpower most spam filters.[41]

According to IT expert Rick Kuwahara, 'Email bombing may be used to hide important notices about account activity from victims in order to make fraudulent online transactions.' In this way the 'spamming' of an individual's inbox can distract them from the actual damage going on out of sight and mind. 'Historically, journalists have found themselves the target of email bombing campaigns in retribution for critical stories.' Moreover the attacks have the ability to interrupt an individual's or group's capacity to communicate.[42]

In the grand scheme of domestic and international terrorism today letter bombs are not among the first choices. Advances in postal security have made postal-related bombs less likely. In recent years it has become more difficult to send weaponized mail through the postal system. In the past, mail addressed to luminaries and government officials was more likely to at least reach their secretaries and offices. These inner sanctums are veritable fortresses today when it comes to security. Any postal materials sent to government officials is 'routinely irradiated to kill live bacillus anthracis spore'. Likewise mail addressed to top secret government installations, such as the Oak Ridge National Laboratory in Tennessee, must undergo some type of X-ray process before winding up on the addressee's desk.[43]

However, there is little doubt that the final words on weaponized mail are yet to be written. It is easy to acquire the necessary components for infernal machines and, whether lethal or not, the mere gesture is enough to provoke terror and anxiety among populations. Over the past 25 years murder by mail has often been attempted by the time-honoured explosive weaponized letters, parcels and packages.[44] Following the 9/11 terrorist attacks, focus on lethal letters was on mail weaponized with toxic substances, most often anthrax and ricin. The following month a batch of letters containing anthrax bacterial spores was placed in a Trenton mailbox. These were sent to several senators on 15 October 2001. Letters were also sent to the offices of news organizations and U.S. Congressional lawmakers. These attacks killed five and injured seventeen. After a seven-year investigation a senior biodefence researcher who had worked with anthrax at the u.s. Army Medical Research Institute of Infectious Diseases came under suspicion for the attacks. However, the motive for the attacks was never substantiated, nor was the suspected scientist, Dr Bruce E. Ivins, convicted. He committed suicide in July 2008.[45]

In January 2019 envelopes believed to be laced with potassium cyanide were sent to more than a dozen Japanese companies. Threats were made of more to come if extortion demands were not met. Targets included newspapers, pharmaceutical companies and a food company. The return addresses on the envelopes had the names of former leaders of the doomsday cult Aum Shinrikyo, who had been executed in 2018 for the 1995 sarin gas attack on the Tokyo subway system.

THIS BOOK IS THE FIRST comprehensive global history of murder by mail. When we began our research we had no idea of its ubiquity over time and did our best to separate the wheat from the chaff, so to speak, by selecting the most germane mail bomb cases for the book. The authors are confident this will not be the last word on the subject and urge future scholars to build on this foundation as the use of infernal devices continues to evolve.

REFERENCES

INTRODUCTION

1 Richard Clutterbuck, *Living with Terrorism* (New Rochelle, NY, 1975), p. 75.
2 'Letter Bombs in Australia: A Psychological Commentary', *International Bulletin of Political Psychology*, V/22 (1998), article 4.
3 Clutterbuck, *Living with Terrorism*, p. 25.
4 Mike Davis, *Buda's Wagon: A Brief History of the Car Bomb* (London, 2008); John Ellis, *The Social History of the Machine Gun* (New York, 1975); Edwyn Gray, *The Devil's Device: Robert Whitehead and the History of the Torpedo* (Annapolis, MD, 1991); Ian Jones MBE, *Malice Aforethought: A History of Booby Traps from World War One to Vietnam* (Yorkshire, 2004); Lydia Monin and Andrew Gallimore, *The Devil's Gardens: A History of Landmines* (London, 2002).
5 Dale Speirs, *The History of Mail Bombs: A Philatelic and Historical Study* (Leeds, 2010), p. 15.
6 Joshua Sinai, 'Weaponized Letter and Package Attacks against Public and Private Sector Targets: Key Takeaways for Security Practitioners', *InfraGard Journal,* II/I (June 2019), pp. 12–23.
7 United States Postal Service, 'Letter or Package Bomb and Bomb Threats', Publication 166, Guide to Mail Center Security, https://aboutusps.com, accessed 1 December 2023.
8 Barry Scott Zellen, *State of Recovery: The Quest to Restore American Security after 9/11* (London, 2013), p. 198.
9 Neil Mackay, 'Murder by Mail Proves Sneakiest Way Known', *Salt Lake Tribune*, 25 July 1952, p. 16.
10 Ibid.
11 Caryl Rivers, 'Murder by Mail', *Boston Globe*, 21 May 1967.
12 Ibid., p. 431.
13 Ibid., p. 433.

1 MAIL BOMBS: THE EARLY YEARS

1 According to a story published in the Tory *Postboy* of 11–13 November, the bandbox was sent to the Earl of Oxford by post on 4 November.
2 This package can be best described as a slight box of cardboard or thin wood typically used for collars, hats, caps and millinery.
3 Paul de Rapin-Thoyras, *History of England*, vol. IV (Lincoln, 1743), p. 297.

4 William Plummer, 'History of Mail Bombings', in 'History of Dangerous Mail Threats Threats', www.raysecur.com/mail-threat-history, accessed 5 March 2024.

5 E. Cobham Brewer, *Dictionary of Phrase and Fable* (London, 1898), p. 6.

6 Jonathan Swift, ed., *The Journal to Stella* (London, 1901), p. 1.

7 Ibid.

8 'Going Postal, A History of Parcel Bombs', *The Economist*, www.economist. com, 6 November 2010.

9 Mary Bellis, 'History of Mail and the Postal System', *ThoughtCo.*, www. thoughtco.com, 4 October 2019.

10 Bryan Burnett and Paul Golubovs, 'The First Mail Bomb?', *Journal of Forensic Sciences*, XLV/4 (2000), pp. 935–6.

11 Ibid.

12 Ibid., p. 935. A horse pistol is a 'long-barreled handgun with a flintlock firing mechanism, carried by cavalrymen and civilians, designed to deliver a larger caliber projectile with greater muzzle velocity at greater effective range than the standard pistol of the era – held and fired with one hand'.

13 Ibid.

14 Ibid.

15 'Southwark', *Morning Chronicle* (London), 15 October 1850, p. 8.

16 Ibid.

17 Dale Brumfield, 'Cincinnati's "Torpedo Man" Was America's First Mail Bomber', *Medium*, https://medium.com, 3 November 2020.

18 Ibid.

19 Ibid.

20 Excellent police work tied the crime to a long-time Cincinnati resident named William H. Arrison who held a personal grudge against Allison. He was convicted of murder after three trials and sentenced to ten years in the Ohio Penitentiary. He only served eight years and was released in 1864. He died around 1900.

21 Brumfield, 'Cincinnati's "Torpedo Man"'.

22 Stephen R. Bown, *A Most Damnable Invention: Dynamite, Nitrates, and the Making of the Modern World* (New York, 2005), p. 19.

23 Laurence Bergreen, *Marco Polo: From Venice to Xanadu* (New York, 2007), p. 321.

24 Adrienne Mayor, *Greek Fire, Poison Arrows and Scorpion Bombs: Biological and Chemical Warfare in the Ancient World* (Woodstock, NY, 2003), p. 17.

25 Bown, *A Most Damnable Invention*, p. 20.

26 Ibid.

27 Mayor, *Greek Fire, Poison Arrows and Scorpion Bombs*, p. 17.

28 'History of Black Powder', adapted from Richard D. Frantz, 'A Chronology of Black Powder', Article 28, https://footguards.tripod.com, accessed 2 January 2024.

29 Simon Webb, *Dynamite, Treason and Plot: Terrorism in Victorian and Edwardian London* (Stroud, Gloucestershire, 2012), p. 13.

30 Ibid.

31 Ibid., p. 14.

32 Ibid.

33 John Merriman, *The Dynamite Club: How a Bombing in Fin-de-Siècle Paris Ignited the Age of Modern Terror* (Boston, MA, 2009), p. 73.

34 Ibid., p. 75.

2 OPENING SALVOS OF THE INFERNAL MACHINES

1 Dale Speirs, *The History of Mail Bombs: A Philatelic and Historical Study* (Leeds, 2010), p. 6.
2 Section 77 of Act 31 Victoria, No. 4, cited ibid., p. 7.
3 Cited in William Oldfield and Victoria Bruce, *Inspector Oldfield and the Black Hand Society: America's Original Gangsters and the U.S. Postal Detective Who Brought Them to Justice* (New York, 2018), p. 152.
4 The owner of the waxworks at that time was a Mr Poyser, who had purchased the exhibition several months earlier and kept on John Tussaud as its manager; *London Times*, 20 July 1889, p. 6.
5 'A Scare at Madame Tussaud's', *London St James Gazette*, 25 June 1889, p. 8.
6 'Dynamite Bombs', *Akron Beacon Journal*, 6 December 1895, p. 1.
7 'Her Minister Lover', *Chattanooga Daily Times*, 9 July 1895, p. 1.
8 Carl Michael von Hausswolff, 'Letter Bombs, 1904–1998: Going Postal', *Cabinet*, www.cabinetmagazine.org, accessed 30 November 2023.
9 'Dr Martin Ekenberg', *London Times*, 8 February 1910, p. 11.
10 Von Hausswolff, 'Letter Bombs, 1904–1998'.
11 'Dr Martin Ekenberg', p. 11.
12 Speirs, *The History of Mail Bombs*, p. 39.
13 The Russo-Japanese War lasted from 1904 to 1905 and resulted in a Japanese victory establishing Japan as a world power. Indeed, it was the first modern war in which an Asian power beat a Western nation. See also Mitchel P. Roth, *The Encyclopedia of War Journalism, 1807–2015* (New York, 2015), p. 311.
14 'Sent a Bomb by Mail', *Parsons Daily Sun* (KS), 28 November 1906.
15 'Mails "Bomb" to Cortelyou', *Weekly Republican* (Plymouth, IN), 5 September 1907, p. 2.
16 'Bomb for Gov. Fort', *Washington Post*, 13 September 1908, p. 3.
17 'Rothschild Letter a Bomb', *Washington Post*, 23 November 1909, p. 11.
18 'Opens Mail – Explodes Bomb', *New York Times*, 10 October 1909, p. C2.
19 Oldfield and Bruce, *Inspector Oldfield and the Black Hand Society*, p. 87.
20 Ibid., p. 93.
21 Ibid., p. 132.
22 'Tried to Blow Up a Judge', *New York Times*, 11 December 1911, p. 1.
23 'Bomb for Judge Injures Officer', *Washington Post*, 17 March 1912, p. 1.
24 'New York's Official Bomb Opener Likes His Gamble with Death', *New York Herald*, 11 May 1919, p. 77.
25 'Bombs in Chicago Mail', *New York Times*, 26 March 1912, p. 1.
26 'Peacock Home Is Threatened by Explosive', *Pittsburgh Daily Post*, 28 April 1912, p. 1.
27 Ibid.; see also 'Dressed in Height of Fashion, Alleged "Black Hand" Specialist Faces Accusers', *Pittsburgh Press*, 1 May 1912, p. 1; 'Prison Sentence for Bomb Sender', *The Dispatch* (Moline, IL), 25 May 1912, p. 1.
28 'Klotz Confessed, Say the Police', *Spokesman-Review* (Spokane, WA), 30 March 1913.
29 Ibid.
30 'New York's Official Bomb Opener Likes His Gamble with Death', p. 77.

31 'This took place on 1 October 1910. The bomb killed scores of workers. Never substantiated, it established in the public mind the connection between terrorists and working-class organizations. The *LA Times* was considered "virulently anti-labor".' Thai Jones, 'Anarchist Terrorism in the United States', in *The Routledge History of Terrorism*, ed. Randall D. Law (London, 2015), pp. 135–6.

32 'Dynamiters Send Bomb to Otis', *Honolulu Advertiser*, 17 September 1913, p. 1.

33 'Quebec Mail Bomb Mystery Unsolved', *The Expositor* (Ontario), 2 February 1935, p. 12.

34 'Sent Bomb That Killed Girl from Bowery Express Office', *New York World*, 12 December 1913, p. 1.

35 'Sent by Mail, Bomb Explodes in Woman's House', *New Orleans Time Democrat*, 24 December 1913.

36 'Woman Gets Bomb by Mail', *New York Times*, 24 December 1913, p. 8.

37 'Sent by Mail, Bomb Explodes in Woman's House'.

38 Ibid.

39 'Fatal Bomb in Mail', *Washington Post*, 2 March 1914, p. 1.

40 'Mailed Bomb Explodes', *Santa Barbara Daily News*, 15 June 1916, p. 1.

41 'u.s. Probe into Mail Box Bomb', *Oakland Tribune*, 28 November 1916, p. 2.

42 'Oregon Officers Hold Man Who Mails Bomb', *Billings Evening Journal* (MT), 29 December 1916, p. 8.

3 SUFFRAGETTE BOMBERS

1 Rebecca Walker, 'Deeds, Not Words: The Suffragettes and Early Terrorism in the City of London', *London Journal*, XLV/1 (2020), pp. 53–64.

2 Simon Webb, *The Suffragette Bombers: Britain's Forgotten Terrorists* (London, 2014), p. 108.

3 See Fern Riddell, *Death in Ten Minutes: The Forgotten Life of Radical Suffragette Kitty Marion* (London, 2018) for more detail on Emily Wilding Davison and the suffragettes.

4 Webb, *The Suffragette Bombers*, p. 81.

5 There are numerous clips on YouTube showing the incident that was recorded that day.

6 Simon Webb, *Dynamite, Treason and Plot: Terrorism in Victorian and Edwardian London* (Stroud, Gloucestershire, 2012), p. 131.

7 Webb, *The Suffragette Bombers*, p. xi.

8 Webb, *Dynamite, Treason and Plot*, p. 130.

9 'Hundreds of Letters Are Damaged', *Dundee Courier*, 29 November 1912; see also 'Suffrage Outrages', *North Devon Journal*, 5 December 1912.

10 Fern Riddell, 'Sanitising the Suffragettes', *History Today*, LXVIII/2 (February 2018), p. 10.

11 Webb, *The Suffragette Bombers*, p. 41.

12 Dale Speirs, *The History of Mail Bombs: A Philatelic and Historical Study* (Leeds, 2010), p. 41.

13 Ibid., p. 43.

14 Ibid., p. 42.

15 Ibid., pp. 41–2.

16 Ibid.

17 Walker, 'Deeds, Not Words', p. 62.
18 Webb, *The Suffragette Bombers*, p. 97.
19 Ibid., p. 41.
20 Ibid., p. 111.
21 'Big Bomb in the Mail', *Washington Post*, 6 May 1913, p. 1.
22 Webb, *Dynamite, Treason and Plot*, p. 135.
23 Webb, *The Suffragette Bombers*, p. 62.
24 Ibid., p. 115.
25 Ibid., p. 118.
26 C. J. Bearman, 'An Examination of Suffragette Violence', *English Historical Review*, cxx/486 (2005), pp. 365–97.
27 Webb, *Dynamite, Treason and Plot*, p. 137.
28 Ibid.
29 Ibid.
30 Walker, 'Deeds, Not Words', p. 61.
31 Webb, *The Suffragette Bombers*, pp. 141–2.
32 Bearman, 'An Examination of Suffragette Violence'.
33 Denmark, 1915; Canada, Estonia, Latvia, Poland, Russia, 1917; Germany, Hungary, Lithuania, 1918; Austria, Netherlands, South Rhodesia, 1919; Czechoslovakia, Albania and the United States, 1920; Burma and Ireland, 1922.

4 MAY DAY AND THE NATIONWIDE PACKAGE BOMB PLOT

1 Robert K. Murray, *Red Scare: A Study in National Hysteria, 1919–1920* (New York, 1955), p. 233.
2 Jeremy Brecher, *Strike!* (San Francisco, CA, 1972), p. 47.
3 Murray, *Red Scare*, p. 72.
4 Quoted in Jeffrey D. Simon, *America's Forgotten Terrorists: The Rise and Fall of the Galleanists* (Lincoln, NE, 2022), p. 203, n. 17. Originally in Andrew Douglas Hoyt, 'And They Called Them "Galleanisti": The Rise of the *Cronaca Sovversiva* and the Formation of America's Most Infamous Anarchist Faction (1895–1912)', PhD dissertation, University of Minnesota, 2018. The newspaper ran from 1903 to 1919.
5 Simon, *America's Forgotten Terrorists*, p. 196.
6 Beverly Gage, *The Day Wall Street Exploded* (New York, 2009), pp. 41–2, quoted in Simon, *America's Forgotten Terrorists*, p. 205, n. 41.
7 Michael Burleigh, *Blood and Rage: A Cultural History of Terrorism* (New York, 2009), p. 72.
8 'The Legacy of Haymarket', *Socialist Worker*, 28 January 2011.
9 Simon, *America's Forgotten Terrorists*, p. 203, n. 17.
10 Ibid., p. 109.
11 Ibid., p. 108.
12 Paul Avrich, *Sacco and Vanzetti: The Anarchist Background* (Princeton, NJ, 1991), pp. 141–2.
13 'Anarchists Planned Reign of Terror for the First Day of May', *Weekly Pioneer-Times* (Deadwood, SD), 1 May 1919, p. 1.
14 'The Hand of the Alien Anarchist', *Spokesman-Review* (Spokane, WA), 2 May 1919, p. 4.
15 Adapted from Simon, *America's Forgotten Terrorists*, pp. 105–6.

16 Avrich, *Sacco and Vanzetti*, pp. 140–43, 147, 149–56, 181–95.
17 Ibid.
18 Simon, *America's Forgotten Terrorists*, p. 179; Mike Davis, *Buda's Wagon: A Brief History of the Car Bomb* (London, 2008), pp. 1–2.
19 'The Bomb Honor List', *New York Tribune*, 2 May 1919, p. 12.
20 'Postal Workers Watch for Three Infernal Machines Remailed at Gimbel Store', *Evening World* (New York), 1 May 1919, p. 1.
21 'New York's Official Bomb Opener Likes His Gamble with Death', *New York Herald*, 11 May 1919, p. 77.
22 Ibid.
23 'Bomb Expert Eagan', *Electrical Experimenter* (August 1919), p. 343.
24 'U.s. Hunts Anarchist as May Day Mail Plot Fails to Gain Victims', *Evening Star* (New York), 1 May 1919, p. 1.
25 Murray, *Red Scare*, p. 67.
26 'Man Who Uncovered Bomb Plot, and Views of the Death Dealing Device', *Evening Star* (New York), 1 May 1919, p. 2; 'U.s. Hunts Anarchist as May Day Mail Plot Fails to Gain Victims', p. 2.
27 Murray, *Red Scare*, pp. 80–81.
28 Simon, *America's Forgotten Terrorists*, p. 199.
29 Ibid., p. 200.
30 'Find More Bombs Sent in the Mails; One to Overman', *New York Times*, 2 May 1919, p. 1.

5 THE ROARING TWENTIES

1 Mike Davis, *Buda's Wagon: A Brief History of the Car Bomb* (London, 2008).
2 'Recognize Anarchist Circulars', *Tacoma Daily Ledger*, 18 September 1920, p. 1.
3 'New York Explosion Work of Anarchists', *Albany Evening Herald* (OR), 17 September 1920, p. 1.
4 'Bomb in Mail Mangles Maine Doctor, Who Loses Right Hand by Explosion', *New York Times*, 16 March 1921, p. 1.
5 'Weekend of Murder, Postal Bomb in Sofia', *Lincolnshire Echo*, 11 July 1922.
6 'Convicted of Murder for Fatal Mail Bomb', *New York Times*, 1 April 1923, p. 17.
7 'Postal Bomb Kills Woman, Injures Man', *Journal and Courier* (Lafayette, IN), 29 December 1922, p. 1; 'Marshfield Farmer Is under Suspicion', *Daily Tribune* (Wisconsin Rapids, WI), 29 December 1922; 'Farmer Arrested as Suspect in Bomb Mailing Outrage', *Austin American Statesman*, 31 December 1922, p. 8; 'Magnuson Bound Over to Circuit Court for Trial', *Daily Tribune* (Wisconsin Rapids, WI), 5 January 1923; 'Convicted of Murder for Fatal Mail Bomb', p. 17; 'Writing Experts Aid in Convicting Bomb Murderer', *Lexington Leader* (KY), 7 May 1923, p. 8.
8 'Another Postal Bomb', *London Evening Standard*, 17 February 1923, p. 7.
9 'Postal Blast Laid to Bomb', *Detroit Free Press*, 14 November 1924.
10 'Postal Authorities Trace Bomb Package', *Salt Lake City Tribune*, 27 December 1924, p. 4.
11 'Postal Employee Admits Sending Bombs in Mail', *Salt Lake City Telegram*, 2 June 1925.
12 'Bomb Sent by Mail, Only Cap Explodes', *Omaha Evening World-Herald*, 15 May 1926.

13 'Constable Gets Life Term for "Bomb" Murders', *Modesto News* (CA), 2 June 1926, p. 9.
14 'Hold Klansman in the Muskegon Mail Bomb Case', *Omaha Evening World-Herald*, 28 May 1926, p. 1; 'Trace Bomb to Mailing Wednesday', *Daily Advertiser* (Lafayette, LA), 28 May 1926, p. 1.
15 'Doctors Examine Mail Bomb Sender', *Chattanooga Daily Times*, 15 December 1929, p. 2; 'Inventor Confesses Mail-Bomb Scheme', *Pittsburgh Sun-Telegraph*, 15 December 1929, p. 36; 'Postal Authorities Seek Bomb Sender', *Argus Leader* (Sioux Falls, SD), 30 November 1929, p. 2.
16 'Postal Employee Sees Bomb in Nick of Time', *Register-Democrat* (Portage, WI), 22 February 1929, p. 1.
17 'Roosevelt Bomb Proves to be "Dud"', *Baltimore Sun*, 9 April 1929, p. 2; 'Bomb Intended for Roosevelt Declared a Dud', *Fresno Bee*, 8 April 1929, p. 1.
18 'Negro Charged with Sending Fake Bomb', *Orlando Evening Star*, 10 April 1929, p. 1; 'Needy Postal Aid Admits Bomb Hoax', *Courier-Journal* (Louisville, KY), 11 April 1929, p. 3.

6 THE 1930S: WAR CLOUDS ON THE HORIZON

1 'Assassination Plot Seen in Mail Bomb', *Wisconsin State Journal*, 4 October 1930, p. 4.
2 'Millionaire Newsie Dead; His Son Hurt', *Chicago Tribune*, 8 December 1930, p. 2.
3 'A Tale of Terrorism: Long List of Outrages in 1931', *Evening Standard*, 14 December 1931, p. 2.
4 'Antifascist Plot Seen as Mail Bombs Kill 2', *Washington Post*, 31 December 1931, p. 1.
5 'Anti-Fascist Probe to be Made in United States', *Urbana Daily Citizen* (IL), 31 December 1931, p. 1.
6 'Antifascist Plot Seen as Mail Bombs Kill 2', p. 1.
7 'Probers Differ on Plot behind Bomb Blast', *Santa Cruz Evening News*, 31 December 1931, p. 1.
8 'Mail Bomb Terror Spreads in East', *Santa Cruz Evening News*, 31 December 1931, p. 1.
9 'Net Believed to Be Tightening in Mail Bomb Plot', *Sacramento Bee*, 1 January 1932, p. 1.
10 'Italy Takes Steps to Intercept Mail Bombs', *Evening Telegraph* (North Platte, NE), 11 January 1932, p. 1.
11 'U.S. Seizes Fascist Foe in Three Mail Bomb Deaths', *Daily News* (New York), 9 March 1932, p. 1.
12 'Suspect Cleared of Mail Bomb Sending', *Alton Evening Telegraph*, 10 March 1932, p. 3.
13 'Three Cubans to Die for Mail Bomb Murder', *Atlanta Constitution*, 29 November 1932, p. 9.
14 'Madison Negro Admits Aiding with Mail Bomb', *Chattanooga Daily Times*, 11 January 1933, p. 4.
15 This refers to Giuseppe Zangara, an anarchist who fired on Franklin D. Roosevelt and Mayor Anton Cermak of Chicago, killing the mayor.
16 'Bomb Clew', *Washington Post*, 3 March 1933.
17 'Mail Bomb to Roosevelt', *Kearny Daily Hub* (NE), 30 March 1933, p. 1.

18 'Crank Mails Bombs to F.D.R. "for Fun"', *Orlando Sentinel*, 22 June 1933, p. 3.

19 'Infernal Machine from Alabama Is Sent to Attorney Leibowitz', *Northwest Enterprise* (Seattle, WA), 4 May 1923, p. 1.

20 'Bomb Wrecks Newspaper Plant at Mansfield, Ohio', *Bangor Daily News*, 13 November 1933, p. 7.

21 'Mail Bomb Shakes Capital Post Office', *Philadelphia Inquirer*, 22 May 1934, p. 1.

22 'Dead Letter Bomb Wounds Postal Clerks', *Daily News* (New York), 22 May 1934, p. 61.

23 'Coal Miner Is Held in Mail Bomb Case', *Billings Gazette* (MT), 10 June 1934, p. 3.

24 'Mail-Bomb Suspect Denies Guilt in Explosion Which Severed Postman's Hand', *Fort Worth Telegram*, 10 June 1934, p. 1.

25 'Terrorists Mail Bombs in Paris in Death Threats', *Reno Gazette Journal*, 14 June 1934, p. 1.

26 'Three Judges of Hell Sought in Mail Bombs', *Knoxville Journal* (TN), 15 June 1934, p. 2.

27 'Terrorists Mail Bombs in Paris', *Miami Herald*, 16 June 1934, p. 12.

28 'Terrorists Continue to Mail Bombs', *Portsmouth Star* (VA), 16 June 1934, pp. 1, 8.

29 'Mail Bomb Maniac Ceases His Attacks', *Indianapolis Star*, 17 June 1934, p. 4.

30 'Satan's Gang Mails Bomb', *Spokane Chronicle*, 22 June 1934, p. 17.

31 'Three Judges of Hell Mail 6 Bombs in Paris', *Baltimore Sun*, 15 December 1935, p. 22.

32 'Farley Aides Guard Long from Any Bombs by Mail', *New York Times*, 23 February 1935.

33 'Mail Bombs Blocked', *Evening Star* (Washington, DC), 20 September 1935, p. 30.

34 Philip Taft and Philip Ross, 'American Labor Violence: Its Causes, Character, and Outcome', in *The History of Violence*, ed. Hugh Davis Graham and Ted Robert Gurr (New York, 1969), p. 281.

35 'Mining Town Terrified by Mail Bombs', *Knoxville Journal* (TN), 11 April 1936, p. 1.

36 Bernadine Elick, 'Maloney Mail Bombing Happened on Good Friday in W-B Township', *Citizen's Voice* (Wilkes-Barre, PA), 17 April 2019.

37 'Man Killed by Mail Bomb', *Journal Gazette* (Mattoon, IL), 10 April 1936.

38 Koehler (1885–1967) was the chief wood technologist at the Forest Products Lab. He reached national prominence for his role in convicting Bruno Richard Hauptmann for the Lindbergh kidnapping in 1932. 'Fugmann Is Linked to Cigar Box Bombs', *New York Times*, 30 September 1936, p. 11.

39 Elick, 'Maloney Mail Bombing Happened'.

40 'Cape Charles Man Victim of Mail Bomb', *Daily Times* (Salisbury, MD), 23 July 1936, p. 1.

41 'Man Charged with Murder Is Suicide', *Index Journal* (Greenwood, SC), 12 October 1936, p. 3.

42 Rupert Allason, *The Branch: A History of the Metropolitan Special Branch, 1883–1983* (London, 1983), p. 97.

43 Edgar O'Ballance, *Terror in Ireland: The Heritage of Hate* (Novato, CA, 1981), p. 57.

44 Allason, *The Branch*, p. 97.

45 Ibid., p. 100.

46 'Bomb Outrages Explosions in Five Towns', *Daily Herald* (London), 5 August 1939, p. 9.

47 'IRA Strikes Five Cities', *Birmingham Gazette*, 10 June 1939, p. 1.

48 'Christmas Letter Bombs Go Off in Six Post Offices', *Birmingham Gazette*, 22 December 1939, p. 1.

49 'IRA Again, Outrages in London and Midlands', *The Guardian*, 22 December 1939, p. 7.

50 Ibid.

51 'Dijon Prosecutor Is Injured by Mail Bomb', *Fresno Bee*, 18 June 1942, p. 19.

52 'Delivered by Mail, Bomb Does Not Go Off', *Big Spring Weekly Herald*, 6 July 1945, p. 9.

53 'Blind Man Mails Bomb to Woman', *Siskiyou Daily News*, 23 October 1945, p. 4.

54 '"Mails Bomb", Gets 20-Year Term', *Daily News* (LA), 24 October 1945.

7 THE STERN GANG PARCEL BOMB CAMPAIGN AND THE POST-WAR WORLD

1 This chapter will use the name 'Stern Gang' interchangeably with 'Lehi', the most radical of the Zionist underground groups that fought the British in the 1940s. The British preferred this as a more pejorative reference. See Ronen Bergman, *Rise and Kill: The Secret History of Israel's Targeted Assassination* (London, 2019), pp. 4–5.

2 Rupert Allason, *The Branch: A History of the Metropolitan Police Special Branch, 1883–1983* (London, 1983), p. 127.

3 Yaacov or Jacob Levstein was known by other names, with his last name typically Eliav, as per his autobiography *Wanted*, trans. Mordecai Schreiber (New York, 1984). Terrorism historian Bruce Hoffman refers to him as Ya'acov Eliav aka Ya'acov Levstein (*Anonymous Soldiers: The Struggle for Israel, 1917–1947* (New York, 2015), p. 406). In this chapter I will refer to him by the more common Yaacov Eliav, especially since that is the name he uses in his 1984 autobiography.

4 Eliav, *Wanted*, p. 246.

5 Hoffman, *Anonymous Soldiers*, p. 406.

6 Colin Shindler, 'Secret MI5 Papers Reveal a Blood-Soaked Struggle for Israel's Future', *Jewish Chronicle*, www.thejc.com, 7 December 2017.

7 Eliav, *Wanted*, p. 246.

8 Ibid.

9 Ibid.

10 Ibid., pp. 246–7.

11 Ibid., p. 247.

12 Ibid., p. 248.

13 Ibid., p. 249.

14 Hoffman, *Anonymous Soldiers*, p. 408.

15 Mallory Browne, 'Bevin and Eden Get "Letter Bombs"; Stern Gang Asserts It Sent Them', *New York Times*, 6 June 1947.

16 Ibid.

17 'Letter-Bombs Received by Eden, Bevin', *Washington Post*, 6 June 1947, p. 22.

18 'Nine More Bombs Found', *Washington Post*, 7 June 1947, p. 4.
19 'British Add Guards against Mail Bombs', *New York Times*, 8 June 1947, p. 29.
20 Ibid.
21 'Genoa Visitor Says He Mailed Bomb', *New York Times*, 9 June 1947, p. 10.
22 Carlo Massaro, 'Man in Genoa Says He Posted Letter Bombs for Stern Gang', *Washington Post*, 9 June 1947, p. 7; 'We Mean to Bring Down the Union Jack', *New York Times*, 9 June 1947, p. 10.
23 '"Letter-Bomb" Raids Net Jews in Belgium', *New York Times*, 16 June 1947, p. 10.
24 Eliav, *Wanted*, pp. 322–6.
25 Eric Pace, 'Letter-Bombs Mailed to Truman in 1947', *New York Times*, 2 December 1972.
26 Mallory Browne, 'British Officials Get Bombs in Mail', *New York Times*, 5 June 1947, p. 1.
27 J. A. Cimperman to J. Edgar Hoover letter, London Embassy, via Air Pouch, 19 June 1947, Freedom of Information Act (FOIA). The materials from my FOIA request in 2002 for records about Jewish terrorist groups in Palestine were received that same year. In 2005 I received more complete and unredacted materials that were from the Office of Strategic Services (OSS) and now held by the CIA. So three years later the FBI located CIA material and referred it to the CIA for review and direct response to the author. Reference F-2005-0125.
28 Through a FOIA request to the FBI, the author was able to get the most detailed information on the intricacies of the bombs.
29 Cimperman to Hoover letter, FOIA.
30 Ibid.
31 Ibid.
32 FBI Document 105-3037, 17 June 1947 (OSS). Declassified January 1992.
33 Ibid.
34 Hoffman, *Anonymous Soldiers*, p. 440.
35 David Cesarani, *Major Farran's Hat: The Untold Story of the Struggle to Establish the Jewish State* (Cambridge, MA, 2009), pp. 1–8.
36 Ibid., p. 254, n. 35.
37 Ibid., p. 195.
38 Ibid.
39 Ibid., p. 196.

8 THE 1950S: AN IRON CURTAIN DESCENDS

1 His former name was Frank Bernard Kuczyinski. He changed it when he moved to California in October 1946 after discharge from prison.
2 '2 Here Targets of Mail Bomb Plot; Man Held', *Citizen News* (Hollywood, CA), 21 September 1950, p. 19.
3 'Mail Bomb Case to Grand Jury, Oct. 2', *Marshall News Messenger*, 22 September 1950, p. 1.
4 'Insanity Plea Drawn in Mail Bomb Case', *Marshall News Messenger*, 4 October 1950, p. 1.
5 'Couple Arrested in Mail-Bomb Plot That Has Killed 2', *Courier-Journal* (Louisville, KY), 1 December 1951, p. 23.

6 'Reich Youth, 24, Held for Mail Bomb Deaths', *Morning News* (Wilmington, NC), 13 December 1951, p. 4.

7 'Mail Bomb Suspect Held', *Spokane Chronicle*, 2 April 1952, p. 2.

8 '1 Killed, 4 Hurt by Package Bomb Sent to Adenauer', *Washington Post*, 28 March 1952, p. 1.

9 'Neo-Nazi Raps Bomb Attempt against Adenauer', *Columbus Ledger* (GA), 2 April 1952, p. 17.

10 'German Anti-Red Leader Target of Mail Bomb Plot', *Fort Worth Star Telegram*, 18 March 1955, p. 11.

11 'Seek Red Agent in Murder Plot', *Daily News* (New York), 27 May 1955.

12 'Mail Bomb Kills Anti-Communist Refugee Leader', *The State* (Columbia, SC), 6 July 1955, p. 7.

13 'Mail Bomb Kills Refugee', *Evansville Courier*, 6 July 1955, p. 5.

14 'Reich Reds Accused of Mail Bomb Plot', *Morning News* (Wilmington, NC), 21 January 1956, p. 2.

15 'Man Is Arrested in "Unbelievable" Mail Bomb Plot', *Buffalo Evening News*, 23 January 1952, p. 1.

16 'Suspect Admits Mail Bomb Plot', *Philadelphia Inquirer*, 26 January 1952, p. 3.

17 'Air Mail Bomb Brings Charge', *Rapid City Journal*, 21 May 1953.

18 'Boys Admit Letter Box "Bomb" Blasts', *Washington Post*, 11 October 1953, p. M8.

19 'Mail Bomb Hurts 2 in New Orleans', *Honolulu Advertiser*, 19 February 1956, p. 97.

20 'Murder by Mail Penalty Boosted', *Atlantic City Press*, 27 August 1957, p. 2.

21 'Bombs in Belfast Mail', *New York Times*, 24 May 1953, p. 72.

22 '6 Mail Bombs Found after Belfast Blast', *Washington Post*, 24 May 1953, p. C5.

23 Ronen Bergman, *Rise and Kill First: The Secret History of Israel's Targeted Assassinations* (London, 2019), p. 50.

24 Ibid., p. 51.

25 'Mail-Bomb Maims Egyptian Official', *Journal Times* (Racine, WI), 16 July 1956, p. 12.

26 'Egyptian Official Dies of Mail-Bomb Injuries', *Courier-Journal* (Louisville, KY), 22 July 1956, p. 32.

27 'Egyptians Charge Israeli Sent Bomb to Embassy', *Washington Post*, 16 July 1956, p. 5.

28 Rupert Allason, *The Branch: A History of the Metropolitan Police Special Branch, 1883–1983* (London, 1983), p. 137.

29 Henry Maule, 'Scotland Yard Bares Plot to Bomb by Mail', *Daily News* (New York), 7 April 1957, p. 83.

30 'Death in French Mails', *Kansas City Star*, 17 May 1957.

31 'Mail Bomb Mystery: Plane Hostess Hurt', *Daily News* (New York), 14 October 1957, p. 154.

32 'Suspect Is Nabbed in Mail Bomb Plot', *The Post* (Covington, KY), 7 November 1957.

33 'Mails Fake Bomb to Ike', *News-Palladium* (Benton Harbor, MI), 23 November 1957, p. 1.

34 'Police Seek Mail Bomb Case Motive', *The Times* (San Mateo, CA), 16 January 1959, p. 528.

35 Ruth Reynolds, 'The Bomb-in-a-Box Mystery', *Daily News* (New York),
   13 September 1959, pp. 114–15.

9 THE 1960S: INTERNATIONAL CONFLICT AND PERSONAL VENDETTAS

1 'Mail Bomb Is Fatal', *Washington Post*, 27 March 1960, A2.
2 'Mail Bomb for Nixon Discovered', *Bristol-Virginian*, 8 November 1960,
   p. 2.
3 'Reds Mail Bombs', *El Paso Herald-Post*, 31 July 1963, p. 1.
4 'Sending Bombs in Mail Annoys Communist China', *Star Tribune*
   (Minneapolis, MN), 3 February 1963, p. 4.
5 Michael Bar-Zohar and Eitan Haber, *The Quest for the Red Prince*
   (New York, 1983), p. 142.
6 Ronen Bergman, *Rise and Kill First: The Secret History of Israel's Targeted
   Assassinations* (London, 2019), p. 61.
7 Nachman Ben-Yehuda, *Political Assassinations by Jews: A Rhetorical Device
   for Justice* (Albany, NY, 1993), p. 307.
8 Bergman, *Rise and Kill First*, p. 62.
9 Ibid., p. 67.
10 Ibid., pp. 67–8.
11 Ibid., p. 68.
12 Ibid.
13 Ibid., p. 69.
14 Michael Karpin, *The Bomb in the Basement: How Israel Went Nuclear and
   What That Means for the World* (New York, 2006), p. 207.
15 '2 Hurt in Cairo by Letter Bomb', *New York Times*, 26 September 1964, p. 2.
16 'Nasser Imports Germans to Build Rockets, Jets', *Spokesman-Review*
   (Spokane, WA), 7 March 1965, p. 10.
17 Ibid.
18 'Letter Bombs and a Zionist Deception', *Arab News*, 1 July 2007.
19 Bergman, *Rise and Kill First*, p. 111.
20 Ibid., p. 112.
21 'Montreal Blast Blows Off Arm of Bomb Expert', *Chicago Tribune*, 18 May
   1963, p. 1.
22 Leon Levinson, 'FLQ Accused Bachand Asks Trial', *Gazette* (Montreal),
   16 October 1963, p. 3.
23 'Capital Man Is Held as Mail Bomb Suspect', *Sacramento Bee*, 24 January
   1962, p. 1.
24 'Mail Bomb Near Fatal', *San Luis Obispo County Telegram-Tribune*,
   19 January 1962, p. 2.
25 'Marital Rift Revealed in Probe of Mail Bomb Blast', *Oakland Tribune*,
   20 April 1963, p. 3.
26 'Wife Denies Mate Sent Mail Bomb', *Oakland Tribune*, 12 April 1963, p. 1.
27 '3 Mail Bomb to Teacher', *Battle Creek Enquirer*, 3 December 1963, p. 9.
28 Bob Hill, '"Mail Bomb" Trial Ordered', *Spokane Chronicle*, 11 December 1965,
   p. 3.
29 'Send Mail Bomb', *Terre Haute Star*, 15 January 1966, p. 1.
30 'Mail Bomb Injures British Aden Envoy', *Vancouver Sun*, 17 January 1966,
   p. 4.
31 'Mail-Bomb Trial Halted for Exam', *Cocoa Tribune*, 27 March 1967, p. 11.

32 'Yule Mail Bomb Probe Clueless', *Edmonton Journal*, 30 December 1966, p. 40.

33 'Man Slays Ex-Wife by Mail Bomb', *Arizona Republic*, 23 February 1967, p. 16.

34 'Housewife Loses Hands in Mail Bomb Blast', *Sydney Morning Herald*, 9 October 1967, p. 28.

35 'Bomb by Mail: Hunt in Vic.', *Sydney Morning Herald*, 9 October 1967, p. 71.

36 'Michigan Mail Bomb Suspect Arrested', *Windsor Star*, 12 October 1967, p. 9.

37 'Mail Bombs Raise Red Hate Theory', *Atlantic City Press*, 9 December 1967, p. 3.

38 'Mail Bomb Sets Fire, Injures Six', *Tampa Times*, 5 December 1967, p. 7.

39 'Peace March Chief Gets Bomb in Mail', *New York Times*, 3 January 1968, p. 3.

40 'Mail Bomb Blast Hurts 5 Cubans', *Philadelphia Inquirer*, 10 January 1968, p. 2.

41 'Cal Bomber Sent Fatal Mail Bomb', *San Francisco Examiner*, 27 March 1968, pp. 1, 21.

42 'Ottawa Police Seek Maker of Mail Box Bomb', *Owen Sound Sun-Times* (Ontario), 2 January 1969, p. 1.

43 'Mail Bomb Linked to W. Germany', *Evening Sun* (Baltimore, MD), 7 February 1969, p. 2.

44 '"Mail" Bombs Rip Post Office in Saigon, 4 Die', *Pittsburgh Post Gazette*, 8 May 1969, pp. 1, 16.

45 'Mail Bomb Injures Employee at College', *Leader Telegram* (Eau Claire, WI), 27 February 1969, p. 8.

46 'Bomb Analysis Admitted as Evidence', *Cincinnati Post and Times Star*, 24 April 1969, p. 29.

47 'Suspect in Mail Bombing Was Quiet, Likeable . . .', *Cincinnati Enquirer*, 26 October 1968, p. 13.

48 'Verdict near in Mail Bomb Murder Case', *Marion Star* (OH), 30 April 1969, p. 2; 'Stifel Found Guilty in Mail Bomb Killing', *Marion Star*, 2 May 1969, p. 16.

49 'Suspect Remains in Jail', *Capital Journal* (Pierre, SD), 30 July 1969, p. 13; 'Mail Bomb Suspect Offers Alibi', *Tacoma News Tribune*, 25 October 1969, p. 23.

10 THE 1970S: MAIL BOMBS GO GLOBAL

1 Samuel M. Katz, *Israel versus Jibril: The Thirty-Year War against a Master Terrorist* (New York, 1993), p. 47.

2 Ibid., p. 48.

3 Bruce Koffler, 'Evidence in Letter Bombs and Parcel Bombs: The Construction of Letter Bombs, Their Wrapping, Labelling, and Other Elements of Evidential Value', *International Journal of Forensic Document Examiners*, II/2 (April–June 1996), pp. 117–43.

4 David Gero, *Flights of Terror: Aerial Hijack and Sabotage since 1930* (Yeovil, 1997), pp. 69–70.

5 Katz, *Israel versus Jibril*, p. 28.

6 Michael Bar-Zohar and Eitan Haber, *The Quest for the Red Prince* (New York, 1983), p. 132.

7 These figures come from Dr Mahmut Cengiz's data set that examined letter bomb attacks between 1972 and 1987 using open sources such as government

reports and reliable media reports. The data set has 28 events with a combined total of 167 letter bomb incidents. Each letter bomb is counted as one incident. However, if the sender mailed more than one letter bomb, those multiple letter bombs are considered as one event. The data fields in the data set are year, month, sender (perpetrator), bomb type, target, number of letter bombs sent in one event, casualties (number killed and wounded), origin city and country, destination city and country of recipients.

8 Lawrence Van Gelder, 'Bombs Mailed to Many Israeli Officials', *New York Times*, 21 September 1972.

9 Bar-Zohar and Haber, *Quest for the Red Prince*, p. 132.

10 Christopher Dobson and Ronald Payne, *The Terrorists: Their Weapons, Leaders and Tactics* (New York, 1979), p. 130.

11 'Flora Lewis, 'Talking of Terror', *New York Times*, 30 November 1988, p. A31.

12 Dobson and Payne, *The Terrorists*, p. 131.

13 Emanuel Perlmutter, 'Mail Clerk Hurt by Letter Bomb', *New York Times*, 15 October 1972, pp. 1, 7.

14 'British Set Probe of Letter Bombs', *Washington Post*, 12 November 1972, p. A18.

15 'Vienna Bombs', *Washington Post*, 5 September 1973, p. 2.

16 'Bomb Kills Pennsylvania Postal Employee', *Washington Post*, 6 December 1974, p. C7.

17 T. A. Sandrock, John Weeks and C. A. Coughlin, 'Life Jail for Paperback Bomber Who Got Too Cocky', *Daily Telegraph*, 11 September 1976, p. 2.

18 Ibid.

19 Robert M. Dudley, *Tragedy on the Prairie: The Story of the 1976 Kimball Post Office Bomb* (Coppell, TX, 2022), p. 9.

20 Ibid., p. 26.

21 Ibid., pp. 31, 42.

22 Kevin Haney, '2 Are Arrested in Mail Bomb Extortion Case', *Clarion-Ledger* (Jackson, MS), 23 May 1981, p. 1.

23 Peter Kihss, 'FBI Links Letter Bombs to 200 Extortion Demands', *New York Times*, 16 June 1976, p. 1.

24 'Parcel Bomb Kills Rhodesian Nationalist', *Washington Post*, 23 January 1977, p. 108.

25 Martin Weil and Glenn Frankel, 'Bomb Parcel Found in Arlington Mail Defused by Army', *Washington Post*, 5 June 1979, p. C1.

26 Robert T. Pienciak, 'Mail Bombs Tied to Anti-Nazi Group', *Philadelphia Inquirer*, 5 June 1979, p. 12; 'Five Mail Bombs Found; More Threatened', *Kansas City Times*, 5 June 1979, p. 4.

27 'Bike Terror Bomb', *Sunday Mirror*, 10 June 1976, p. 5.

28 Paul Hofmann, 'Scotland Yard Will Coordinate Investigation of Bombs by Mail', *New York Times*, 23 September 1972, p. 11.

29 'Britons Are Warned by the Police on Letter Bombs in Holiday Mail', *New York Times*, 19 December 1979, p. A9.

30 'Christmas Letter-Bomb Blitz Traced to European IRA Cell', *Sacramento Bee*, 24 December 1979, p. 4.

11 THE 1980S: WE ARE ALL, I'M AFRAID, VULNERABLE

1 'Terror in the Mails', *Intelligencer Journal* (Lancaster, PA), 1 January 1980, p. 14.
2 'Mail Bomb Destined for Thatcher's Home', *Fort Worth-Star Telegram*, 8 January 1981, p. 5.
3 George Ramos, 'U.S. Seeks Extradition of Bomb Suspect in Israel', *Los Angeles Times*, 14 July 1988, p. 30.
4 John Spano, 'Not-Guilty Plea in Bombing Case', *Los Angeles Times*, 17 August 1988, p. 64.
5 Randy Collier, '5 Years of Surgery Await Disfigured Mail-Bomb Victim', *Arizona Republic*, 7 November 1980, p. 23.
6 Gail Reid, 'Mail Bomb Victims Struggle with Injuries to Body and Spirit', *Arizona Republic*, 27 April 1981, p. 15.
7 The police were never able to positively establish the IRA link. An obscure group calling itself the English Republican Party later claimed responsibility. Police were unable to connect it.
8 'Mail Bomb Sent to Woman MP', *St Joseph News-Press* (MO), 25 March 1981, p. 3.
9 'Prominent Britons Warned of Mail Bombs', *Austin American-Statesman*, 7 May 1981, p. 5.
10 'Of 76 Threats, 4 Bombs Found since N.Y. Blast', *Courier-Post* (Camden, NJ), 19 May 1981, p. 6.
11 Tom Kaser, 'Mail-Bomb Labels Traced to UH Typewriter', *Honolulu Advertiser*, 29 May 1982, p. 3.
12 'Police Seeking Clues in Mail Bomb Death', *Herald Statesman* (Yonkers, NY), 9 May 1982, p. 10.
13 'Son, 28, Accused in Slaying of Mother with Mail Bomb', *Newsday* (Melville, NY), 9 August 1982, p. 3.
14 'Parcel Bomb Kills S. African Opposition Figure in Mozambique', *Washington Post*, 18 August 1982, p. A24.
15 Judith Imel Van Allen, 'Ruth First', www.britannica.com, accessed 13 August 2022.
16 Adekeye Adebajo, 'The First Pan African Martyr', *Mail and Guardian* (Johannesburg), 25 August 2010.
17 'Coal Broker Files Suit in Mail Bomb Attack', *Park City Daily News* (Bowling Green, KY), 7 September 1983, p. 7.
18 'Deadlocked Mail Bomb Jury to Try Again Today', *Courier-Journal* (Louisville, KY), 2 September 1983, p.1.
19 John Stevens, 'Firebomb inside No 10', *The Standard*, 30 November 1982, pp. 1, 2.
20 Gerald Bartlett and John Weeks, 'Bomb Sent to Thatcher Goes Off in No 10', *Daily Telegraph* (London), 1 December 1982, p. 1.
21 Bill Bleyer, 'Mail Bomb Is Called New, Lethal', *Newsday* (Melville, NY), 15 September 1983, p. 21.
22 'Mail Bomb Protest over Visit', *South Wales Echo*, 17 February 1983, p. 1.
23 Deirdre Carmody, 'Mail Bomb Hurts Teacher at Sheepshead Bay High', *New York Times*, 15 February 1984, p. B3.
24 'Mail Bomb Kills Two in Exile', *Fort Worth-Star Telegram*, 30 June 1984, p. 41; 'Mail-Bomb Kills White Foe of Apartheid, Father Says', *Miami Herald*, 30 June 1984, p. 160.

25 'Man Executed for Planting Mail Bomb', *Columbus Enquirer* (GA), 11 October 1984, p. 10.

26 'Violence Resumes, Intensifies in War on Abortion', *Miami Herald*, 6 December 1985, p. 30.

27 David Sheppard, 'Postal Agents Check Defused', *El Paso Times*, 22 August 1985, p. 1.

28 'Libya Mails Bombs to 100 Journalists', *Morning Call* (Allentown, PA), 29 September 1985, p. 8.

29 'Officials Arrest Florida Man in Connection with Mail Bomb', *Vero Beach Press Journal*, 20 October 1985, p. 8.

30 Douglas Lavin, '2-Year Job of Tracing Mail Bomb', *The Record* (Hackensack, NJ), 24 May 1985, p. 24.

31 Brian Ford, 'Postal Inspectors Tracing Origins of 2 Mail Bombs', *Tulsa World*, 11 May 1986, p. 18.

32 'Mail Bomb Hurts 6', *Tucson Citizen*, 19 January 1987, p. 13.

33 'Obituary', *New York Times*, 4 July 1992.

34 'Love Triangle Cited in Case of Mail Bomb', *Austin American-Statesman*, 27 February 1987, p. 30.

35 Robert Joffee, 'Bomb Squad Destroys Videotape to Mas Corona', *Miami News*, 1 April 1987, p. 9.

36 Kim Crompton, 'Mail Bomb Defendant Pleads Guilty', *Spokesman-Review* (Spokane, WA), 16 July 1987, p. 6.

37 'Man Convicted for Mail Bomb', *Daily Herald* (Provo, UT), 2 August 1987, p. 5.

38 'Witness Testifies in Mail Bomb Trial', *Pittsburgh Press*, 12 November 1987, p. 65.

39 'IRA Blamed for Letter Bombs', *Calgary Herald*, 16 April 1987, p. 9.

40 Robby Trammell, 'Man Convicted in Mail Bomb Case', *Daily Oklahoman*, 22 January 1988, p. 66; 'Mail Bombs Credited to Sallisaw Resident', *Sequoyah County Times*, 6 September 1987, p. 1.

41 Ed Asher, 'Mail Bomb Had Return Address in Nevada', *Albuquerque Tribune*, 26 October 1988, p. 1; 'Suspect in Mail Bombing Graduated from NMSU', *El Paso Times*, 4 November 1988, p. 10.

12 FROM JUNKYARD BOMBER TO UNABOMBER

1 Robert Graysmith, *Unabomber: A Desire to Kill* (Washington, DC, 1997), p. 60.

2 Nancy Gibbs et al., *Mad Genius: The Odyssey, Pursuit, and Capture of the Unabomber Suspect* (New York, 1996), p. 71; Graysmith, *Unabomber*, p. xiv.

3 Graysmith, *Unabomber*, p. xiv.

4 Ibid., p. 51.

5 Ibid.

6 Quoted in Alston Chase, *Harvard and the Unabomber* (New York, 2003), p. 52.

7 Graysmith, *Unabomber*, p. 60.

8 Robert Graysmith, *Amerithrax: The Hunt for the Anthrax Killer* (New York, 2003), p. 206.

9 John Douglas and Mark Olshaker, *Unabomber: On the Trail of America's Most Wanted Serial Killer* (New York, 1996), p. 159.

10 Kelly Stoner and Gary Perlstein, 'Implementing "Justice" through Terror and Destruction: Ecoterror's Violent Agenda to "Save" Nature', in

Lynne L. Snowden and Bradley C. Whitsel, *Terrorism: Research, Readings, and Realities* (Upper Saddle River, NJ, 2005), pp. 90–133.
11 Ron Arnold, *Ecoterror: The Violent Agenda to Save Nature* (Bellevue, WA, 1997), p. 104.
12 Ibid.
13 Gibbs et al., *Mad Genius*, p. 27.
14 Ibid.
15 Ibid., p. 70.
16 Graysmith, *Amerithrax*, p. 206.
17 Gibbs et al., *Mad Genius*, pp. 70–71.
18 Graysmith, *Amerithrax*, p. 206.
19 Douglas and Olshaker, *Unabomber*, p. 157.
20 Gibbs et al., *Mad Genius*, pp. 67–8.
21 Quoted in Chase, *Harvard and the Unabomber*, p. 52.
22 Gibbs et al., *Mad Genius*, pp. 67–8.
23 Graysmith, *Amerithrax*, p. 203; USPS, *The History of the Postal Inspection Service*, Publication 259, January 1982.
24 John N. Makris, *The Silent Investigators: The Great Untold Story of the U.S. Postal Inspection Service* (New York, 1959), p. 19.
25 Eric Hickey, *Serial Murderers and Their Victims* (Belmont, CA, 2009), p. 268.
26 Ibid.
27 Douglas and Olshaker, *Unabomber*, p. 169.
28 Ibid., p. 170.
29 Chase, *Harvard and the Unabomber*, p. 66.
30 Gibbs et al., *Mad Genius*, p. 81.
31 Douglas and Olshaker, *Unabomber*, p. 170.
32 Ibid., p. 171.
33 Ibid.
34 Chase, *Harvard and the Unabomber*, p. 66.
35 Douglas and Olshaker, *Unabomber*, p. 172.
36 Chase, *Harvard and the Unabomber*, p. 75.
37 Ibid.
38 Douglas Long, *Ecoterrorism* (New York, 2004), p. 51.
39 Ibid.
40 Hickey, *Serial Murderers and Their Victims*, p. 268.
41 Chase, *Harvard and the Unabomber*, p. 69.
42 Gibbs et al., *Mad Genius*, p. 75.

13 VANPAC: THE ROY MOODY MAIL BOMB MURDERS

1 Mark Winne, *Priority Mail: The Investigation and Trial of a Mail Bomber Obsessed with Destroying Our Justice System* (New York, 1995), p. 25.
2 Alex Alvarez and Ronet D. Bachman, *Violence: The Enduring Problem* (Thousand Oaks, CA, 2021), p. 43.
3 Ray Jenkins, *Blind Vengeance: The Roy Moody Mail Bomb Murders* (Athens, GA, 1997), p. 268.
4 Ibid., pp. 184–5.
5 Ibid., p. 185.
6 Jenkins, *Blind Vengeance*, p. 190.
7 Winne, *Priority Mail*, p. 12.

8 Jenkins, *Blind Vengeance*, p. 198.
9 Winne, *Priority Mail*, p. 24.
10 Ibid.
11 Ibid, p. 25.
12 Jenkins, *Blind Vengeance*, p. 91.
13 Ibid., p. 26.
14 Ibid. Other accounts suggest his right arm was blown off just below the shoulder and his left hand mangled.
15 Athan G. Theoharis, ed., *The FBI: A Comprehensive Reference Guide* (New York, 2000), pp. 98–9.
16 Jenkins, *Blind Vengeance*, p. 215.
17 Ibid., p. 229.
18 Ibid., p. 305.
19 Ibid., p. 230.
20 Alan Blinder, 'Alabama Executes Mail Bomber, 83, the Oldest Inmate Put to Death in Modern Era', *New York Times*, 19 April 2018.

14 THE 1990S: MAYHEM BY MAIL IS NOW A FACT OF LIFE

1 David Rose, 'Police Warn of New IRA Letter Bomb Campaign', *The Guardian*, 17 January 1990, p. 24.
2 'Mail Bomb Injures CBN Guard', *Charlotte Observer*, 28 April 1990, p. 55; 'Texas Mail Bomb Linked to Other Blast?', *Tyler Courier Times*, 30 April 1990, p. 17.
3 'Letter Bombs Blamed on Welsh Group', *Derby Evening Telegraph*, 21 June 1990, p. 2.
4 Jeff Strickler, 'A Story of Healing', *Star Tribune* (Minneapolis, MN), 25 August 2007.
5 Oscar Hedin, 'In the Interest of the Nation', *Uppdrag Granskning*, 27 May 2006.
6 'Efat Ghazi', *Free Journal*, 16 May 2020.
7 'Reza Taslimi', People Pill, https://peoplepill.com, accessed 24 April 2021.
8 'France Bomb Plot: Iran Diplomat Assadollah Assadi Sentenced to 20 Years', BBC News, www.bbc.co.uk, 4 February 2021.
9 Mahmut Cengiz interview with bomb disposal expert, 11 May 2021.
10 'Hamido 'yu Kim Oldurdu', *TRT Haber*, 16 August 2011.
11 'En Yetkili Agizdan hamido Suikasti', *Hurriyet*, 10 March 2008.
12 Mahmut Cengiz interview with terrorism expert, 18 May 2021; 'Mumcu, Kisla li, Ana fartalardaki ile Avni: RDX Pat la yici', *Milliyet*, 28 July 2008.
13 Aytunç Erkin, 'Bahriye Üçok'u kim/ler öldürdü?', *Sozcu*, 6 October 2020.
14 'Mumcu, Kisla li, Ana fartalardaki ile Avni'.
15 'Turkiye'de Yasanan Teror Olaylari, 1993–2018', *Indigo Dergisi*, 8 January 2018.
16 Sydney Young, 'Di's Letter Bomb Menace', *Daily Record* (Glasgow), 20 July 1990, p. 1.
17 Natalie Phillips, 'Trial in Alaska Murder-by-Mail Case Unfolds in Tacoma', *News Tribune* (Tacoma, WA), 13 February 1995, pp. 7, 9.
18 Natalie Phillips, 'Murder-by-Mail Trial Unfolds in Tacoma', *News Tribune* (Tacoma, WA), 13 February 1995, p. 5.
19 Ibid.

20 'Letter Bomb Kills Journalist at Lima Paper', *Arizona Daily Star*, 11 October 1991, p. 12.

21 He was released in 1999 and died in 2004.

22 'Army's Standard Strategy', *The Journal* (Newcastle upon Tyne), 13 March 1995.

23 Lawrence Van Gelder, 'Plea Bargain in Mail Bombings That Killed 5 Upstate', *New York Times*, 9 February 1995.

24 'Letter Bomb Explodes at Home of Yugoslavs', *Times and Democrat* (Orangeburg, SC), 19 December 1993, p. 8.

25 'Escobar's Brother Wounded in Blast', *Oshkosh Northwestern*, 19 December 1993, p. 20.

26 John Wade, 'Bombs, Political Intrigue Are Shaking Caracas', *Miami Herald*, 19 August 1993, p. 250.

27 Robert Cotterill, 'Letter Bombs Sent . . .', *Evening Sentinel* (Stoke-on-Trent), 23 December 1993, p. 3.

28 'Austria Hit by Wave of Letter Bombs', *Gazette* (Montreal), 7 December 1993, p. 3; 'Letter Bombs Blamed on the Right Wing', *Vancouver Sun*, 7 December 1993, p. 10.

29 'Bombs Injure Two in Anti-Foreigner Attacks', *Fort Worth Star Telegram*, 17 October 1995, p. 10.

30 'Vienna: Austrian Police Accuses Suspect of Unabomber-Like Attacks', *Tennessean* (Nashville, TN), 11 October 1997, p. 87.

31 'Austrian Unabomber Sentenced to Life in Prison', *Great Falls Tribune*, 11 March 1999, p. 5.

32 'Austrian Bomb Victim Gets Two New Hands', *Fort McMurry Today* (Canada), 9 March 2000, p. 2.

33 'Mail Bomb Kills Man in Colorado Springs', *New York Times*, 26 April 1994, p. A20.

34 Wendell Jamieson, Julio Laboy and Joseph A. Gambardello, 'Woman, 75, Wounded by Letter Bomb', *Newsday* (Melville, NY), 6 April 1994; 'Letter-Bomb Victim Remains "Critical"', *Asbury Park Press* (NJ), 8 April 1994, p. 117.

35 Gef White, 'Bomb Suspect in Court', *Heartland Evening News*, 6 June 1994, p. 1.

36 Mark Honigsbaum, 'Trolley Terrorism', *The Observer*, 8 March 1998, p. 74.

37 'Brothers Held over Mardi Gra Bombings', *Richmond and Twickenham Informer*, 8 May 1998, p. 1.

38 'The Cashline Trap', *The Mirror*, 30 April 1998, p. 5.

39 'Accused Brothers Facing Fresh Charges', *Southall Gazette*, 31 July 1998, p. 20.

40 'Letter Bomb Explosion Keeps Japanese Jittery', *Jackson Sun* (TN), 17 May 1995, p. 8.

41 'Aum's Kikuchi to Be Indicted for Attempted Murder', *Kyodo News*, 4 August 2012.

42 Phil Green, 'Hunters Prey to Deadly Hate Mail', *Chronicle* (Chester), 7 July 1995, p. 3.

43 Michael Dekker, 'Murder by Mail Bomb Attempt Nets Charges', *Lawrence Journal* (KS), 2 March 1996.

44 'Man Sends Singer Bomb, Then Tapes Suicide', *Spokesman-Review* (Spokane, WA), 18 September 1996.

45 Lizette Alvarez, 'Police Pursue Varied Leads in Inquiry on Mail Bomb', *New York Times*, 29 December 1996, p. 30.

46 David Taylor, 'British Sports Star on Letter Bomb Alert', *Evening Standard*, 20 January 1997.
47 James Rowley, 'Followers of Egyptian Cleric Linked to Letter Bombs', *News Tribune* (Tacoma, WA), 4 January 1997, p. 8.
48 'Eighth Letter Bomb Surfaces at Leavenworth Post Office', *Daily Spectrum* (St George, UT), 4 January 1997.
49 Cassandra Burrell, 'Semtex Suspect in Letter Bombs', *Wisconsin State Journal*, 5 January 1997.
50 Sarah Lyall, '2 Hurt at Arabic Paper as Bombs Are Mailed to London and U.N.', *New York Times*, 14 January 1997, p. AI.
51 'Parcel Bomb Kills Daughter of Ranking Official in Burma', *Washington Post*, 8 April 1997, p. AII.
52 Bill McAllister, 'Postal Service to Tighten Security with Parcel Mail', *News Tribune* (Tacoma, WA), 8 August 1996, p. 8.
53 Gabrielle Costa and Les Kennedy, 'Device Exploded by Police', *The Age* (Melbourne), 3 December 1998, p. 6.
54 'How Terror Arrived in the Mail', *The Age*, 3 December 1998, p. 6.
55 Les Kennedy and Brendan Nicholson, 'Massive Hunt for Revenge Bomber', *The Age*, 3 December 1998, p. 6.
56 'Women Targets for Postal Bomb Attacks', *The Age*, 3 December 1998, p. 6.
57 Doug Conway, 'Australia's Short, Violent History of Terror by Post', *The Age*, 3 December 1998, p. 6.
58 John Lang, 'Mayhem by Mail Is Now a Fact of Life', *Honolulu Star Bulletin*, 5 February 1999, p. 6.
59 Ibid.

15 THE MAGABOMBER: CESAR SAYOC JR'S WAR ON THE DEMOCRATIC PARTY

1 Kyra Gurney et al., 'Sayoc Lived a Bizarre and Scattered Life in South Florida', *Miami Herald*, 27 October 2018, p. 2A.
2 Martin Vassolo, Sarah Blaskey and Linda Robertson, 'Cesar Sayoc, Lost and Angry, Found His Tribe with Trump', *Miami Herald*, 28 October 2018, pp. AI, A8.
3 Ibid.
4 Faith Karimi, 'Pipe Bomb Suspect Cesar Sayoc Describes Trump Rallies as "New Found Drug"', CNN, https://edition.cnn.com, 24 April 2019.
5 Vassolo, Blaskey and Robertson, 'Cesar Sayoc, Lost and Angry, Found His Tribe with Trump', pp. AI, A8.
6 Gurney et al., 'Sayoc Lived a Bizarre and Scattered Life in South Florida', p. 2A.
7 Ibid.
8 Larry Neumeister, 'His Mail Bombs Didn't Detonate but They Spread Fear; He Cried as He Pleaded Guilty', *Miami Herald*, 22 March 2019, p. A4.
9 Eric Tucker, Michael Balsamo and Colleen Long, 'Pipe Bomb Suspect Was Spinning Records as FBI Closed In', *Bradenton Herald*, 29 October 2019, p. A7.
10 Benjamin Weiser, 'Guilty Plea for Trump Supporter Who Mailed Bombs to Democrats', *New York Times*, 22 March 2019, p. AI9.
11 Vassolo, Blaskey and Robertson, 'Cesar Sayoc, Lost and Angry, Found His Tribe with Trump', p. A8.

12 Philip Bump and Devlin Barrett, 'Florida Man Who Sent Bombs to Dems, Media Gets Twenty Years', *Orlando Sentinel*, 6 August 2019, p. A3.
13 Devlin Barrett, Mark Berman and Matt Zapotosky, 'Man in Florida Arrested, Charged in Connection with Mail Bombs Sent to Public Figures', *Washington Post*, 26 October 2018.
14 Weiser, 'Guilty Plea for Trump Supporter Who Mailed Bombs to Democrats', p. A19; Neumeister, 'His Mail Bombs Didn't Detonate but They Spread Fear', p. A4.
15 Larry Neumeister, 'His Mail Bombs Sent to Public Figures', *Miami Herald*, 22 March 2019, p. A19.
16 Ibid.
17 Karimi, 'Pipe Bomb Suspect Cesar Sayoc Describes Trump Rallies as "New Found Drug"'.
18 Weiser, 'Guilty Plea for Trump Supporter Who Mailed Bombs to Democrats', p. A19.

16 THE MODERN ERA

1 Richard Savill, 'Bungling Letter Bomber Put on Too Few Stamps', *Daily Telegraph*, 6 May 2001.
2 Richard Savill, 'Tesco Bomb Blackmailer Is Jailed for 16 Years', *Daily Telegraph*, 12 June 2001.
3 Kay Luna, 'Morrison-Area Victims Recall Pipe Bomb Blast', *Quad-City Times* (Davenport, IA), 4 May 2003, p. A4.
4 Todd Ruger, 'Engelbrechts Too Busy to Dwell on Bombings', *Quad-City Times* (Davenport, IA), 4 May 2003, p. A4.
5 Ann McGlynn, '5 Days of Terror', *Quad-City Times* (Davenport, IA), 4 May 2003, pp. A1, A4.
6 Ibid., p. A4.
7 Stephen Castle and Ian Herbert, 'Anarchy in the EU: Labour MEP Is the Letter Bombers' Latest Target', *The Independent*, 6 January 2004, p. 3.
8 'Iowa Man Arrested in Janus Threats', *Denver Post*, 25 April 2007.
9 Nick Britten, 'Letter Bomber Driven by Anger over Father's DNA Police Record', *Daily Telegraph*, 28 September 2007.
10 Ibid.
11 'Scottsdale Touts Commitment to Gay Community', *Arizona Republic*, 16 August 2007.
12 Chris Wattie, 'Mystery Bomb Maker May Be Honing Skills: Experts', *National Post* (Toronto), 25 August 2007, p. 15.
13 'Letter Bomb Suspect Charged with Attempted Murder', *Times Colonist* (British Columbia), 7 November 2007.
14 Megan O'Toole, 'Only Meant to "Scare" Accused', *National Post* (Ontario), 23 March 2010; Sam Pazzano, 'Toronto Letter Bomber Found Guilty', *North Bay Nugget*, 26 June 2010.
15 Nicholas Paphitas, Elena Becatoros and Melissa Eddy, 'Mail-Bomb Campaign in Athens Reaches Germany', *Newark Advocate*, 3 November 2010, p. 11.
16 'Mail Bomb Plot Targets European Destinations', *Tulsa World*, 3 November 2010, p. 12.

17 'Italian Letter Bombs Linked to Anarchists', *News and Record* (Greensboro, NC), 29 December 2010, p. 14.
18 Jeffrey Fleischman, 'Yemeni Hunts for Bomb Maker', *Dayton Daily News*, 30 November 2010.
19 John F. Burns and Ravi Somaiya, 'Mail Bombs Are Prelude to a Soccer Showdown', *New York Times*, 24 April 2011, p. SP1.
20 'Muirhead and McKenzie Jailed for Neil Lennon Parcel Bomb Plot', BBC News, www.bbc.co.uk, 27 April 2012.
21 Nicholas Kulish, 'Letter Bomb Targets Powerful German Banker', *Houston Chronicle*, 9 December 2011, p. A12.
22 Leigh Phillips, 'Nanotechnology: Armed Resistance', *Nature* (August 2012), p. 577.
23 'Letter Bombs in N. Ireland', *Bismarck Tribune* (ND), 8 March 2014.
24 'Mail Bombs Lay Ruin to Chinese County as 7 Killed, Dozens Injured in 17 Sites across Guangxi's Liucheng', *South China Morning Post*, 30 September 2015.
25 Michaela Winberg, 'Old Friend Steps Up for Bombing Victim', *Philadelphia News*, 28 November 2016, p. 39.
26 'Letter Bomb Injures Worker at IMF Bureau in France', *Los Angeles Times*, 17 March 2017.
27 'Athens Terror as Bomb Explodes', *Daily Star*, 25 May 2017; 'Blast in Car Injures Greek ex-PM', BBC News, www.bbc.co.uk, 26 May 2017.
28 Roberto Villapando et al., 'FBI Confirms Package in SE Austin FedEx Is a Bomb Connected to Previous Explosions', *Austin American-Statesman*, 20 March 2018.
29 John C. Moritz and Doug Staglin, 'SWAT Team Members Moved in on His Car', *Corpus Christi Caller-Times*, 22 March 2018.
30 Kelly Geraldine Malone, 'Manitoba Man Convicted over Letter Bombs', *The Province* (Vancouver), 18 May 2018.
31 Craig Gibson, 'Swede Who Sent Pipe Bombs in Mail Jailed', *Sunday Herald* (Glasgow), p. 17.
32 'London Transit Bombs?', *New York Times*, 5 March 2019.
33 Justin Davenport, 'Police Issue Alert over Possible Missing Letter Bomb', *Evening Standard*, 12 March 2019.
34 Jose Bautista, Isabella Kwai and John Ismay, 'U.S. and Ukrainian Embassies in Spain Targeted by Letter Bombs', *Buffalo News*, 2 December 2022, p. A3.
35 Jennifer O'Mahony, 'Spain Letter Bomb Suspect Charged with Terrorism', *The Journal* (White Plains, NY), 28 January 2023.
36 Edward Wong, Julian E. Barnes and Eric Schmitt, 'Russian Agents Linked to Mail Bombs in Spain', *Boston Globe*, 23 January 2023.
37 'At Least 5 News Stations Receive Letter Bombs in Ecuador, One Explodes: "Clear Message to Silence Journalists"', CBS News, www.cbsnews.com, 21 March 2023; 'Ecuador Opens Terrorism Investigation after Journalists Receive Explosive Devices in Mail', CNN, https://edition.cnn.com, 23 March 2023.
38 'Pipe Bomb Scare Raises New Questions About Mail Safety', *Associated Press*, https://apnews.com, 25 October 2018.
39 National Consortium for the Study of Terrorism and Responses to Terrorism, 'Terrorist Attacks Involving Package Bombs, 1970–2017', University of Maryland, 2018, p. 1.

40 Ibid.
41 Rick Kuwahara, 'How to Survive an Email Bomb Attack', www.paubox.com, 7 September 2022.
42 Ibid.
43 Ben Marks, 'You've Got Mail Bombs: Tracking Down the Most Dangerous Letters in the World', *Collector's Weekly*, www.collectorsweekly.com, 16 October 2015.
44 Between 1970 and 2017 there were 39 terrorist attacks 'involving dangerous substances sent through the mail. Of these, 21 were with anthrax, 6 with ricin, 4 with 1080 pesticide and 3 with cyanide. The rest were unidentified.' National Consortium for the Study of Terrorism and Responses to Terrorism, 'Terrorist Attacks Involving Package Bombs', p. 2.
45 For more on bioterrorism attacks by mail, see Leonard A. Cole, *The Anthrax Letters: A Medical Detective Story* (Washington, DC, 2003); Robert Graysmith, *Amerithrax: The Hunt for the Anthrax Letter* (New York, 2003); David Willman, *The Mirage Man: Bruce Ivins, the Anthrax Attacks, and America's Rush to War* (New York, 2011).

BIBLIOGRAPHY

Allason, Rupert, *The Branch: A History of the Metropolitan Special Branch, 1883–1983* (London, 1983)

Arnold, Ron, *Ecoterror: The Violent Agenda to Save Nature* (Bellevue, WA, 1997)

Avrich, Paul, *Sacco and Vanzetti: The Anarchist Background* (Princeton, NJ, 1991)

Bar-Zohar, Michael, and Eitan Haber, *The Quest for the Red Prince* (New York, 1983)

Bearman, C. J., 'An Examination of Suffragette Violence', *English Historical Review*, CXX/486 (2005), pp. 365–97

Ben-Yehuda, Nachman, *Political Assassinations by Jews: A Rhetorical Device for Justice* (Albany, NY, 1993)

Bergman, Ronen, *Rise and Kill First: The Secret History of Israel's Targeted Assassinations* (London, 2019)

Bishop, Patrick, *The Reckoning: Death and Intrigue in the Promised Land: A True Detective Story* (New York, 2014)

'Bomb Expert Eagan', *Electrical Experimenter* (August 1919), pp. 296–7, 341–4

Bown, Stephen R., *A Most Damnable Invention: Dynamite, Nitrates, and the Making of the Modern World* (New York, 2005)

Brodie, Thomas G., *Bombs and Bombings: A Handbook to Detection, Disposal and Investigation for Police and Fire Departments* (Springfield, IL, 1972)

Brumfield, Dale M., 'Cincinnati's "Torpedo Man" Was America's First Mail Bomber', *Medium*, https://medium.com, 3 November 2020

Burleigh, Michael, *Blood and Rage: A Cultural History of Terrorism* (New York, 2009)

Burnett, Bryan, and Paul Golubovs, 'The First Mail Bomb?', *Journal of Forensic Sciences*, XLV/4 (2000), pp. 935–6

Cannell, Michael, *Incendiary: The Psychiatrist, the Mad Bomber, and the Invention of Criminal Profiling* (New York, 2017)

Cesarani, David, *Major Farran's Hat: The Untold Story of the Struggle to Establish the Jewish State* (Cambridge, MA, 2009)

Chase, Alston, *Harvard and the Unabomber* (New York, 2003)

Clutterbuck, Richard, *Guerrillas and Terrorists* (London, 1983)

Davis, Mike, *Buda's Wagon: A Brief History of the Car Bomb* (London, 2008)

Dillon, Brian, *The Great Explosion: Gunpowder, the Great War, and a Disaster on the Kent Marshes* (New York, 2015)

Dobson, Christopher, and Ronald Payne, *The Terrorists: Their Weapons, Leaders and Tactics* (New York, 1979)

Douglas, John, and Mark Olshaker, *Unabomber: On the Trail of America's Most Wanted Serial Killer* (New York, 1996)

Dudley, Robert M., *Tragedy on the Prairie: The Story of the 1976 Kimball Post Office Bomb* (Coppell, TX, 2022)

Eagan, Sean P., 'From Spikes to Bombs: The Rise of Eco-Terrorism', *Studies in Conflict and Terrorism*, XIX/1 (1996), pp. 1–18

Eliav, Yaacov, *Wanted*, trans. Mordecai Schreiber (New York, 1984)

FBI FOIA, 'The Use of Mail to Send Bombs: Hearing before the Subcommittee on Postal Operations and Services of the Committee on Post Office and Civil Service', House of Representatives, 103rd Congress, Second Session, 22 March 1994; Serial No. 103–38

Gage, Beverly, *The Day Wall Street Exploded: A Story of America in Its First Age of Terror* (New York, 2009)

Gibbs, Nancy et al., *Mad Genius: The Odyssey, Pursuit, and Capture of the Unabomber Suspect* (New York, 1996)

Graysmith, Robert, *Amerithrax: The Hunt for the Anthrax Killer* (New York, 2003)

—, *Unabomber: A Desire to Kill* (Washington, DC, 1997)

Greenburg, Michael M., *The Mad Bomber of New York: The Extraordinary True Story of the Manhunt That Paralyzed a City* (New York, 2011)

Hoffman, Bruce, *Anonymous Soldiers: The Struggle for Israel, 1917–1947* (New York, 2015)

Hoyt, Andrew Douglas, 'And They Called Them "Galleanisti": The Rise of the *Cronaca Sovversiva* and the Formation of America's Most Infamous Anarchist Faction (1895–1912)', PhD dissertation, University of Minnesota, 2018

Jenkins, Ray, *Blind Vengeance: The Roy Moody Mail Bomb Murders* (Athens, GA, 1997)

Jones, Ian, *London: Bombed, Blitzed and Blown Up: The British Capital Under Attack since 1867* (Barnsley, 2016)

Katz, Samuel M., *Israel versus Jibril: The Thirty-Year War against a Master Terrorist* (New York, 1993)

Lee, Martha F., *Earth First: Environmental Apocalypse* (Syracuse, NY, 1995)

Leslie, David, 'Inside a Terrorist Group – The Story of the SNLA', *Electric Scotland*, https://electricscotland.com (2006)

Liddick, Donald R., *Eco-Terrorism: Radical Environmental and Animal Liberation Movements* (Westport, CT, 2005)

Long, Douglas, *Ecoterrorism* (New York, 2004)

Lowenthal, Max, *The Federal Bureau of Investigation* (New York, 1950)

Mahan, Sue, and Pamela L. Griset, *Terrorism in Perspective* (Los Angeles, CA, 2013)

Makris, John, *The Silent Investigators: The Great Untold Story of the U.S. Postal Inspection Service* (New York, 1959)

Merriman, John, *The Dynamite Club: How a Bombing in Fin-de-Siècle Paris Ignited the Age of Modern Terror* (Boston, MA, 2009)

Missliwetz, J., et al., 'Injuries Due to Letter Bombs', *Journal of Forensic Sciences*, XLII/6 (1977), pp. 981–5

—, 'Post Parcel and Letter Bombs (PPLBS)', *Proceedings of the Institute of Electrical and Electronic Engineers*, 29th Annual Conference of Security Technology (October 1995), pp. 230–31

Murray, Robert K., *Red Scare: A Study in National Hysteria, 1919–1920* (New York, 1955)

O'Ballance, Edgar, *Terror in Ireland: The Heritage of Hate* (Novato, CA, 1981)

Oldfield, William, and Victoria Bruce, *Inspector Oldfield and the Black Hand Society: America's Original Gangsters and the U.S. Postal Detective Who Brought Them to Justice* (New York, 2018)

Pedahzur, Ami, and Arie Perliger, *Jewish Terrorism in Israel* (New York, 2009)

Phillips, Leigh, 'Nanotechnology: Armed Resistance', *Nature*, CDLXXXVIII (30 August 2012), pp. 576–9

Riddell, Fern, *Death in Ten Minutes: The Forgotten Life of Radical Suffragette Kitty Marion* (London, 2018)

Rothschild, M. A., and H. Maxeiner, 'Death Caused by a Letter Bomb', *International Journal of Legal Medicine*, CXIV (2000), pp. 103–6

Schmidt, Regin, *Red Scare: FBI and the Origins of Anti-Communism in the United States, 1919–1943* (Copenhagen, 2000)

Simon, Jeffrey D., *America's Forgotten Terrorists: The Rise and Fall of the Galleanists* (Lincoln, NE, 2022)

—, 'The Forgotten Terrorists: Lessons from the History of Terrorism', *Terrorism and Political Science*, XX (2008), pp. 195–214

Sinai, Joshua, 'Weaponized Letter and Package Attacks against Public and Private Sector Targets: Key Takeaways for Security Practitioners', *InfraGard Journal*, II/I (June 2019), pp. 12–23

Speirs, Dale, *The History of Mail Bombs: A Philatelic and Historical Study* (Leeds, 2010)

Stoner, Kelly, and Gary Perlstein, 'Implementing "Justice" through Terror and Destruction: Ecoterror's Violent Agenda to "Save" Nature', in Lynne L. Snowden and Bradley C. Whitsel, *Terrorism: Research, Readings, and Realities* (Upper Saddle River, NJ, 2005), pp. 90–133

Swift, Jonathan, ed., *The Journal to Stella* (London, 1901)

Talty, Stephan, *The Black Hand: The Epic War between a Brilliant Detective and the Deadliest Secret Society in American History* (Boston, MA, 2017)

Van Dijken, Lara, 'The Scottish National Liberation Army: Marzipan Gang or Real Terrorist Threat? A Case Study of the Scottish National Liberation Army and the Reasons Why They Did Not Become a Large Terrorist Movement during the Years 1979–1997', MA Thesis, University of Leiden, June 2016

Walker, Rebecca, 'Deeds, Not Words: The Suffragettes and Early Terrorism in the City of London', *London Journal*, XLV/I (2020), pp. 53–64

Webb, Simon, *Dynamite, Treason and Plot: Terrorism in Victorian and Edwardian London* (Stroud, Gloucestershire, 2012)

—, *The Suffragette Bombers: Britain's Forgotten Terrorists* (London, 2014)

Winne, Mark, *Priority Mail: The Investigation and Trial of a Mail Bomber Obsessed with Destroying Our Justice System* (New York, 1995)

INDEX